IMAGES of America

RAILROADS OF SOUTHWEST FLORIDA

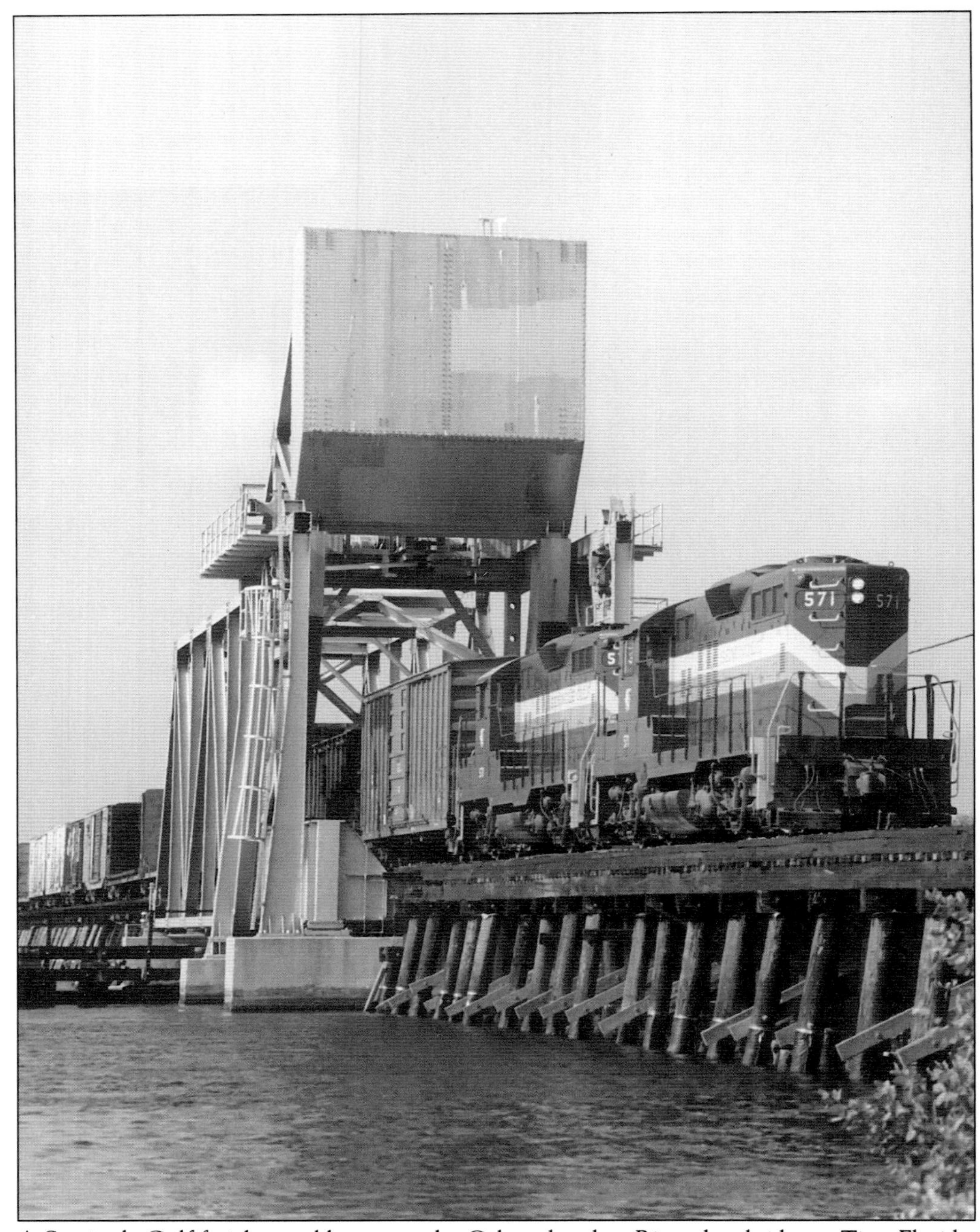

A Seminole Gulf freight rumbles across the Caloosahatchee River drawbridge at Tice, Florida, near Fort Myers. Trains have been crossing this important waterway ever since Atlantic Coast Line arrived in 1904. Seminole Gulf is one of two shortline railroads that currently serve the region. Farther inland is South Central Florida Express, another prosperous shortline. (Photo by Jeanne Hickam.)

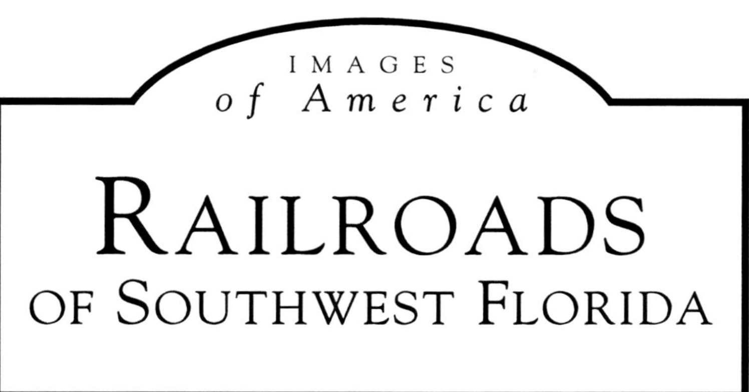

Gregg M. Turner

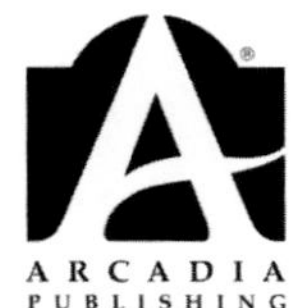

ISBN 978-0-7385-0349-3

Published by Arcadia Publishing,
Charleston, South Carolina

Printed in the United States of America

Library of Congress Catalog Card Number: 2005921751

For all general information contact Arcadia Publishing at:
Telephone 843-853-2070
Fax 843-853-0044
E-mail sales@arcadiapublishing.com
For customer service and orders:
Toll-Free 1-888-313-2665

Visit us on the Internet at www.arcadiapublishing.com

For Nancy, Anne, and Koko

Cover Image: A Seaboard Airline Railway train arrives in Boca Grande, Florida, on May 27, 1926. (Florida State Archives.)

CONTENTS

ACKNOWLEDGMENTS

With much pleasure I acknowledge the following individuals and organizations who made this work possible:

Joan Morris and Jody Norman, Florida State Photo Archives; Cynthia Wise, Florida State Library; Dr. Lewis Wynne, The Florida Historical Society; Mark Smith, Historical Resources, Sarasota County Government; Nancy Olson and David Southall, Collier County Museum; Stan Mulford, Fort Myers Historical Museum; John McCarthy, Sarasota County Historical Society; U.S. Cleveland, Charlotte Harbor Area Historical Society; Dr. and Mrs. Theodore VanItallie, Boca Grande Historical Society; Dorothy Korwek of the Venice Archives & Area Historical Collection; Larry Goolsby and Joseph Oates, Atlantic Coast Line and Seaboard Air Line Railroads Historical Society (POB #325, Valrico, FL 33595); Jeanne Hickam and Mike Mulligan, The Railroad Museum of South Florida (POB #7372, Fort Myers, FL 33911); William Dixon, Suncoast Chapter, National Railway Historical Society (POB #15828, Sarasota, FL 34277); and the Railway & Locomotive Historical Society; Patricia Aftoora and Michael Lee, CSX Transportation; Bureau of Railroads, Florida Department of Transportation; L. Craig Simmons, Alico; Richard Conley of South Central Florida Express; Dr. Canter Brown Jr.; Sherrie Stokes; Ailsa Dewing; Don Hensley Jr.; Larry Luckey; Jim Herron; Clifford Lund; Howard Melton; Bill Donahue; Rollins Coakley; Fred Clark Jr.; Scott A. Hartley; Kent Chetlain; William Griffin Jr.; Prudy Taylor Board; Judy Harmon; Ed Kelly; and Dr. Karen Walker.

To one and all I extend a sincere word of thanks!

—G.T.

INTRODUCTION

"Without doubt the greatest factors in Florida's progress are her railroads."
—Governor Perry's message to the Legislature, 1887

Railroads achieved almost overnight success because they supplied the traveler and shipper with a new and much-needed service: fast, regular, dependable, all-weather transportation. In the process they became America's first big business.

In Florida, their story proved both decisive and historic. Railroads conquered the state's vast interior, linked population centers, brought in tourists, and carried off the wealth of mines, factories, forests, and agriculture. New life sprang up at almost every railroad stopping place; energy, enterprise, and progress followed their course. As historian Oliver Jensen reminds Americans, "Behind the chuffing locomotives and little wooden cars followed the farmer, the miner, the merchant, the immigrant, and all that adventurous company who laid the rails, filled the empty lands, and made the desert . . . blossom like a garden."

Southwest Florida—land of tropical flowers and royal palms—was actually one of the last regions in the South to get railroad service. When, in fact, the first Iron Horse arrived in the region at Charlotte Harbor in 1886, nearly 150,000 miles of railroads existed in America. The transcontinental route to the Pacific was open; the Westinghouse air brake was in use; and Pullman sleeping cars were making long distance travel pleasurable. Area citizens and communities wanted railroads sooner, but a sparse population and lack of big freight markets retarded their arrival. And from a railroad point of view, it was in freight traffic that the real money was made.

Another impediment had been the state itself. Since 1855 trustees of the Internal Improvement Fund had dispensed free land grants for railroad construction, and they endorsed railroad bonds. But most of Florida's railroads were in bankruptcy after the Civil War. To extricate itself, the state tried to sell huge tracts of land to redeem the Fund and make good on the defaulted securities. Efforts though were proving futile, until a white knight stepped across the stage.

Hamilton Disston was a wealthy young industrialist from Philadelphia who came to Florida to fish and hunt. Governor William Bloxham learned of this and joined Disston at one of his outings. There, he pitched the state's dilemma—that if certain tracts could be sold, then the indebtedness of the Fund could be erased and the land grants resumed. Miraculously, Disston saw great potential in the so-called swamp and overflow lands, and, in 1881, his syndicate purchased some four million acres—at 25¢ each! The sale refreshed the state treasury, bankruptcy was averted, and the land grants resumed at record levels. The resources of Florida then attracted two spectacular developers: Henry Bradley Plant and Henry Morrison Flagler. Thanks to Plant, the Iron Horse came to Charlotte Harbor.

Railroad fever gripped the state after the Disston transaction, and, in time, Southwest Florida became the objective of many proposals. Though some lines got built, most never saw the light of day because of finances or folly. Even a line contained on a barrier island was unhatched. The Sanibel Island Railway and Construction Company of 1897 was to have constructed a railroad from "a point known as Reeds Landing . . . on the northern shore . . . to the extreme western end . . . with all necessary branches and side tracks." It was never built.

Henry Plant died in 1899 and the huge Plant System of railroads was sold to the Atlantic Coast Line in 1902. Shortly before that event, another prominent carrier achieved a toehold in the region—the Seaboard Air Line. For nearly seven decades thereafter, the Coast Line and Seaboard firms would compete for the freight and passenger traffic of Southwest Florida.

Both railroads rendered yeoman service to the country during the First World War. After the hostilities came the incredible Florida land boom of the 1920s. Railroad traffic surged as never before, new lines appeared, and millions were spent on improvements and new equipment. Many projects arose in Southwest Florida, and when completed in 1928, the rail map of the region stood at its greatest extent. The golden age of railroading had arrived.

Unfortunately, the cost of expansion and a business downturn threw the Seaboard right into bankruptcy where it remained until 1946. The Coast Line fared the Depression years better, but neither could escape the competitive nature of cars, buses, trucks, boat lines, and airplanes. In response the railroads slashed expenses, cut fares, introduced new services, air conditioned coaches, and ordered fast diesel engines and streamlined cars. This helped, as did profits from a Second World War. But the era in Southwest Florida also witnessed many service curtailments and track abandonments.

After decades of being rivals, the Coast Line and Seaboard firms merged as the Seaboard Coast Line Railroad in 1967. Redundant routes and facilities were at last rationalized and many operational efficiencies were subsequently achieved. The merged firm then became a part of CSX Corporation in November 1980.

In time, CSX began shedding many of its lightly used lines to smaller railroad companies called shortlines. Today, Seminole Gulf and South Central Florida Express ably serve the rail requirements of Southwest Florida, and both carry on a heritage that began just over a century ago.

One

Rails to Charlotte Harbor

"We need something to cheer us up, as we have looked so long for the proposed Rail-road, that we have come to the conclusion that there will never be one."

—comment of Ft. Ogden resident, *Sunland Tribune*, December 13, 1879

Railroads were first proposed to the Charlotte Harbor area after the Civil War. Though none were built then, promoters kept dreaming of the day when trains would arrive here and connect with ships bound for New Orleans, Cuba, the West Indies, and perhaps South America.

The Florida Southern Railway was one of many firms that comprised the Plant System of railroads. Its route began at Palatka and ran down the peninsula to Pemberton Ferry by way of Gainesville, Ocala, and Leesburg. Another Plant enterprise, the South Florida, advanced its sibling to Bartow, where rails arrived in September 1885. There the Florida Southern embarked upon its last big construction effort: the 75-mile Charlotte Harbor Division down the Peace River Valley. The project launched the railroad story of Southwest Florida.

The Florida Southern actually began life in 1879 as the Gainesville, Ocala and Charlotte Harbor Railroad. In the early 1880s, a reorganization of the firm took place, Henry Plant got control and the Florida Southern name was adopted. Legislators looked kindly upon the enterprise and endowed it with a generous land grant. In the end the Florida Southern received the biggest handout of any Florida railroad—2.58 million acres!

In the interest of saving money, the railroad's directors had the line built with a narrow gauge track; that is, one measuring three feet between the rails instead of the standard gauge dimension of 4 feet, 8 1/2 inches. Engines and cars therefore were smaller than their standard gauge counterparts and less costly to purchase. Because the narrow gauge line passed through many citrus areas, the Florida Southern became known as "The Orange Belt Route."

A six percent bond issue, totaling $807,900, helped finance the Charlotte Harbor Division, which meant the new line cost about $11,000 a mile to construct and equip. Surveyors began to locate the right-of-way in May 1885, and among those employed for the task was Albert Gilchrist—a civil engineer from Punta Gorda and future Florida governor. By fall, nearly 1,500 laborers were at work grading the line, building bridges and trestles and laying track.

A subject of much speculation was where the new division would actually terminate. Naturally the Charlotte Harbor area was widely spoken of, but other objective points were rumored such as Boca Grande, Pine Island, Fort Myers, Punta Rassa, even Marco Island. Railroad officials remained conveniently mum on the subject for they were busy extracting "inducements" from area communities and individuals. (Donations of land and cash helped decide where the route would go.) Case in point was Isaac Trabue, who owned prime parcels of land on the southern side of Charlotte Harbor. Trabue realized early on that only a railroad could make his hamlet of "Trabue" prosper. The Kentucky lawyer ended up giving the Florida Southern half of his holdings, and it was here that the Charlotte Harbor Division ultimately terminated. A year after the railroad arrived, "Trabue" became Punta Gorda.

The Florida Southern opened for business between Bartow and Arcadia in March 1886. That month, railroad officials toured Governor Edward Perry and state officials over the new line. At Zolfo Springs, the Pullman car special halted on the Peace River Bridge. There the governor's entourage supped on cold turkey and Mumm champagne while a "saucy mockingbird swayed and sang in a tree-top close by."

Construction halted at Arcadia allowing time for the town "to commence." Prior to the railroad's arrival, about 16 families resided in the area. But by autumn, thanks to the Iron Horse, Arcadia boasted nearly forty homes, four stores, three boarding houses, two drugstores, and two sawmills.

This interlude, however, infuriated folks who lived below Arcadia, many of whom had waited years for railroad service as our opening quotation suggests. The *Fort Myers Press* newspaper asked a correspondent for an explanation: "No train to Fort Ogden yet; still at Arcadia; cause unknown. We are now having transportation by schooners as of old. There is a dead dog under the house as regards the railroad movements."

Construction resumed in May 1886, and in the following months trains were at last seen at Fort Ogden. When Cleveland was reached, the Peace River steamboat *Alice Howard* arranged to meet trains and supplied a boat connection to Fort Myers. Then, on July 24, 1886, the first through train was run from Bartow to Trabue. Other trains brought in supplies and materials for the new Punta Gorda Hotel, being built by the railroad's real estate division. Laborers also toiled on the 4,200-foot "Long Dock" at the end of the Punta Gorda peninsula, where in time trains met connecting steamboats.

In 1892, the railroad's narrow-gauge track was converted to standard gauge, which greatly facilitated the interchange of cars. An uptick in traffic also occurred about this time thanks to the pebble phosphate industry in the Peace River Valley. On balance, though, the Florida Southern was not a huge Plant money-maker. In Poor's *Manual of Railroads* for 1902, we learn that the 243-mile company incurred a loss of $78,796. In fact, the deficit carried forward that year amounted to $1.2 million. Nevertheless, the Charlotte Harbor Division stimulated the Peace River Valley. It conveyed travelers, tourists, and settlers, plus it was a commercial artery to the outside world.

Henry Bradley Plant never allowed Punta Gorda or the Charlotte Harbor area to rival his beloved Tampa, where he built the sumptuous Tampa Bay Hotel and the world's largest marine phosphate terminal. After his death, the Plant system of railroads was sold to the Atlantic Coast Line. The Coast Line, however, had ambitions for its Charlotte Harbor Division, which we will explore in Chapter Three.

Henry Bradley Plant became one of the richest and most powerful men in the South. The Connecticut native started his career as a lowly cabin boy on a steamboat. After mastering the express business, he entered the railroad field and acquired some 14 separate railroad companies. When sold in 1902, the Plant System of rails boasted some 2,235 miles of lines. (Florida State Archives.)

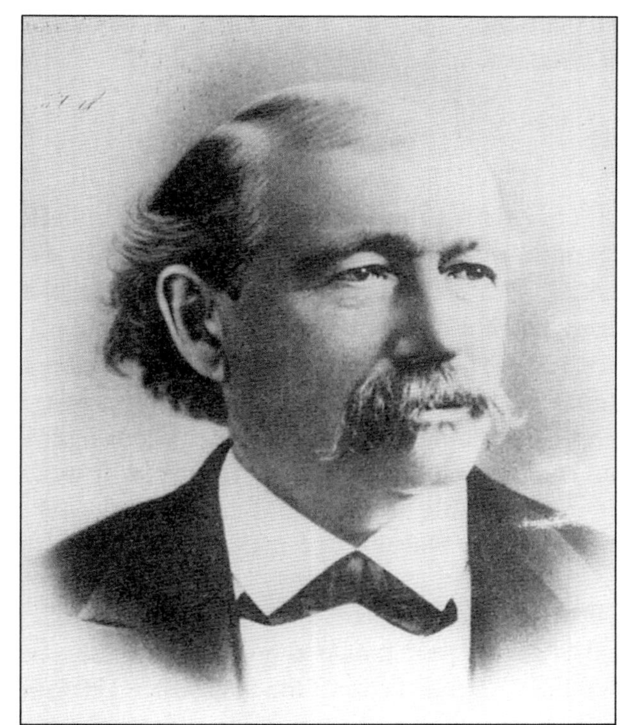

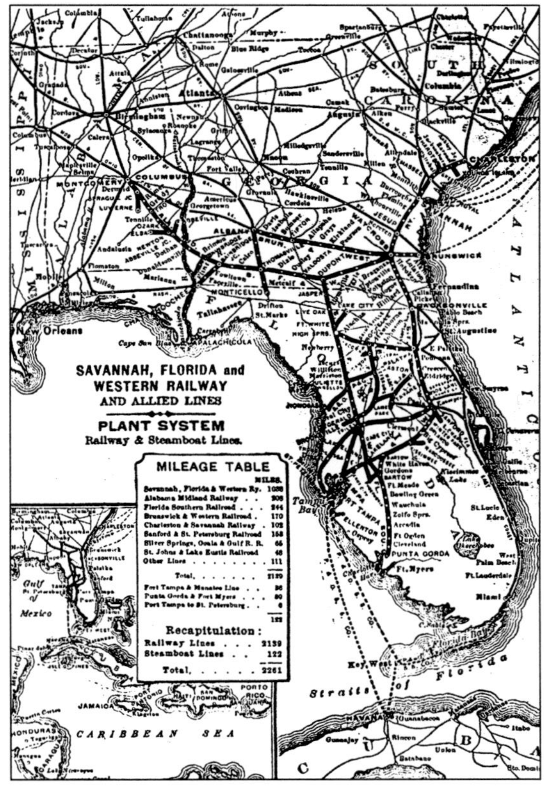

The Charlotte Harbor Division of the Florida Southern is clearly evident in this Plant System map. Plant toured his empire using Pullman Palace Car No. 100, with an interior of fitted carved mahogany and rich blue velvet. The master maintained a suite in his sumptuous Tampa Bay Hotel, but his real home was on Fifth Avenue in New York City.

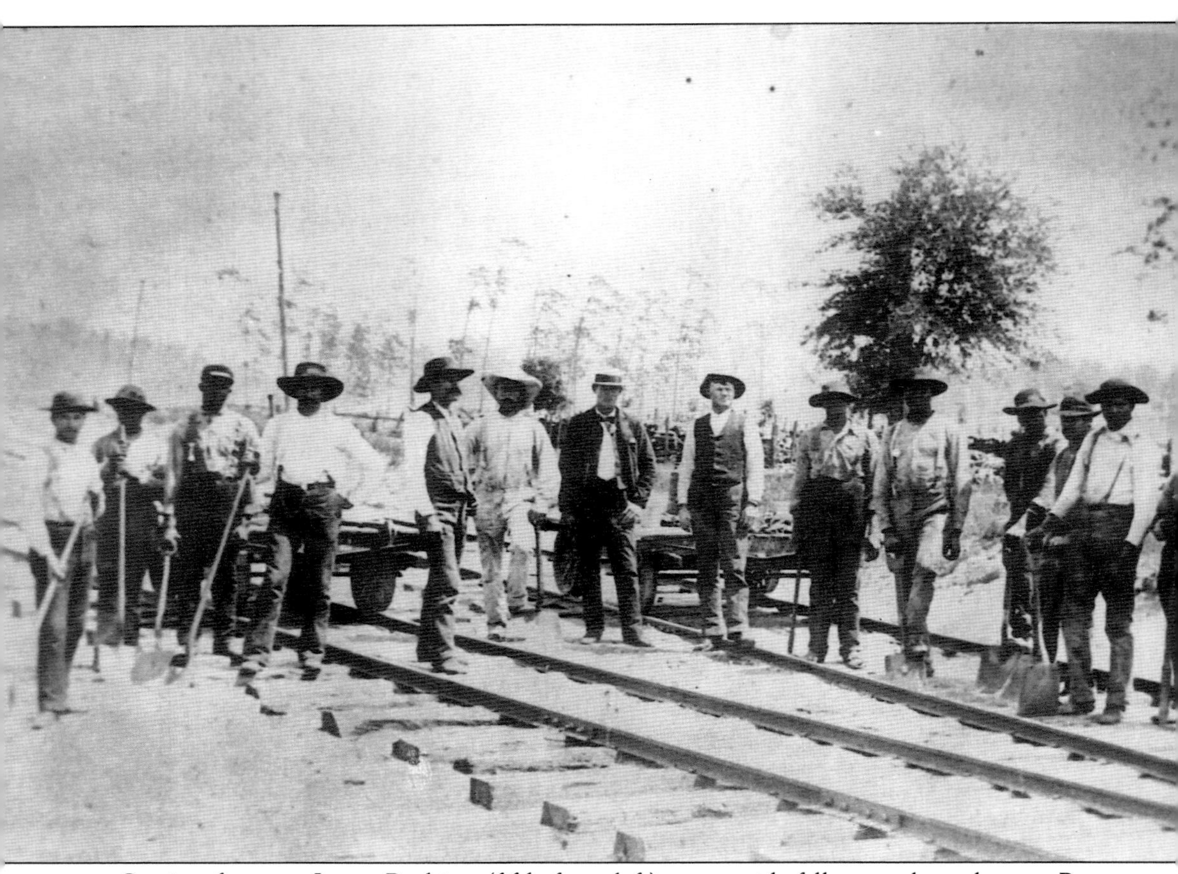

Section foreman James Rushing (fifth from left) poses with fellow track workers at Bartow. Two Plant railroads converged here: the narrow gauge Florida Southern (seen at left) and the standard gauge South Florida Railroad. Locomotives had to be built for one gauge or the other, but the interchange of cars was interestingly handled. A standard gauge car arriving in Bartow destined down the Charlotte Harbor Division was shuttled into a three-rail siding. There, it was jacked-up, the standard gauge wheel sets removed, and narrow gauge ones inserted. Thus, a standard gauge car—passenger or freight—could travel all the way to Punta Gorda. (Charles Rushing photo courtesy of Dr. Canter Brown Jr.)

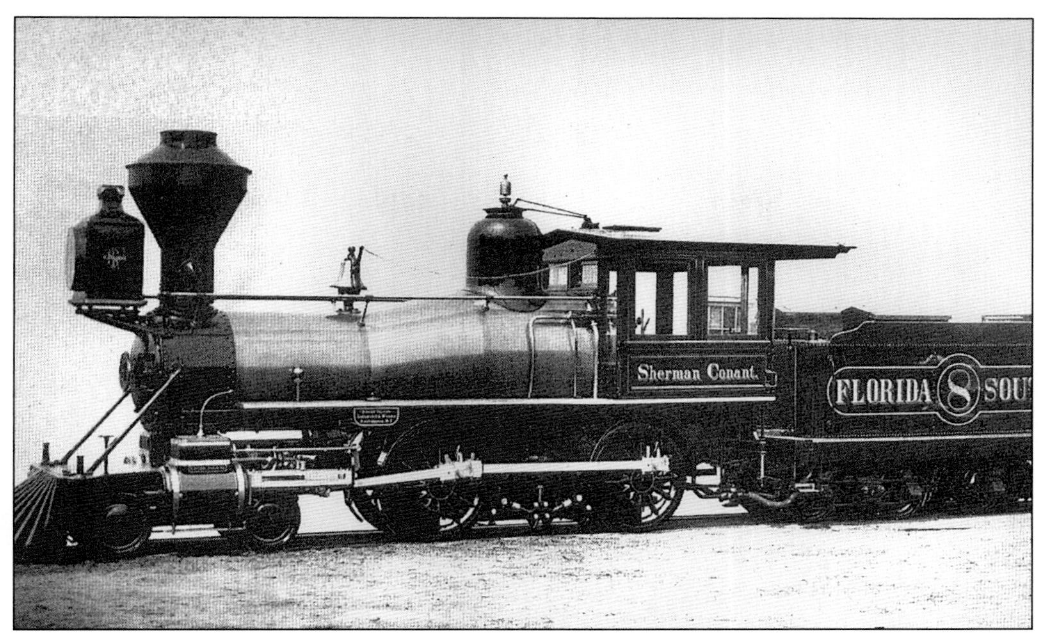

The Rhode Island Locomotive Works, like many builders, photographed their products after completion. No. 8 for the Florida Southern Railway was an "American" type locomotive (4-4-0 wheel arrangement) that burned wood and featured a large oil-lit headlight and cowcatcher. This particular example lacked a sand dome, but not a name. Sherman Conant was the railroad's general manager. (Railway & Locomotive Historical Society.)

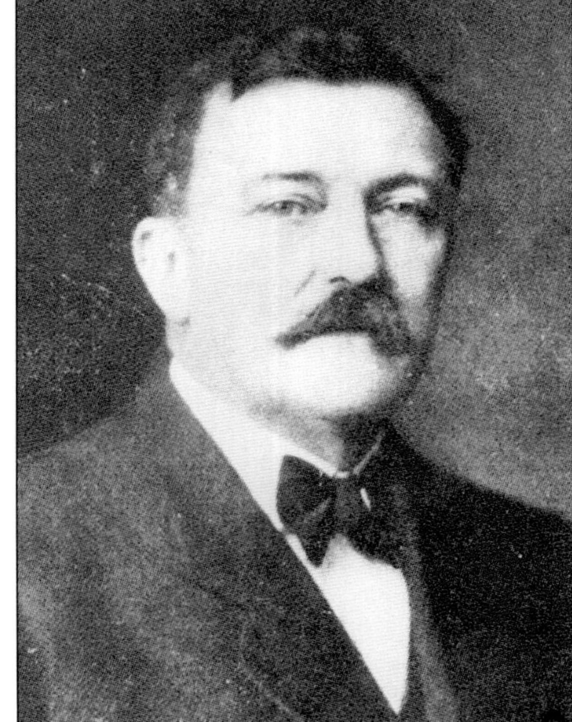

The hero of Punta Gorda was Albert W. Gilchrist. Trained at West Point, the future governor (1909–1913) dabbled in civil engineering, citrus, and real estate. When not surveying railroads, he was busy plotting the town of Boca Grande on Gasparilla Island. A life-long bachelor, he accumulated a small fortune which, upon his demise, benefited many organizations. (Florida State Archives.)

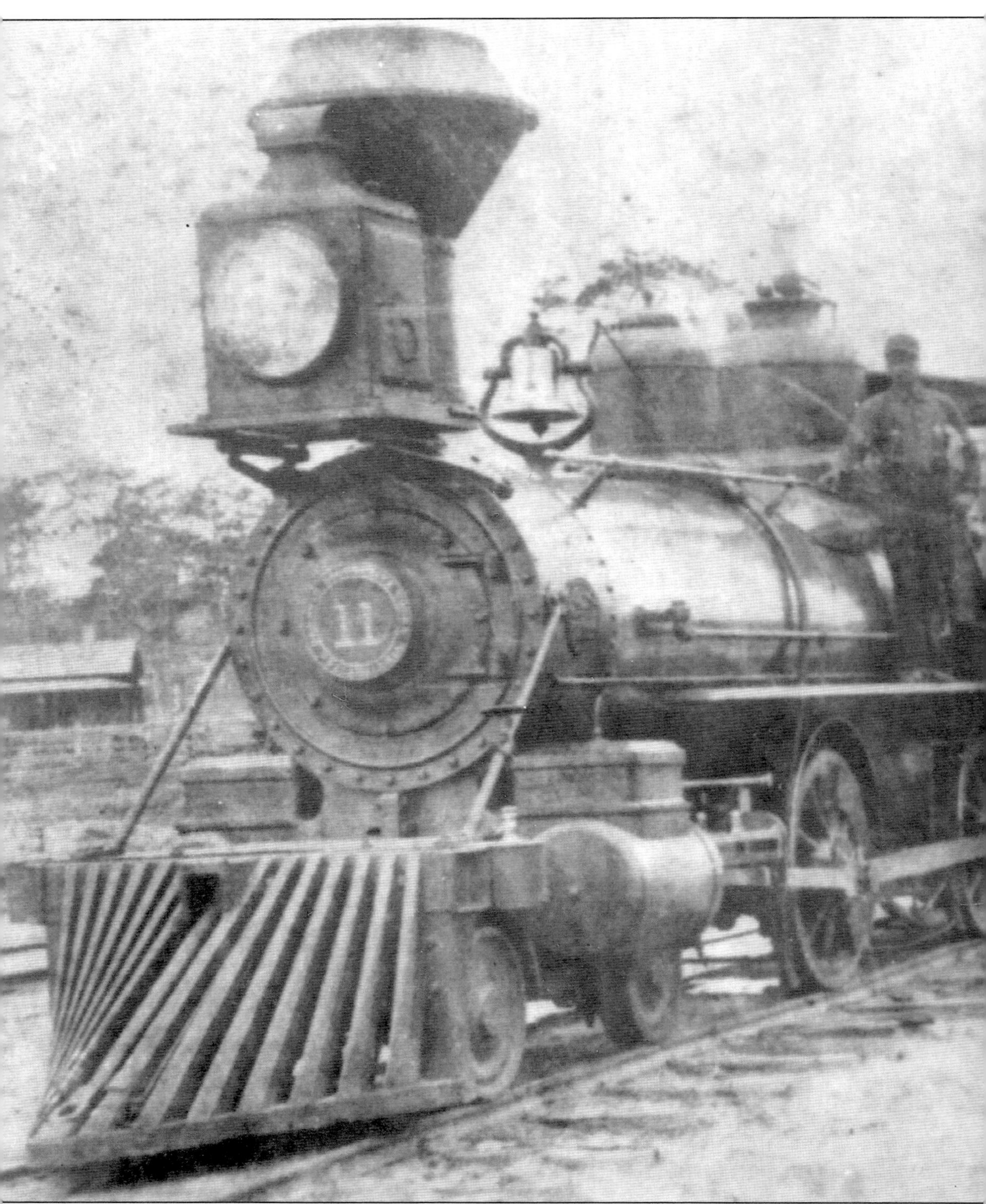

Employees pose next to the first through passenger train that ran between Bartow and Trabue (Punta Gorda). No crowds greeted the consist at the latter point—no parade, no public ceremony. In fact, Trabue was a rough and ready outpost "overrun with bums, toughs, gamblers,

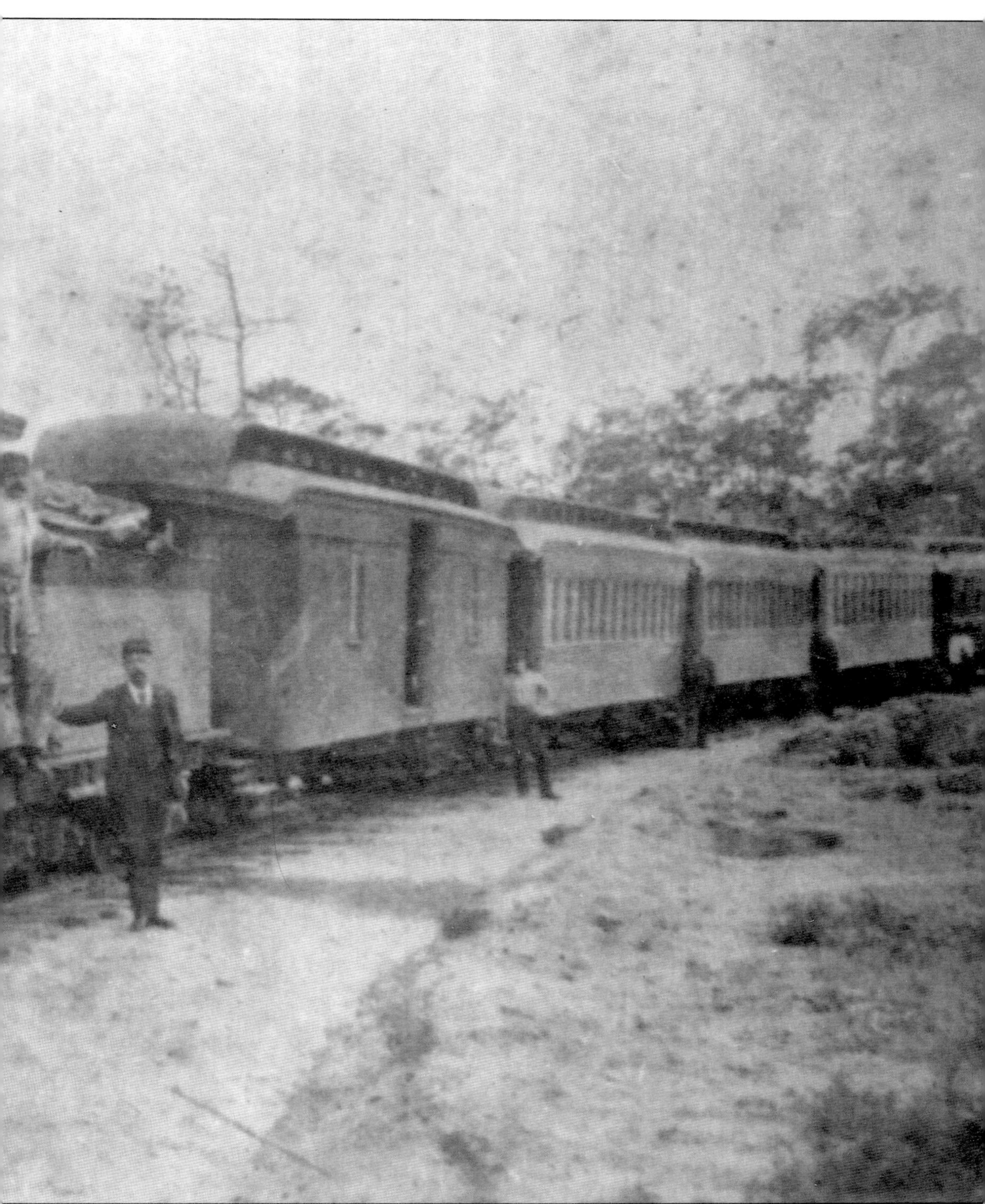

adventurers and fugitives from justice." High sawgrass, palmetto, and pine woods abounded; absent were paved streets and sidewalks. When "Trabue" became Punta Gorda, the town started to clean up its act. (Florida State Archives.)

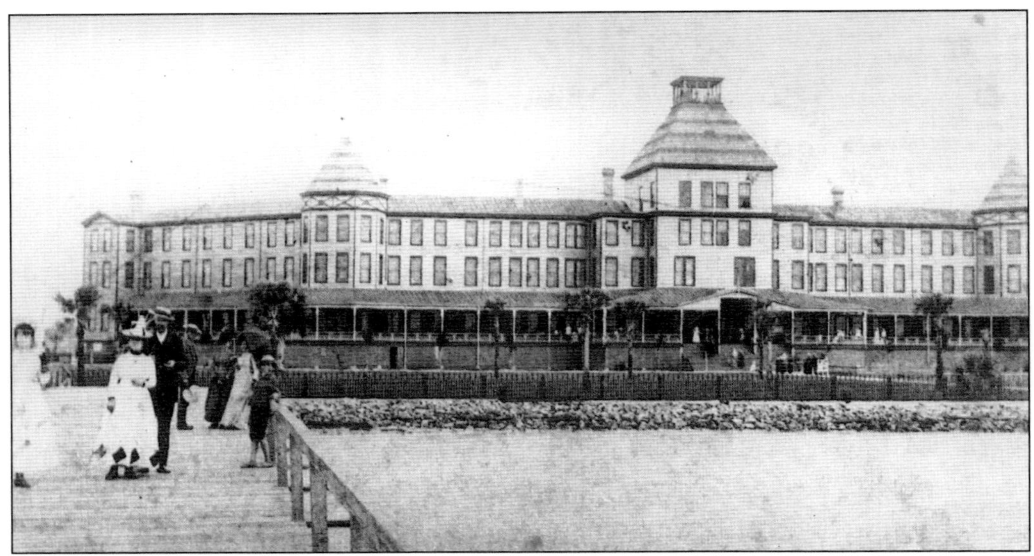

The railroad's real estate division—the Florida Commercial Company—built the 150-room Punta Gorda Hotel which, in time, became a watering hole for the rich and famous. Guests arrived by train, including John Wanamaker, Harvey Firestone, Andrew Mellon, and President Teddy Roosevelt. The edifice, open only in winter, pre-dated Henry Plant's magnificent Tampa Bay Hotel by several years. (Florida State Archives.)

Florida Southern Railway.

ORANGE BELT ROUTE.

AUGUST 12, 1886.

CHARLOTTE HARBOR DIVISION.

GOING SOUTH.

Leave	Bartow	6 30 a m
Arrive	Homeland	6 52 a m
"	Fort Meade	7 16 a m
"	Bowling Green	7 38 a m
"	Wachula	8 06 a m
"	Zolfo Springs	8 22 a m
"	Charlie Apopka	8 58 a m
"	Arcadia	9 12 a m
"	Nocatee	10 10 a m
"	Fort Ogden	10 34 a m
"	Cleveland	11 15 a m
"	Punta Gorda	11 45 a m

Close connection made with steamer Tuesday, Thursday and Saturday for Punta Rassa, FORT MYERS, etc.

GOING NORTH.

Leave	Punta Gorda	12 05 p m
"	Cleveland	12 30 p m
Arrive	Fort Ogden	1 09 p m
"	Nocatee	1 34 p m
"	Arcadia	1 [illegible] p m
"	Charlie Apopka	2 36 p m
"	Zolfo Springs	3 10 p m
"	Wachula	3 26 p m
"	Bowling Green	3 53 p m
"	Fort Meade	4 19 p m
"	Homeland	4 42 p m
"	Bartow	5 05 p m

Slightly more than five hours was required for the 75-mile train trip between Bartow and Punta Gorda. At first, trains were not punctual and the steamboat connection was occasionally missed at Long Dock in Punta Gorda. Nevertheless, the Florida Southern provided transportation to the outside world, and for this the Peace River valley was grateful. (Railway & Locomotive Historical Society.)

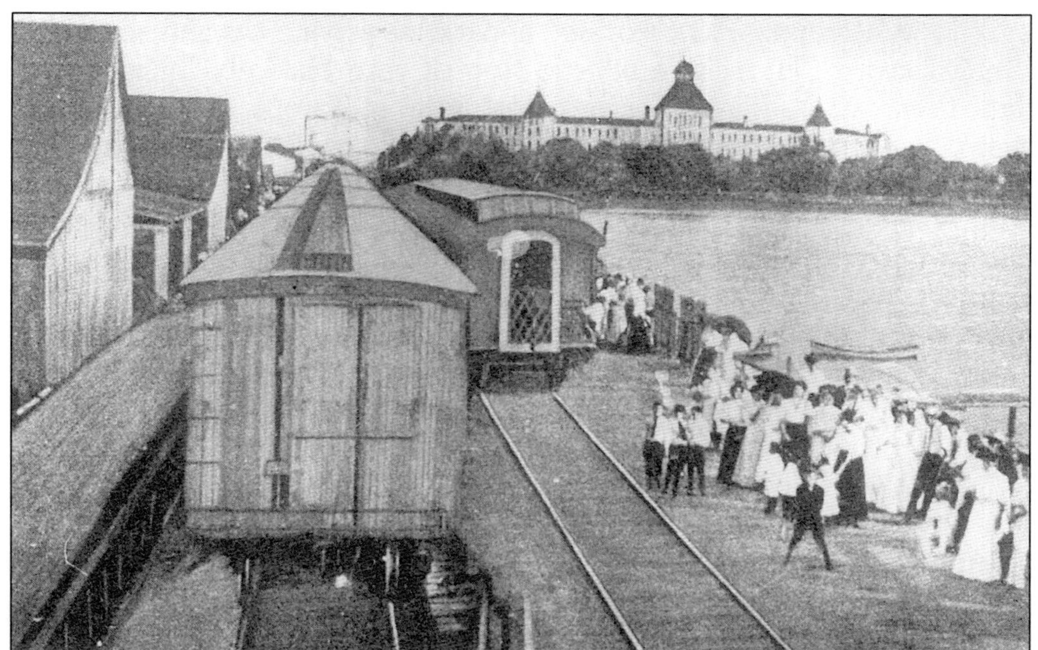

To discourage competitor boats from touching in at Long Dock, Henry Plant had a smaller, shallow-water one built at King Street in front of the Punta Gorda Hotel. Florida Southern trains ran out on it, and patrons could directly board Plant steamboats. Millionaire Barron Collier eventually purchased and renovated the hotel in the 1920s. Then it burned. Today, the Punta Gorda Mall occupies the site. (Florida State Archives.)

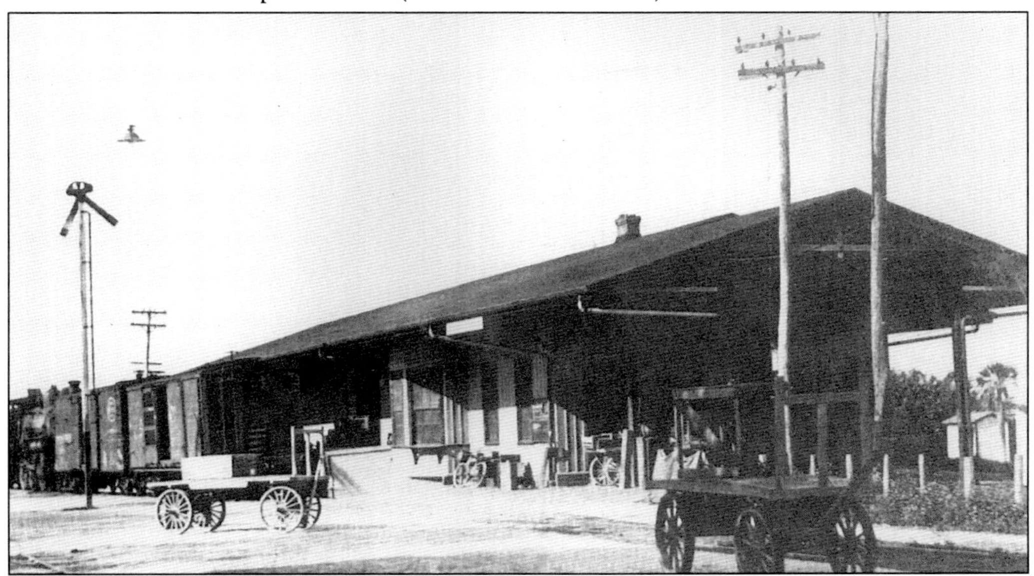

The second depot at Punta Gorda sat next to the hotel on King Street. A considerable amount of freight was run out onto the King Street dock and loaded into steamboats. In this scene, a switch engine of the Atlantic Coast Line Railroad shuttles several ventilated box cars, which were used for vegetable and citrus shipments. A third depot was later built at Taylor Street in the 1920s. (Florida State Archives.)

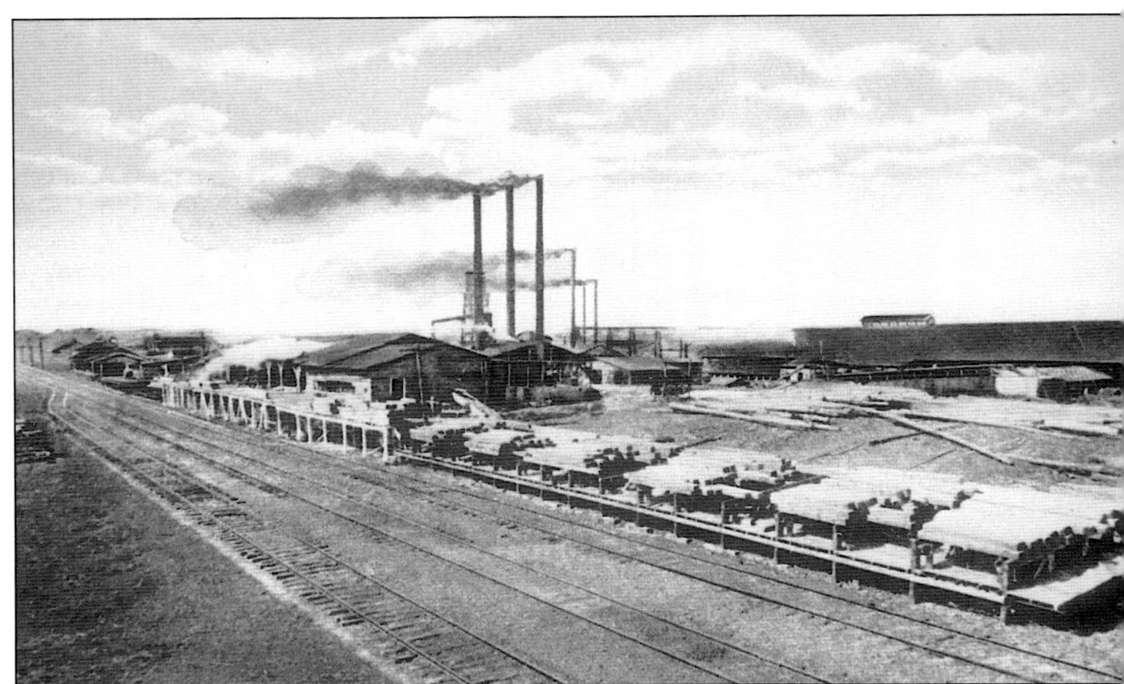

Albert Gilchrist helped in founding Nocatee, a community five miles south of Arcadia. From humble beginnings there arose this century the huge King Lumber works. For many years logs and milled lumber provided important revenue for Atlantic Coast Line, as this postcard scene suggests. (Florida State Archives.)

Two

AROUND SARASOTA AND VENICE

"The country traversed by the Florida West Shore Railway is exempt from frost, and is admirably adapted for the growing of oranges, lemons, grapefruit, pineapples, bananas and early fruits and vegetables of all kinds."

—Annual Report, Seaboard Air Line Railway, 1903

Sarasota's first railroad project was to have revived two land companies. Its promoters believed that a rail line would enhance land values, attract settlers, and the newcomers would end up buying acreage from the land firms. Such was the strategy behind the Manatee & Sarasota Railway and Drainage Company of 1890.

Unfortunately, the railroad started with little cash, hoping that the sale of bonds would raise the real funds for construction. But in the end, even with the land firms chipping in property for the route, no market could be found for the securities. Thus, the company flickered out of existence and the directors assigned their interests to another firm.

A year later the curtain went up on the Arcadia, Gulf Coast & Lakeland. Spearheaded by Boston capitalists, the company had the right to construct a rail line from Lakeland to Gasparilla Island and install branches where needed. The firm managed to open a small stretch of track between Braidentown and Sarasota. On May 16, 1892, the company's first train chugged into Sarasota whereupon passengers made a mad dash to the DeSoto Hotel and Captain Bacon's Oyster House for food and refreshment. The 9-mile trip, which passed through piney woods and orange groves, had taken one hour and nine minutes.

The new line was not very well constructed. In fact, cars rocked and lurched over the poorly constructed track which prompted locals to nickname it the "Slow & Wobbly." A used engine of Civil War vintage served as the prime mover, which was named "Old Pete" in honor of the line's president, Anthony Peters. Passengers rode in a crude "day coach" that was really a built-up flat car with wood benches and canvas top awning.

Without question the Slow & Wobbly was a unique and colorful operation. No employee of the railroad, for instance, received a salary, which prompted the conductor and engineer to pocket most of the fares. Trains were actually run on an as-needed basis. On one trip, the conductor's lunch pail flew off the illustrious day coach. No problem! A solicitous engineer backed his train some 4 miles so it could be retrieved and enjoyed. Occasionally "Old Pete" derailed, and it did so one day at Braidentown where it demolished the water tank. The crew, unfazed, managed to rerail the engine and siphon water from a nearby pond. Of course taxes were never paid, and at one point the sheriff actually chained "Old Pete" to the rails until bills were paid. Last but not least was the fact that the little line connected with no other railroad.

The Slow & Wobbly was reorganized in 1893 as the Florida, Peninsula & Gulf. Armed with a generous land grant and the right to construct new lines, the picture looked encouraging. But the auspicious start was short lived. The company failed for lack of business and was sold under foreclosure to a private party in Georgia. Area loggers ended up using the line without the owners permission, and occasionally daring blades fired up "Old Pete" and ran it as a lark. The track was ultimately sold and the decrepit cars were left to rust on a siding near Braidentown.

Upon the Sarasota scene there now appeared Ralph Caples, Ohio native and railroad executive. Caples had fallen in love with the Sarasota area while on his honeymoon, and was convinced that all the area needed was a railroad connection to Tampa. Quietly he approached other investors about the idea, and with the backing of a Tampa banker, the Florida West Coast Railway was unhatched in 1901. Surveys and plans were subsequently prepared, but just before construction began, the Seaboard Air Line Railway swung into action for it too desired a presence in Sarasota. Realizing his firm was no match against the Seaboard, Caples capitulated.

Actually, it was a subsidiary of the Seaboard that obtained a presence in Sarasota. The United States & West Indies Railroad and Steamship Company was empowered to build a rail line from Plant City to Gasparilla Island, plus it could install branches where necessary. In August 1901, under the Seaboard's direction, construction began on a 51-mile line from Durant to Sarasota by way of Parrish, Manatee, and Oneco. Some of the line actually traversed the old roadbed of the Slow & Wobbly. The company's first passenger train—supplied by the Seaboard—arrived at Sarasota on the evening of March 23, 1903. The company's track, however, continued past the freight depot and headed west along Strawberry Avenue to Hog Creek, where the railroad constructed a dock facility.

The company with the imposing name reorganized itself in 1903 as the Florida West Shore Railway. Another lease and traffic agreement was signed with the Seaboard, and in return the latter guaranteed the former's first mortgage construction bonds. The reorganized firm built a 3-1/2-mile branch from Sarasota to the agricultural district of Fruitville, which opened July 1, 1905. Four years later, the Seaboard officially acquired the Florida West Shore, and its corporate identity came to a close.

Bertha Honore Palmer, a wealthy and prominent Chicago widow, convinced the Seaboard to extend its track south of Fruitville to Venice, where she owned extensive land holdings. Work commenced on the 16-mile extension in January 1910, by way of Osprey and Laurel. The project was completed in fall, 1911. Palmer arranged to have the Venice post office moved to the station grounds at Venice. Where the post office formerly stood, citizens eventually renamed the area Nokomis.

Huge stands of timber existed in the Venice area, and logging railroads emerged to transport the forest products. Of significance was the Gulf Coast Railway, which had been incorporated in 1915 by the Manasota Land & Timber Company. Its standard gauge track began at the Seaboard connection in Venice and meandered down to the company town of Manasota, which in 1921 became Woodmere. Here, a four-story mill house existed as well as 1,500 homes, a commissary, a movie house, and two churches. A network of company-owned narrow-gauge tracks penetrated the piney woods, over which the firm operated its own engines and cars. Another area logging firm of note was the J. Ray Arnold Company at Laurel, which at one time operated nearly 30 miles of railroad tracks.

Extraordinary events occurred in Venice during the Florida land Boom of the 1920s. The Brotherhood of Locomotive Engineers of Cleveland, Ohio, purchased over 50,000 acres of Venice land, and began to create a city of beautiful homes, hotels, apartments, and shops. Parks, boulevards, and paved streets were included, as well as utilities and demonstration farms. It was a huge speculative venture that, regrettably, failed because of poor timing and mismanagement. Nevertheless, investors and the curious came across the country to see the wonders of Venice. The Brotherhood paid to have the Seaboard tracks moved a quarter-mile east in order to accommodate the unfolding city, plus it funded a new station. The latter still stands, as do many other Brotherhood buildings, reminding residents and tourists of a bygone era.

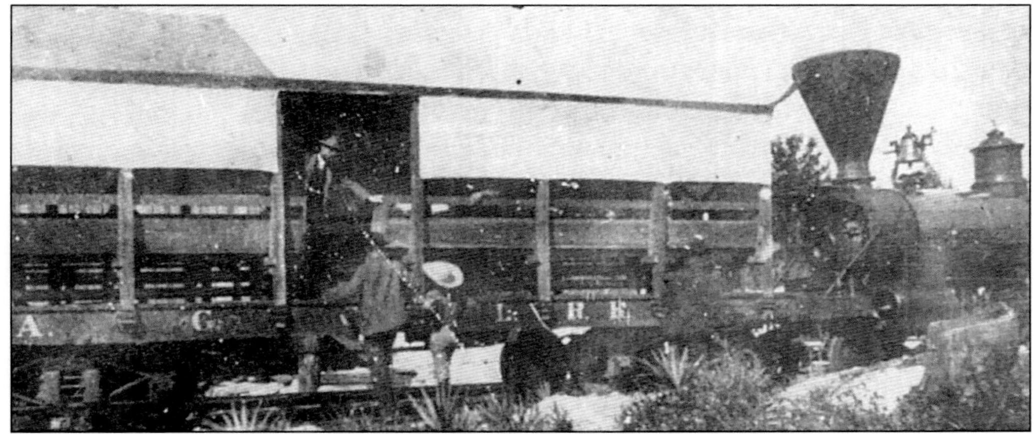

Passengers are helped into the illustrious "day coach" of the Arcadia, Gulf Coast & Lakeland. Wood benches awaited inside, and the canvas top cover shielded patrons from rain, sun, and embers that spewed out of the balloon smokestack of "Old Pete." Because train service was slow and sporadic, many Sarasotans found a horse and buggy more expedient. (Historical Resources, Sarasota County Government.)

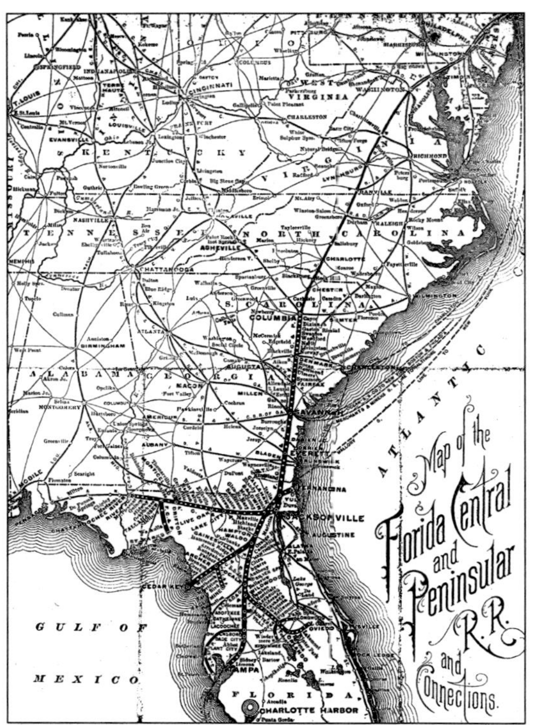

In 1899, the Seaboard Air Line syndicate obtained control of the 940-mile Florida Central and Peninsular Railroad. The Seaboard began through train service the following year from Richmond, Virginia, to Tampa. At Durant, a branch to Sarasota would one day diverge. (Florida State Archives.)

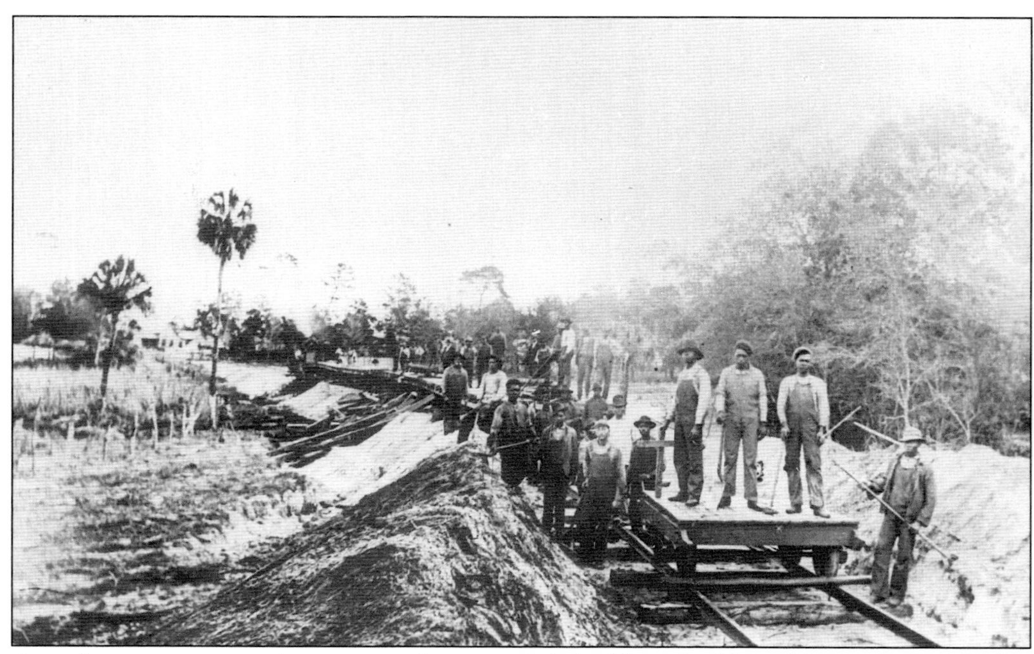

A track crew momentarily pauses at Sarasota while building the United States & West Indies Railroad. Ties, rails, and spikes are being slid off the slow-moving train. Whereas mechanized machinery makes the going easier today, in 1903 it was backbreaking work and not for the faint of heart. (Historical Resources, Sarasota County Government.)

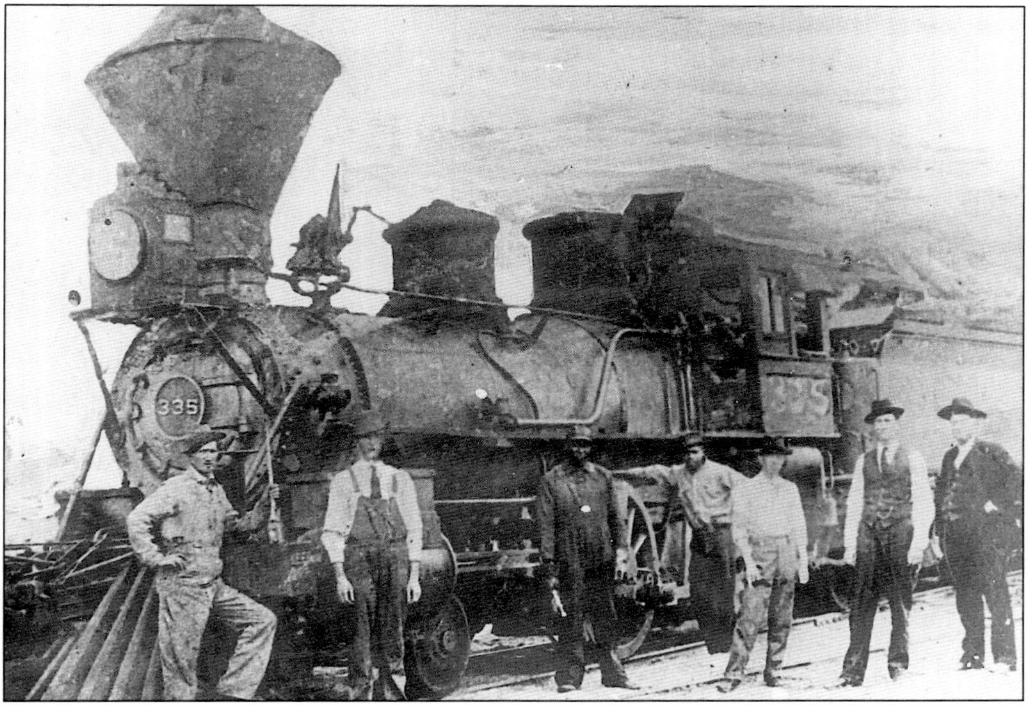

The Seaboard furnished engines and cars for the United States & West Indies subsidiary, and one of the first work trains at Sarasota (c.1902) is pictured here. On March 23, 1903, the first passenger train arrived with baggage car, day coach, and Pullman. About 50 Sarasotans witnessed the event. (The Venice Archives & Area Historical Collection.)

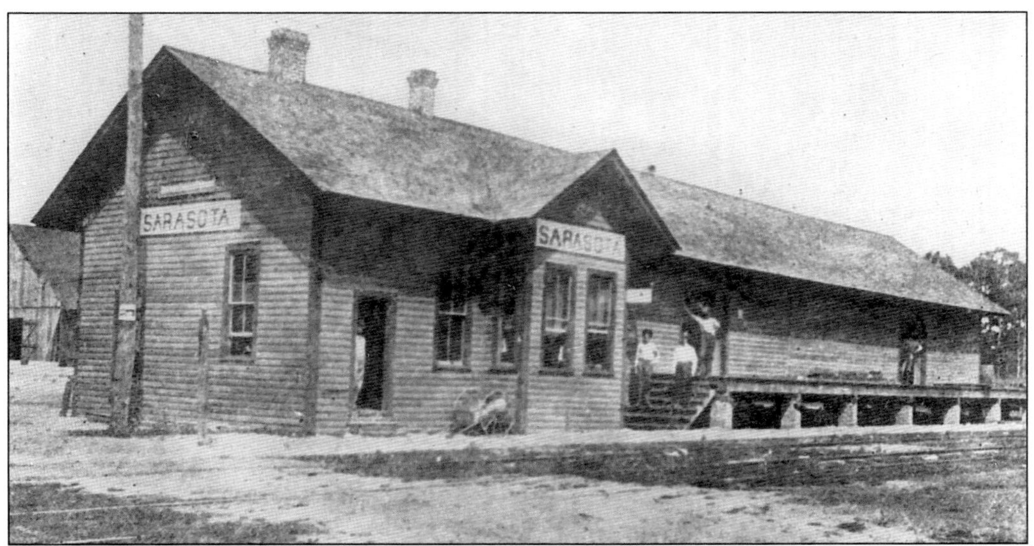

The Seaboard's freight depot at Sarasota was located "in the woods" at 7th and Lemon. When completed, only a telegraph table with instruments existed inside. A clever freight agent fashioned a desk from a bacon box and a chair from a nail keg. Armed with blankets and a kerosene lamp, he also lived in the wood structure. (Historical Resources, Sarasota County Government.)

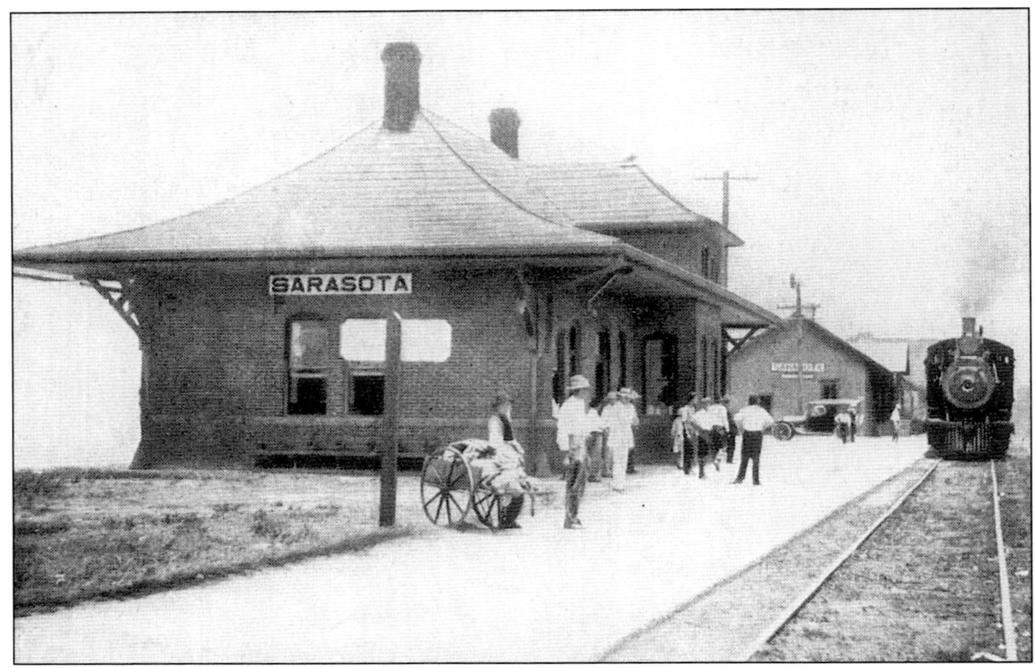

The Seaboard erected a splendid brick station at Sarasota in 1912, and in this view the freight house seen in the previous photograph is in the distance. The land upon which the buildings stood was donated, courtesy of the civic-minded Grantham family. (Historical Resources, Sarasota County Government.)

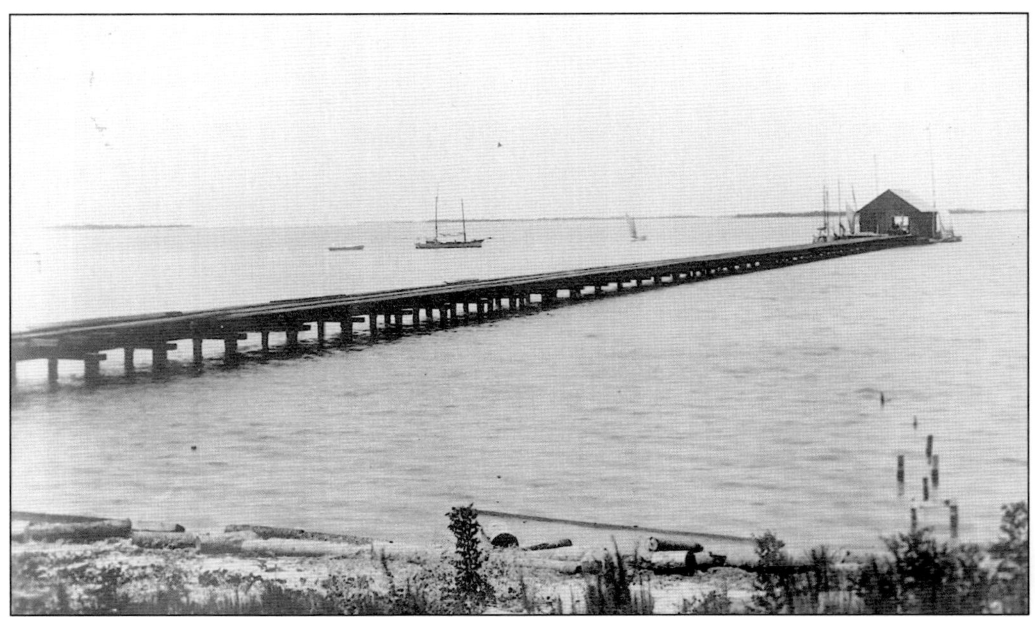

Eager to have a boat connection, the Seaboard's track at Sarasota was extended past the depot grounds to Hog Creek, where a dock was installed. Carloads of fish, vegetables, citrus, and lumber were shipped or received. (Historical Resources, Sarasota County Government.)

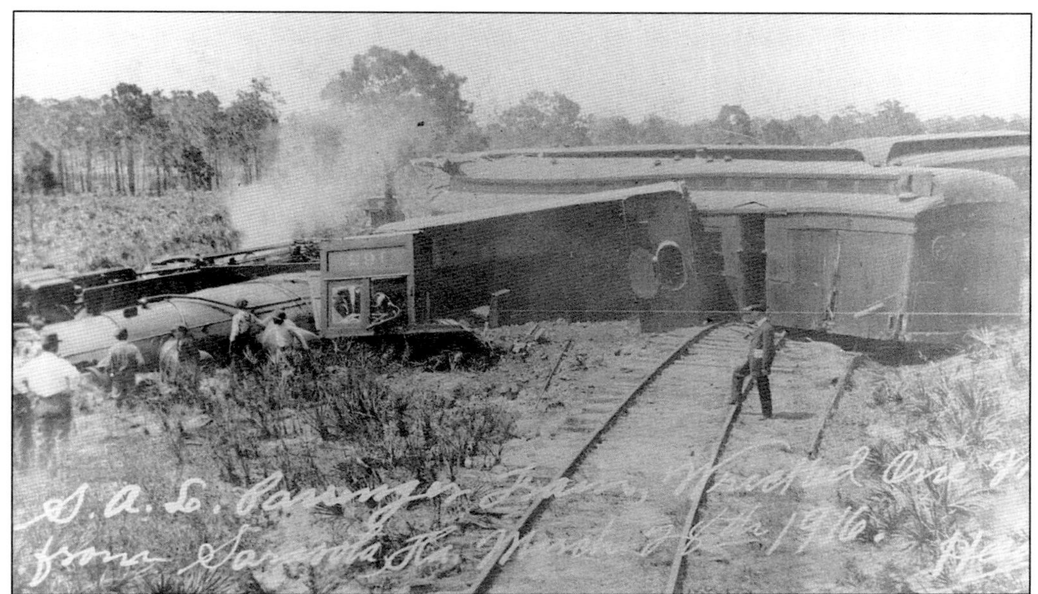

Seaboard train No. 501 was wrecked at Sarasota on March 28, 1916, because someone left a switch half-opened. Result? The front of the engine went one way, the driving wheels went another. Then, the engine lurched over on its side and coaches jacknifed. Whereas the engineer escaped serious injuries, the fireman, pinned under the engine's firebox, was badly scalded. Miraculously, no one was killed. (Historical Resources, Sarasota County Government.)

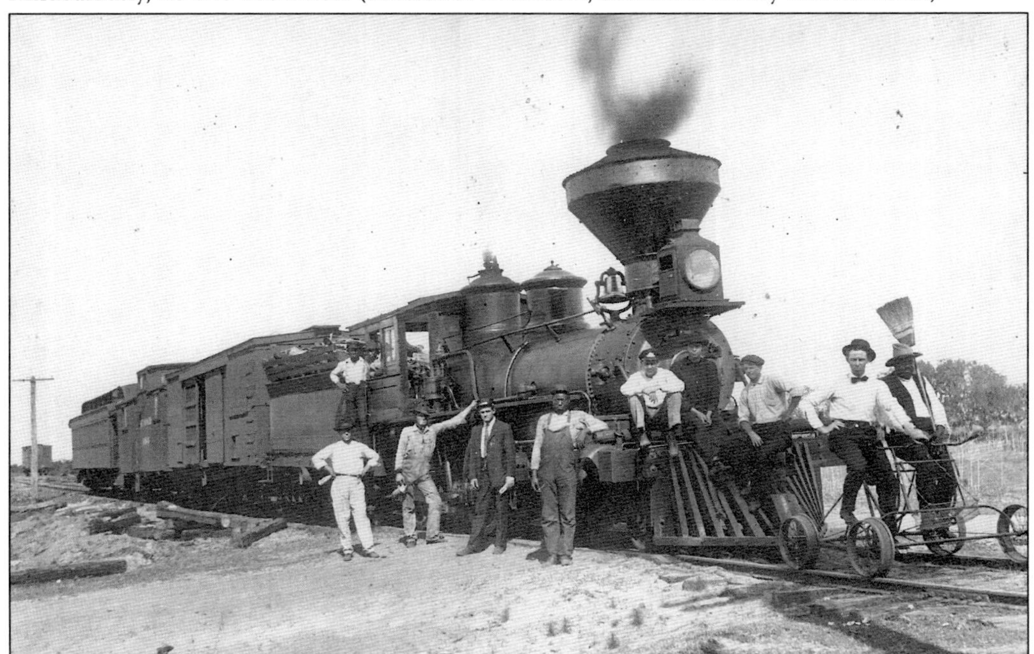

Both freight and passengers were carried on Seaboard's "Vegetable Mixed." It stopped at farm fields and platforms for carts of vegetables. In this 1908 scene, a velocipede precedes the slow-moving consist. At road crossings, the track employee with a broom would jump off and sweep debris off the rails. (Historical Resources, Sarasota County Government.)

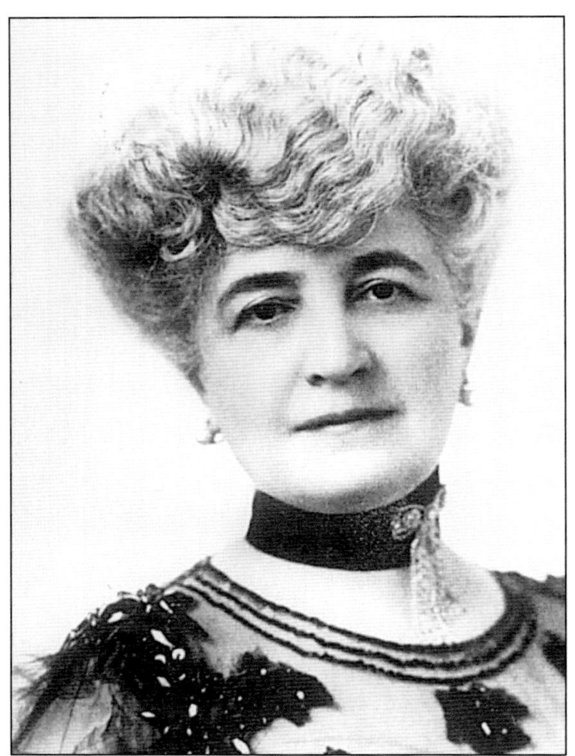

Bertha Honore Palmer chartered a Pullman car and came to Sarasota from Chicago in 1910. So impressed with the region, she purchased more than 60,000 acres of land, much of it bayfront, including what is now Venice Beach. But the sale hinged on the Seaboard extending itself from Sarasota to Venice. The request, once received, was instantly approved. (Historical Resources, Sarasota County Government.)

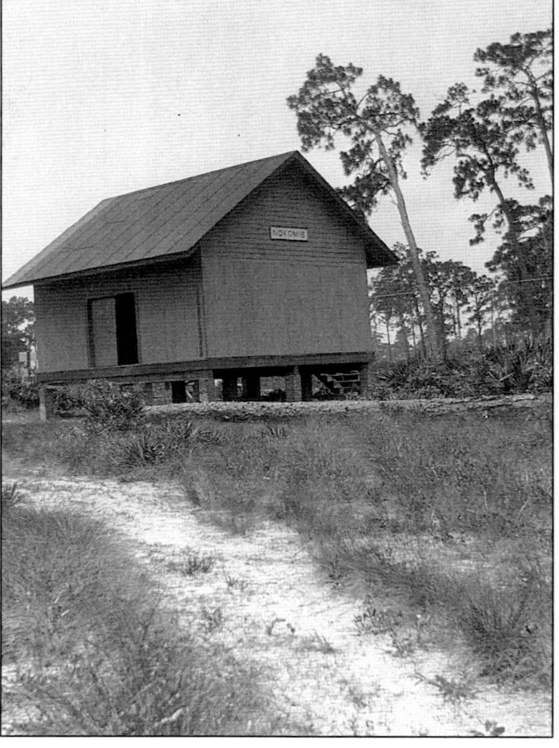

Functional structures dot every railroad landscape, and the freight house at Nokomis, located on Colonial Lane East, was no exception. Boxes, crates, and packages, containing all manner of goods, were both shipped and received. In reality, it was in freight traffic that the Seaboard made its real money, not in passengers. (The Venice Archives & Area Historical Collection.)

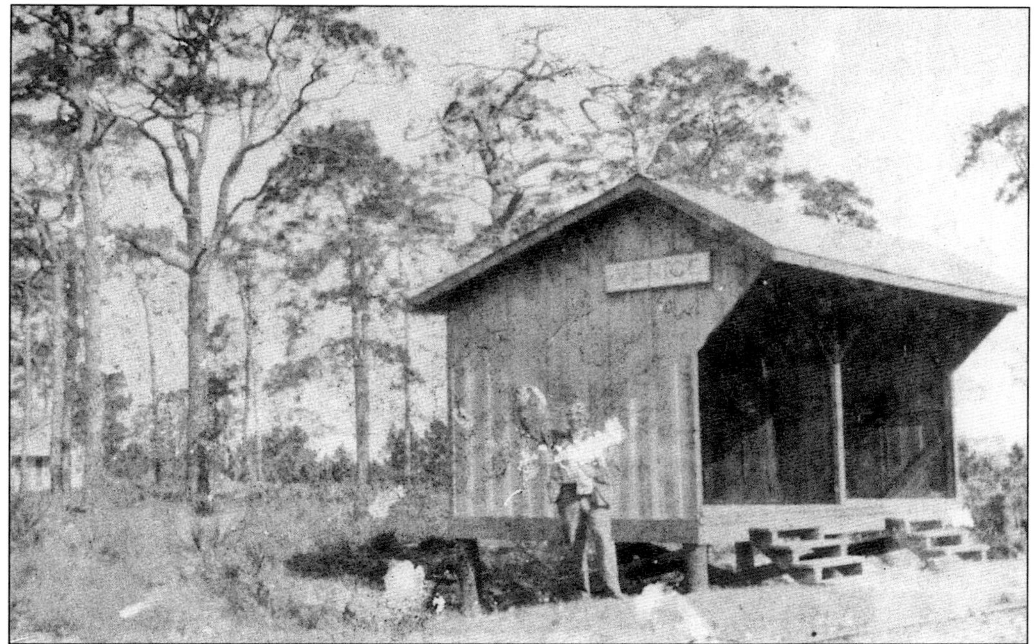

Hard to imagine today, the first Venice depot sat in a veritable wilderness. About 25 families resided in the area when the Seaboard Railroad arrived. The small, shed-like structure had two sets of steps and a partition, which separated white and black passengers. (The Venice Archives & Area Historical Collection.)

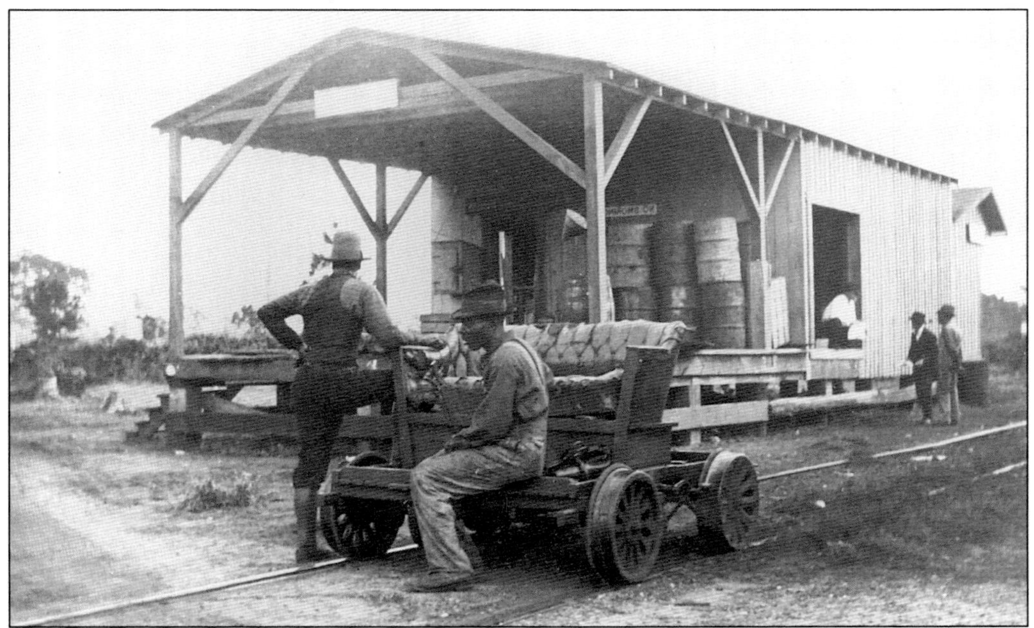

As Venice expanded, so did the depot. A freight shed and platform has been grafted onto the backside of the structure seen in the previous image. Track workers are seen resting after pumping the velocipede. Seaboard officials—likely on an inspection visit—chat in the background with the station agent. (The Venice Archives & Area Historical Collection.)

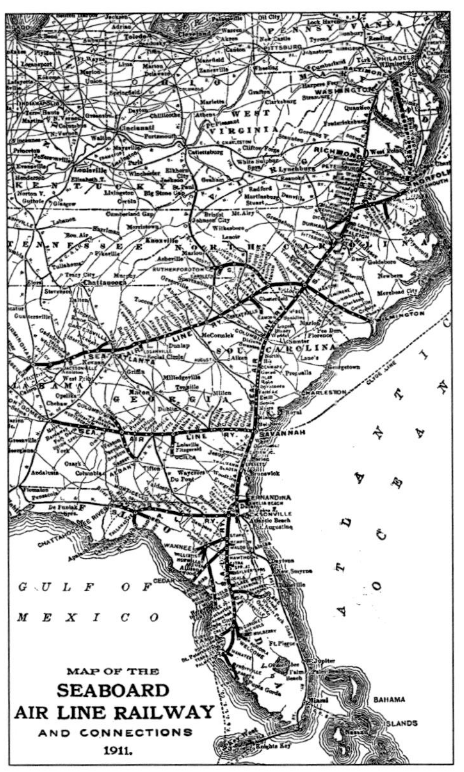

The Seaboard's extension to Venice is evident in this system map of 1911. At the moment, Venice is the southernmost point of the railroad, however all of this will change during the Florida land Boom of the 1920s. On the opposite side of the state, the Florida East Coast continues to dominate rail affairs, and the careful observer will see its rails marching across the Florida Keys.

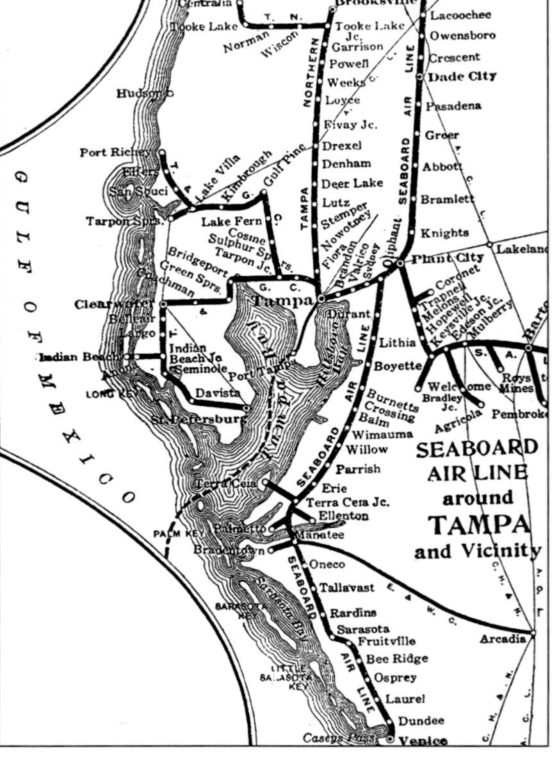

Upon this local Seaboard map is the station of "Dundee." Originally this locale was called Venice. But Bertha Honore Palmer wanted her new community—at the end of the rail line—named Venice as well. Residents of "old" Venice saw red. Mrs. Palmer suggested that they use the name "Potter." It briefly stuck, but was later changed to Dundee. Finally, after years of haggling, townspeople chose the name "Nokomis."

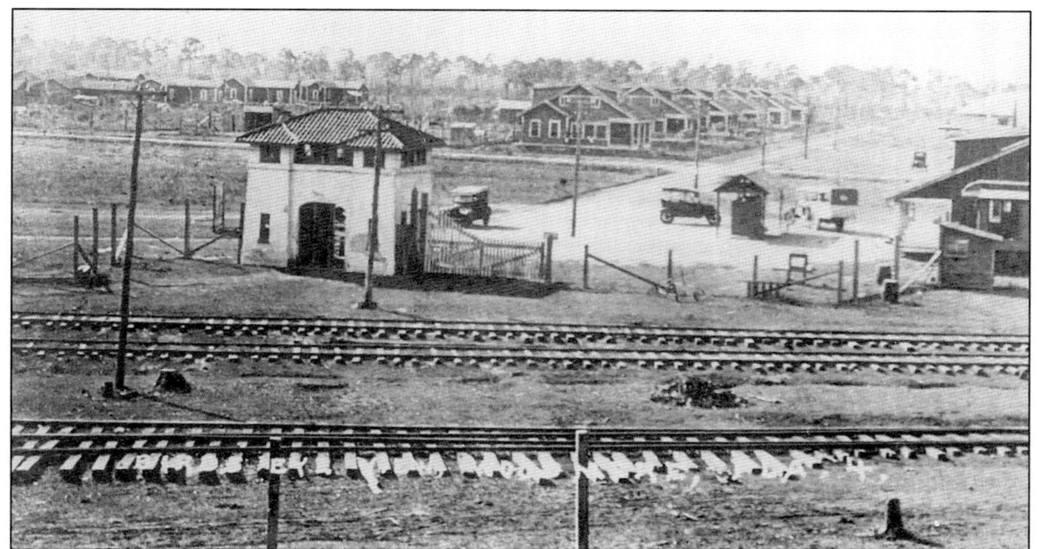

An electric fence surrounded the logging town of Woodmere, and workers could not leave or enter the property after 9 p.m. Long-leaf pine was harvested and milled, then sent over Seaboard rails to Tampa where ships awaited. The complex was located off state route 776, near today's Englewood Disposal Company. (The Venice Archives & Area Historical Collection.)

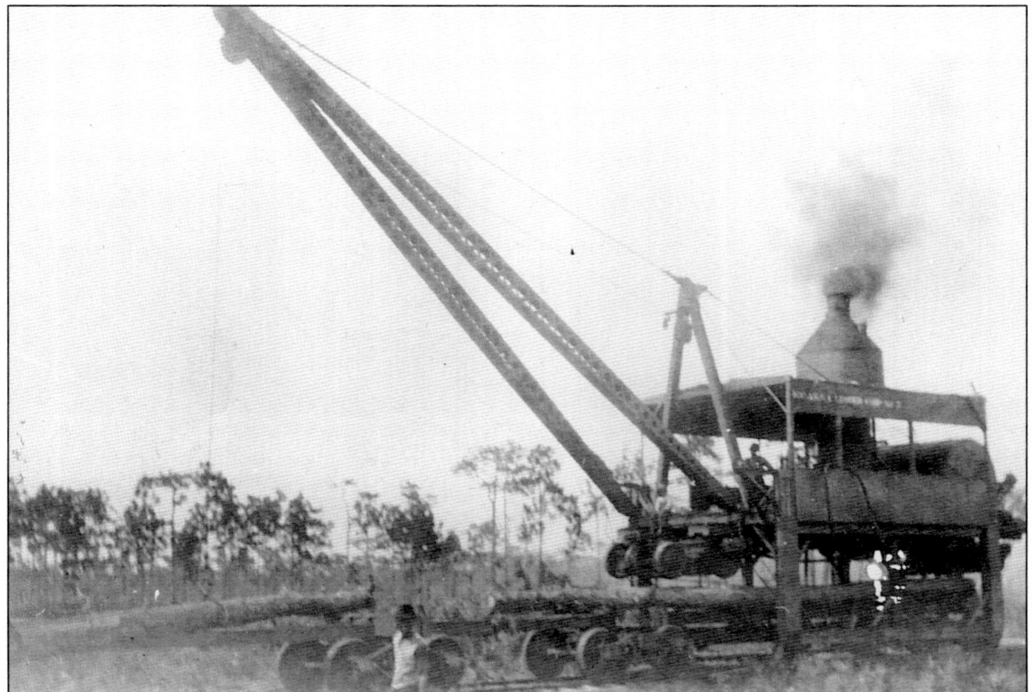

A steam-operated McGifford Log Loader at Woodmere is arranging logs on wheel sets. Once loaded, a narrow gauge engine will couple on and take the consist to the millhouse. In 1921, Manasota Lumber sold out to Nocatee-Manatee Lumber and the mill town of Manasota became known as Woodmere. (The Venice Archives & Area Historical Collection.)

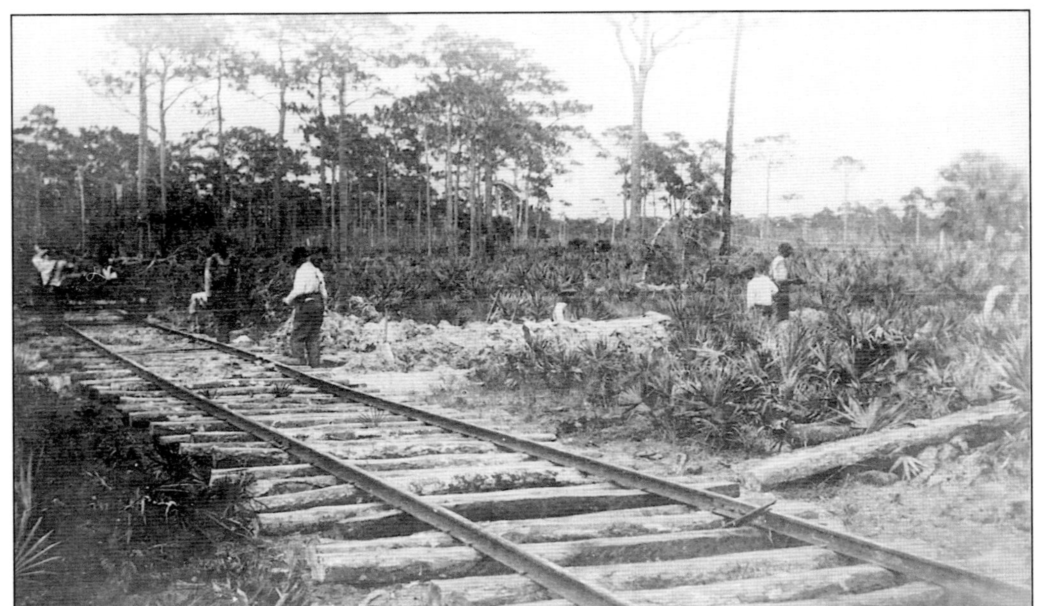

Logging tracks penetrated the piney woods around Woodmere. After an area was exhausted ("cutover"), the tracks were taken apart and laid anew elsewhere. Dimensioned cross-ties (under the rails) were infrequently used since a ready supply of rough-hewn timber was at hand, as this picture suggests. Rails were directly spiked to the ties without a metal tie plate in between. (The Venice Archives & Area Historical Collection.)

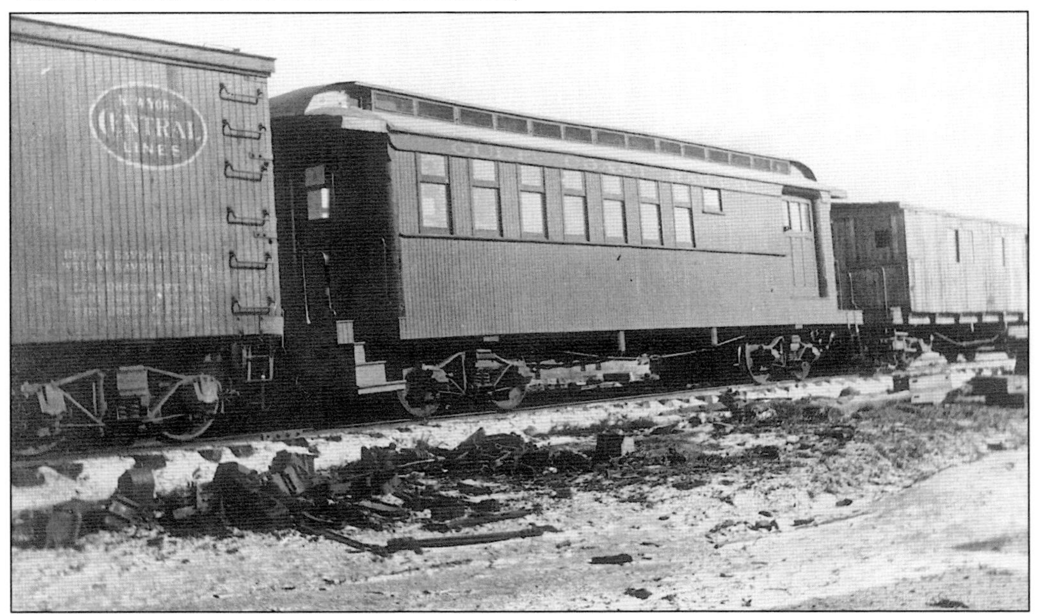

On Saturday nights a passenger train would depart Woodmere for Sarasota in order that workers could enjoy a night out and shopping. The combination coach and baggage car they rode in is pictured here. In 1930, fire destroyed the Woodmere mill. That event, along with little demand for lumber during the Depression, spelled doom. The complex was abandoned. (The Venice Archives & Area Historical Collection.)

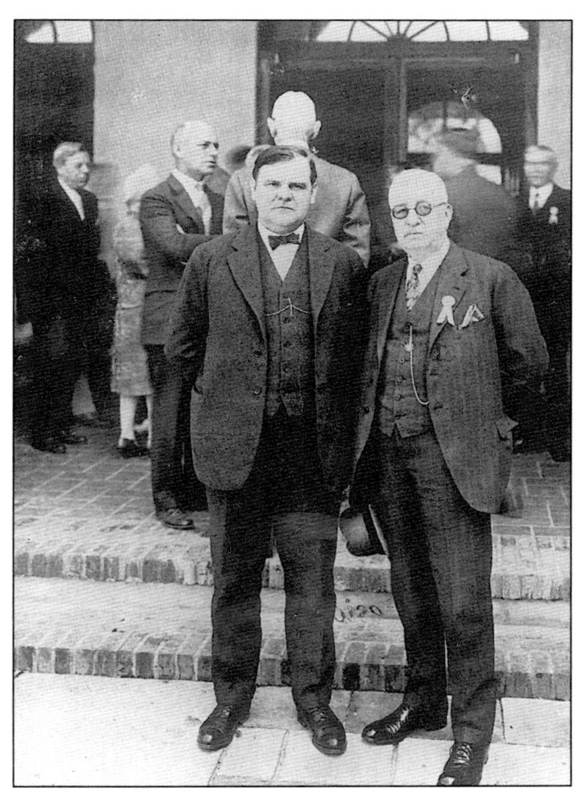

Florida Governor John W. Martin (left) poses with William B. Prenter, president of the Brotherhood of Locomotive Engineers. In 1927, when this picture was taken at Hotel Venice, serious financial problems were plaguing the Brotherhood's "ready-made" city. Later, at a union convention, Prenter was removed from office. (The Venice Archives & Area Historical Collection.)

New York architects Walker and Gillette drew plans for a new Venice station, paid for by the Brotherhood. The Mediterranean Revival building cost $47,500, and was built by Fuller Construction Company. Timbers came from Brotherhood holdings in Venice. Seaboard trains arrived the new structure March 27, 1927. (Betty Arnall, Creator of the City of Venice Archival Collection.)

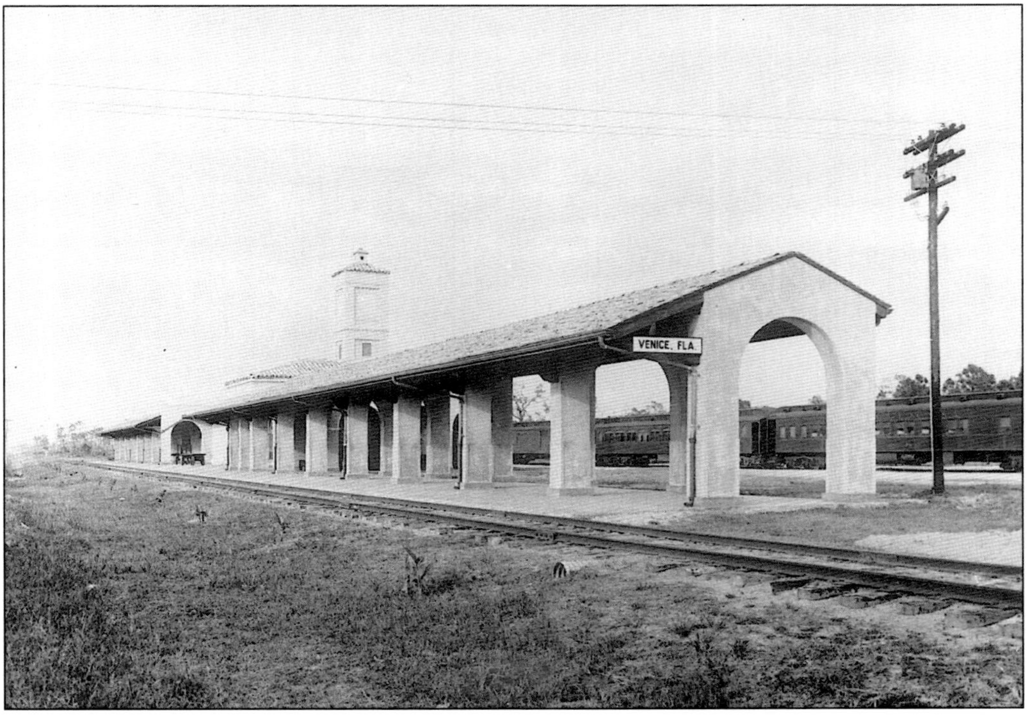

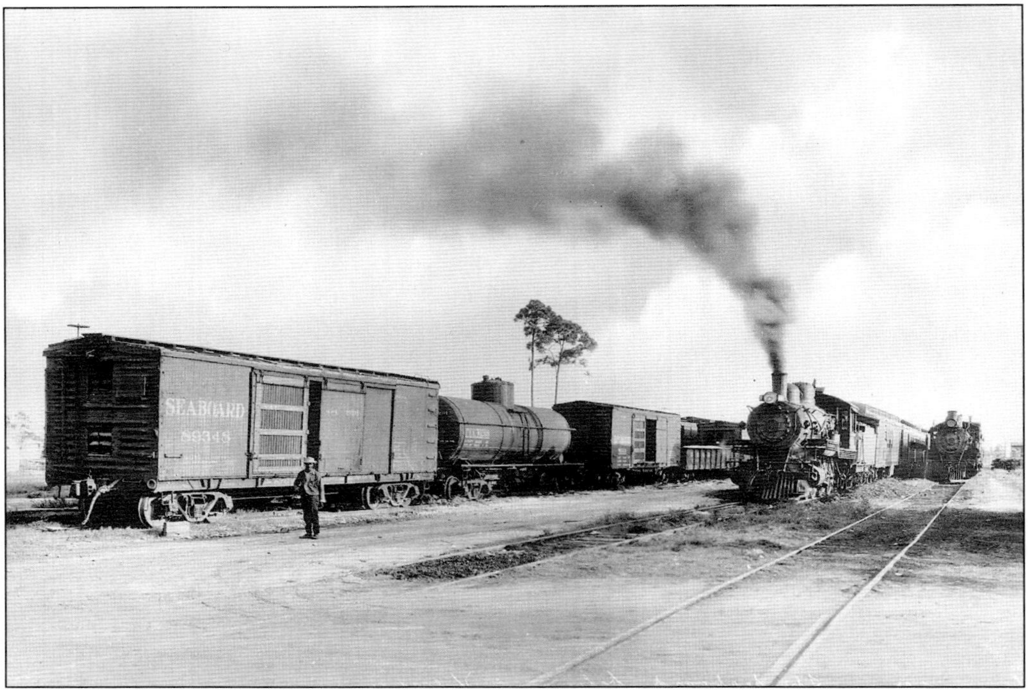

A Seaboard passenger train leaves the Venice rail yards in this 1927 scene. South of the complex and city proper was a wye track, which permitted engines to be turned around for the run back to Sarasota. The box car at left is equipped with ventilated slats and accommodated vegetables or citrus. (The Venice Archives & Area Historical Collection.)

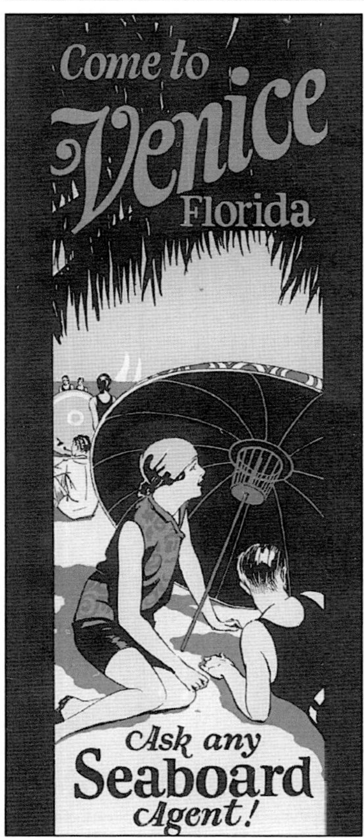

Railroads distributed countless travel brochures to the public that focused on a particular area served by the company. They contained pictures, historical sketches, information about attractions, and train schedules. Today, such "paper" is highly prized by collectors, and a single piece can often fetch hundreds of dollars. (Railway & Locomotive Historical Society.)

Three

Finally Fort Myers

"A great many of our citizens have lost faith in the building of the extension of the Atlantic Coast Line Railroad from Punta Gorda to this place. Don't be in too much of a hurry, gentlemen, the road is coming all right."

—*Fort Myers Press*, September 25, 1902

The history of Fort Myers has been forever linked with the gently curving Caloosahatchee River. Sloops, schooners, and steamboats once called in here, and often departed with cargoes of sugar, molasses, alligator and animal hides, bird plumes, and even cigars. Down river, at Punta Rassa, countless cattle were once coaxed into ships and sent to the Confederate war machine, Cuba, and northern markets.

Vessels also conveyed people. At Punta Rassa you could board a schooner for Key West, then take a Mallory Line boat up the Atlantic seaboard. Schooners also sailed to Tampa, where a mail boat awaited for Cedar Key. There, a train of the cross-state railroad conveyed passengers to Fernandina where northern connections could be made. Although a vessel—sail or steam—might leave when scheduled, its actual arrival at another port was always subject to conditions at sea and the vagaries of weather.

What the City of Palms lacked in the 19th century was railroad service. Town fathers tried to convince the Florida Southern to terminate here in 1885, but Henry Plant selected Trabue (Punta Gorda) instead. In May 1889, the DeSoto, Fort Myers and Gulf promised to link DeSoto County with Fort Myers and "some point on the Gulf in said Lee County." Colonel W.N. Haldeman, publisher of the Louisville *Courier-Journal*, championed its cause and believed that a rail line would help his struggling colony of Naples. But it was never built. Neither was the DeSoto, Lee and Gulf, or the Jacksonville and Tampa Bay Improved Railway, nor the Southern Florida & Gulf Coast. The latter, promoted by Chicago streetcar millionaire John A. Roach, would have connected Punta Rassa and Fort Myers with Lake Okeechobee and Fort Pierce.

In January 1896, an executive of the Plant System hinted that if Lee County would donate $40,000, a railroad might be provided. "I believe that Mr. Plant would entertain such a proposition," said Vice-President D.F. Jack, "as he has already acted favorably on such an inducement in Alabama." But a youthful Lee County could not afford such a sum.

Plant died in 1899, and three years later the 2,235-mile Plant System of rails was sold to the Atlantic Coast Line. The latter ended up paying Plant's heirs $17,657,398, plus it assumed all Plant System debt, which amounted to $28,906,500.

Sensing a propitious moment, Fort Myers banker Walter G. Langford started writing Coast Line officials about extending their Charlotte Harbor Division. The persistence paid off, and in July 1902, the company's construction engineer visited the City of Palms "to look the situation over." A favorable report was subsequently transmitted to the railroad's directors, who, in early August, announced that they would extend the line if Fort Myers would furnish a right-of-way through town plus a depot site. A Board of Trade was promptly formed for the tasks, and a depot and wharf site was secured at Monroe Street, Fort Myers, for $6,000.

G.S. Baxter & Company of Jacksonville was named general contractor for the $309,000 project. In March 1903, the cutting of vegetation began along the 28-mile line, and by June 12 carloads of rails had arrived at Punta Gorda.

A subject of no little importance was how the Coast Line would cross the wide expanse of the Caloosahatchee River. Several approaches were examined, but the one selected was located upstream using Beautiful Island. Bridge crews were dispatched to the scene and a pile driver was brought in from Tampa. Because the island lay in the middle of the river, extensive trestle work was required on both sides of the drawbridge. The American Bridge Company built the 138-foot swing span, which was made of steel. The railroad itself was actually completed to the river before the drawbridge was ready. By building a temporary pier on the north bank, the citrus harvest of 1903 was accepted at the structure and placed into awaiting rail cars.

Four depots were constructed on the Fort Myers extension: Alligator Creek (near Acline Road), Daughtrey Creek (Slater), Tice (East Fort Myers), and the one at Monroe Street.

Rails reached the Monroe Street depot on February 20, 1904. That day jubilant citizens draped the town flag on engine 499 of the Coast Line work train together with bunches of flowers. In fact, several ladies made their way into the locomotive cab and pulled the bell rope and whistle cord. The last spike was tapped into place by Mrs. James E. Hendry Sr., whereupon the crowd cheered, boat whistles blew, church bells rang, and a cannon was fired. Mrs. T.J. Evans distributed sandwiches to the railroad workers along with sausages, cookies, and homemade candy while area businessmen handed out oranges, cigars, and cheroots.

The first regularly scheduled train on the Coast Line arrived from Punta Gorda on May 10, 1904, and consisted of three passenger coaches and two flat cars of lumber. Twenty-five people stepped off, and in the late afternoon it left for Charlotte Harbor with 80 boxes of fruit and the first northbound passenger, who got off at nearby Tice. Mail started to arrive by train in mid-June, about the time the new railroad wharf was completed near Monroe Street. On July 11, a gala excursion train from Bartow arrived in town with over 1,700 people. Later in the year, circus trains and theater companies started to roll in by rail.

The "Coming of the Railroad" sparked a renaissance in Fort Myers. New buildings were erected and residents agitated for paved streets, sidewalks, a fire engine company, sewers, and water mains. The railroad also spurred new industry. Freshwater fish caught in Lake Okeechobee was brought to Fort Myers, and sent north by rail. Later, saltwater varieties were dispatched. The railroad also proved a blessing to citrus and vegetable growers as trains could convey products faster and farther than any boat line. Prior to the Coast Line's arrival, the population of Fort Myers was 943 persons; by 1910 it stood at 2,463.

It took the Atlantic Coast Line several years to perfect the routes and facilities of the Plant System in Florida. During that time, the company occasionally heard from disgruntled persons, such as Philip Isaacs, editor of a Fort Myers newspaper and secretary of the Fort Myers Board of Trade. In 1905, Isaacs reprimanded officials about the general condition of the Charlotte Harbor Division. Too many crossties, he said, were rotten and rail spikes could be pulled out "with the fingers." He also fumed about the dirty and dusty condition of passenger coaches. Frequently they lacked lights and drinking water, making it "intolerable for ladies to be compelled to ride in."

Fortunately an ambitious program was already underway to improve Coast Line properties in Florida, including the Charlotte Harbor Division. But the railroad story of Fort Myers did not cease then. A new chapter would be written in the Florida land Boom of the 1920s.

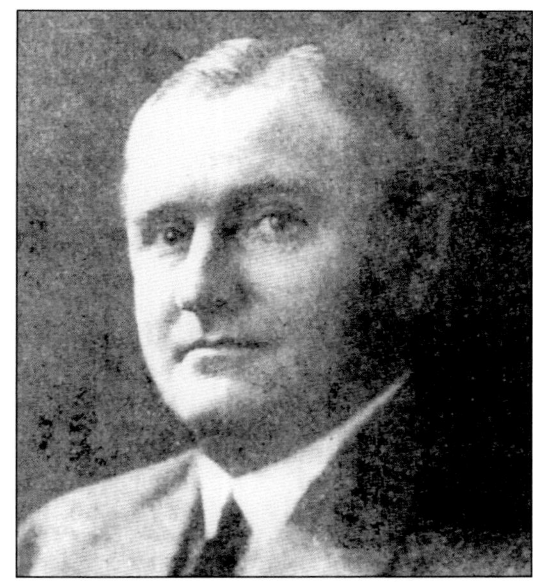

Walter G. Langford helped develop extensive grapefruit groves at Deep Lake in Collier County. But he is best remembered as having convinced officials of the Atlantic Coast Line Railroad to extend its line from Punta Gorda south to the City of Palms. He also organized the First National Bank of Fort Myers. (Fort Myers Historical Museum.)

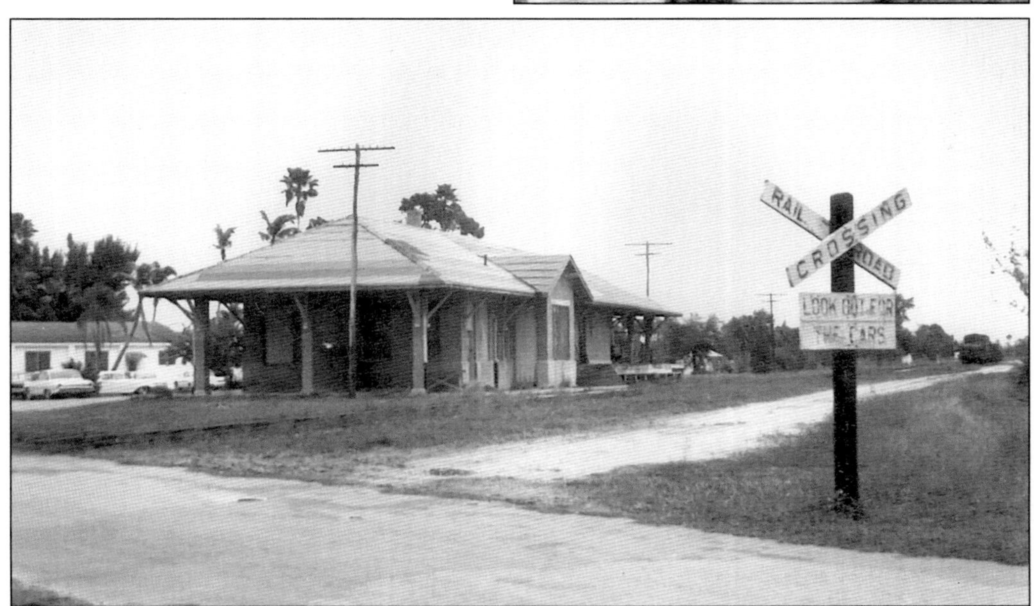

Acline station, formerly called Alligator Creek, was located in South Punta Gorda. The name was an acronym for Atlantic Coast Line. In days of old a turpenstine still existed in the area as well as a sawmill, citrus groves, and the "Bloody Bucket" speakeasy. The structure seen here burned in 1964, but Acline Road survives. (Fort Myers Historical Museum.)

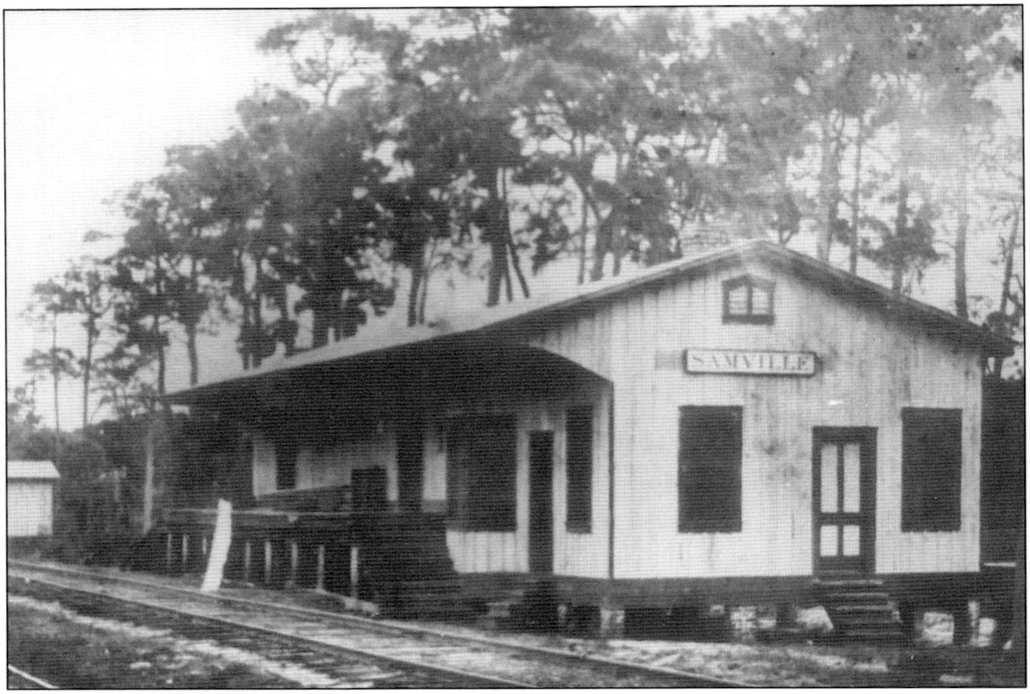

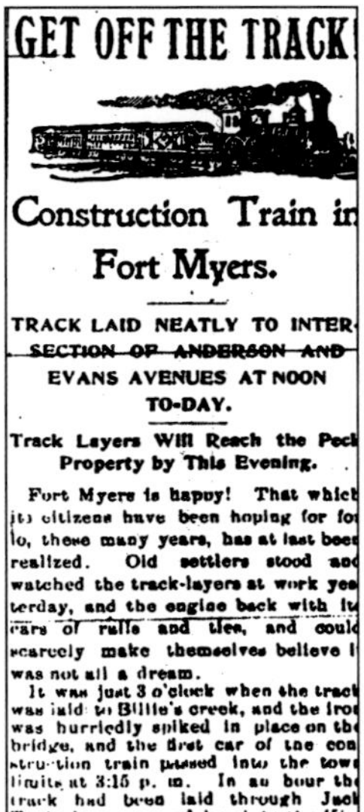

GET OFF THE TRACK!

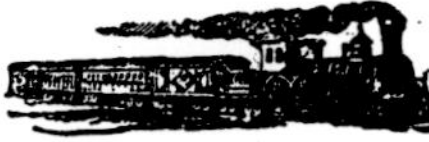

Construction Train in Fort Myers.

TRACK LAID NEATLY TO INTERSECTION OF ANDERSON AND EVANS AVENUES AT NOON TO-DAY.

Track Layers Will Reach the Peck Property by This Evening.

Fort Myers is happy! That which its citizens have been hoping for lo, these many years, has at last been realized. Old settlers stood and watched the track-layers at work yesterday, and the engine back with its cars of rails and ties, and could scarcely make themselves believe it was not all a dream.

It was just 3 o'clock when the track was laid to Billie's creek, and the iron was hurriedly spiked in place on the bridge, and the first car of the construction train passed into the town limits at 3:15 p. m. In an hour the track had been laid through Jack Taylor's grove, and by night the Kinze property had been reached.

This morning the crew were at work again, and at noon the track and train were within a quarter of a mile of the intersection of Evans and Anderson avenues, at which corner the line curves, and comes down to Monroe street, parallel with Anderson avenue. The track layers will reach the Peck property by night, and should reach the heart of town on Monroe street by to-morrow night, at which time it is proposed to drape the engine with the stars and stripes. Conductor Hugh A. Simmons has the honor of running the first train into Fort Myers, and M. E. Moye is at the throttle of the locomotive. Capt. Kilpatrick is chief foreman of the construction gang. It is likely that there will be an impromptu celebration when the train reaches

Samville was named for North Fort Myers cattleman Samuel Williams. It was briefly known as "Woodrow" in honor of president Woodrow Wilson, then reverted to Samville by 1925. Later, the name "Bayshore" was adopted. Three miles north of the Samville depot was Slater (Daugherty Creek). Both station buildings were built by the Coast Line in 1905 as well as the one at Tice. (Railroad Museum of South Florida Collection.)

There was a time when newspapers chronicled most any railroad event, as this *Fort Myers Press* article of February 11, 1904, attests. Progress reports of a new line were rendered on a weekly basis, and of course the railroads rarely objected to the free publicity. Because Fort Myers had waited decades for the Iron Horse, the excitement reached fever pitch.

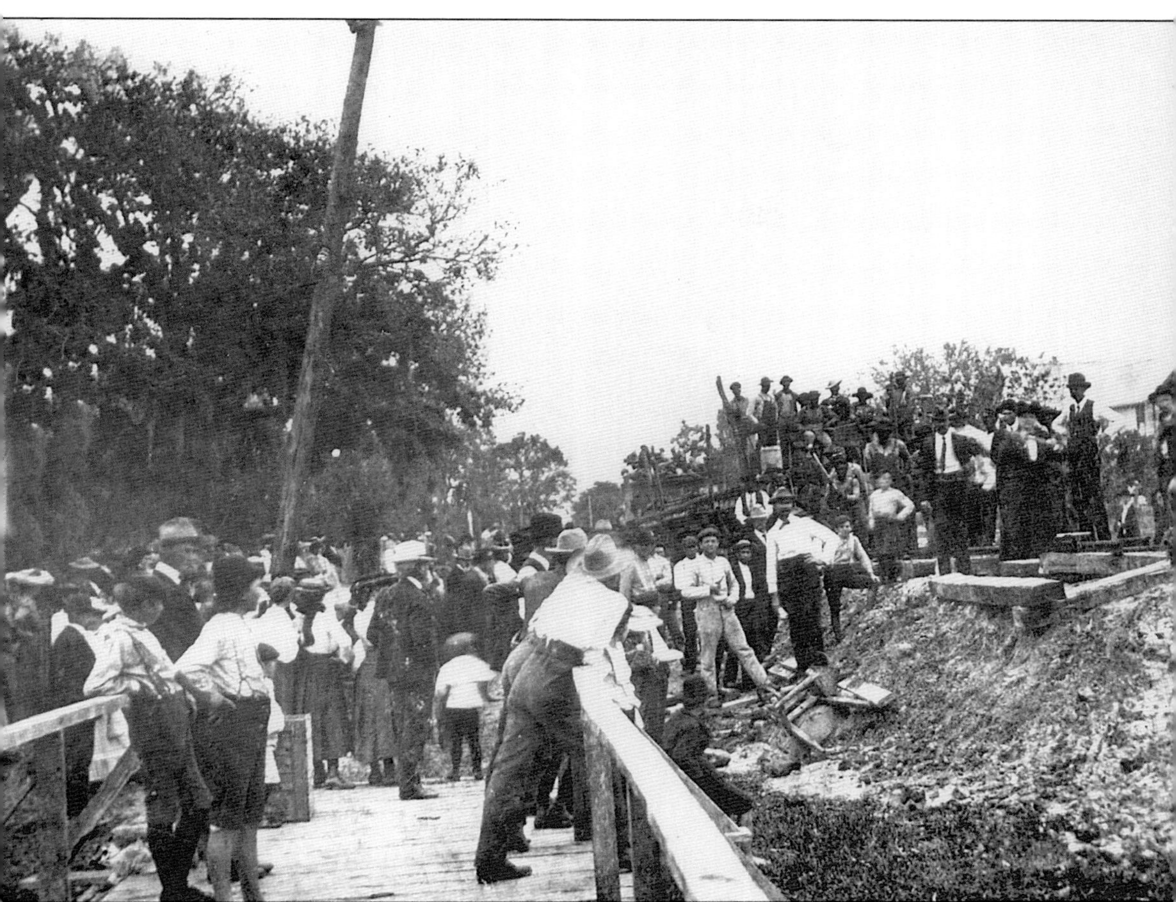

Mrs. James (Julia) Hendry, Sr.—a former "Miss Tampa"—drove home the last spike at Fort Myers, and the crowd approved. Church bells rang; a cannon boomed. Celebrants then clamored aboard flat cars of the construction train, and an obliging crew treated all to a free jaunt. (Fort Myers Historical Museum.)

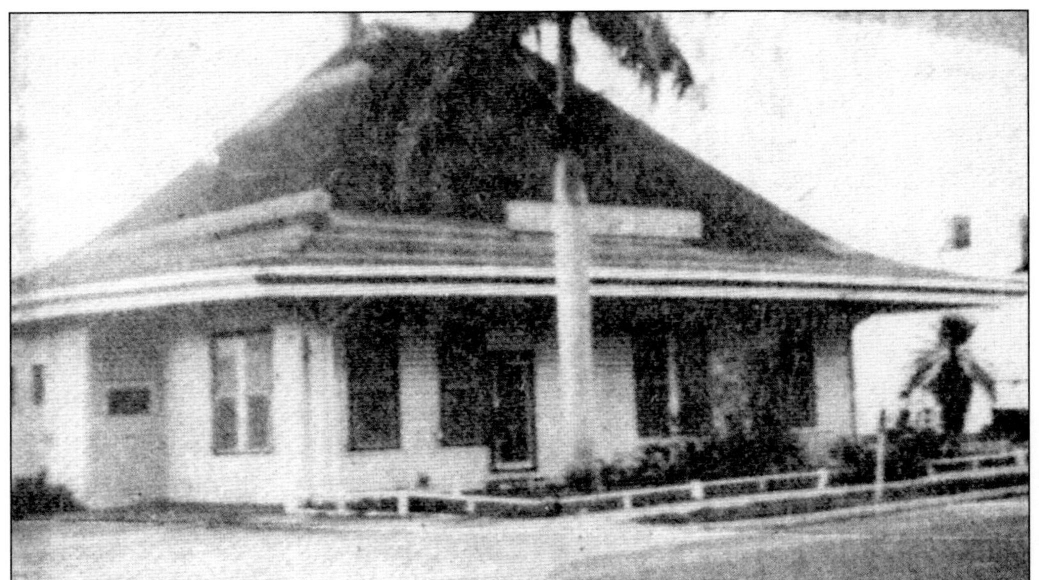

At Main and Monroe Streets in Fort Myers the Atlantic Coast Line built the above depot. Near it, freight facilities were erected plus docks on the Caloosahatchee River. The pagoda-like building stood until the 1960s. (Fort Myers Historical Museum.)

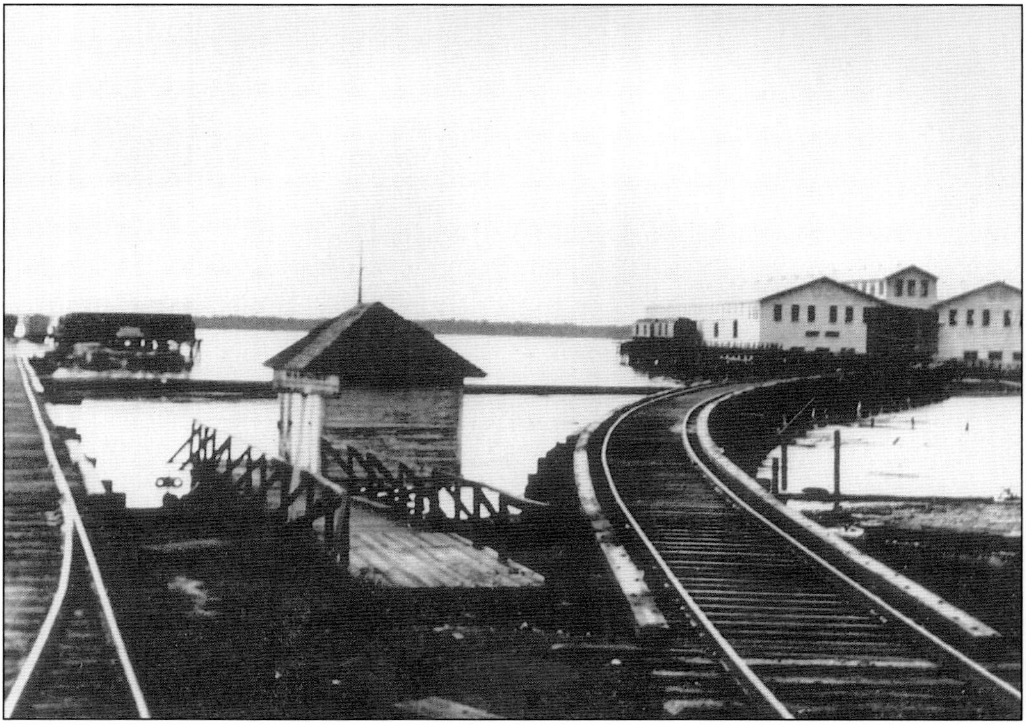

A network of rails serviced the Caloosahatchee River waterfront at Fort Myers. Some tracks were installed on piling and made their way to packing houses. In decades past, a considerable traffic of citrus and fish arrived by water and left by rail. (Fort Myers Historical Museum.)

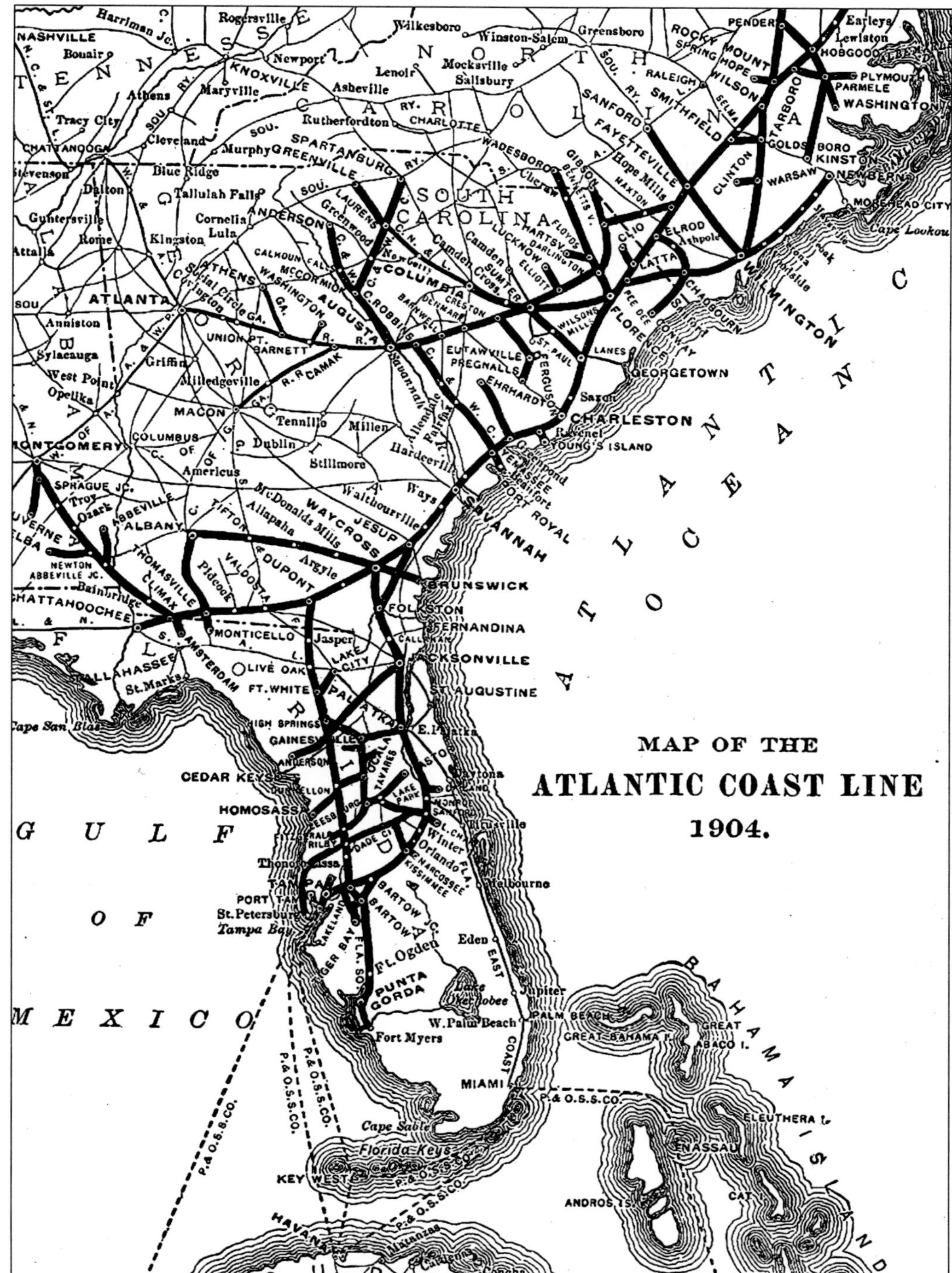

Until the Florida land Boom of the 1920s, Fort Myers was the southernmost point of the Atlantic Coast Line system. The company itself was a consolidation of over 100 railroads. William Walters and Benjamin Newcomer, merchant and banker respectively of Baltimore, had carefully assembled the empire, which now included the Plant System of rails.

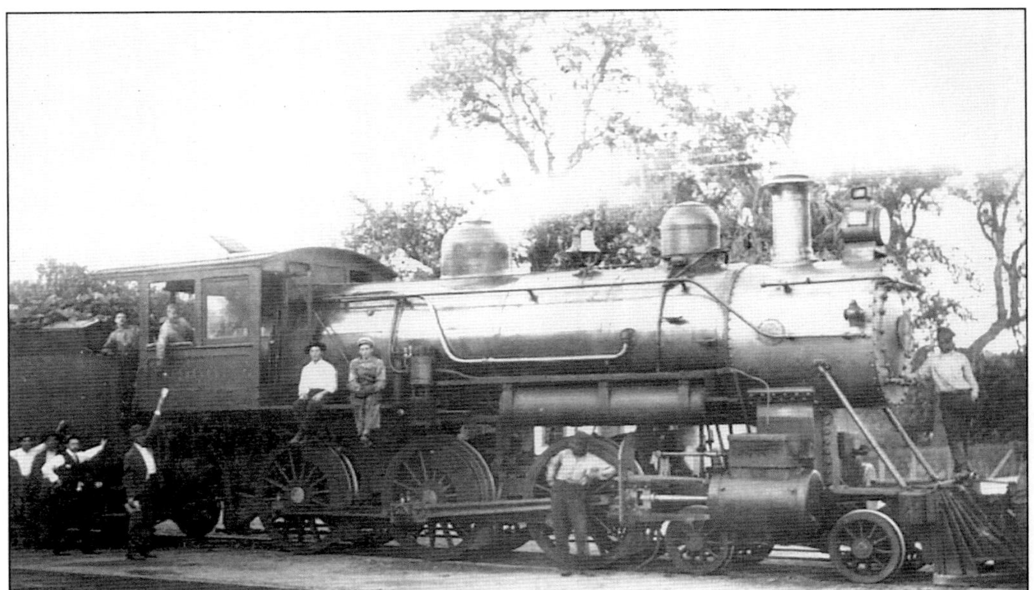

Coast Line employees gather around a Baldwin-built, 70-ton, coal-burning locomotive, the first of its kind to arrive in Fort Myers. Nicknamed a "copperhead" because its smokebox area was sheathed in copper, it represented the latest and fastest passenger engine design.

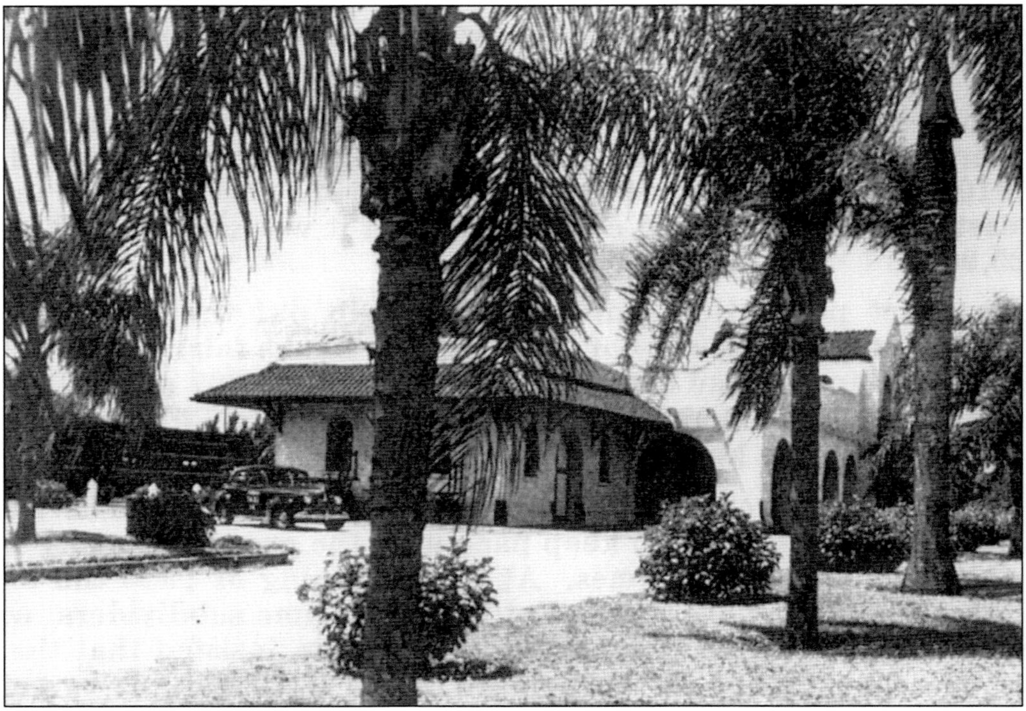

The Peck Street, Fort Myers station—designed by Coast Line architect Alpheus M. Griffin—opened in 1924 and cost $48,293 to construct. Inside this "little temple of commerce" there were waiting rooms and bathrooms for white and black patrons. Today it houses the Fort Myers Historical Museum, which supplied this image.

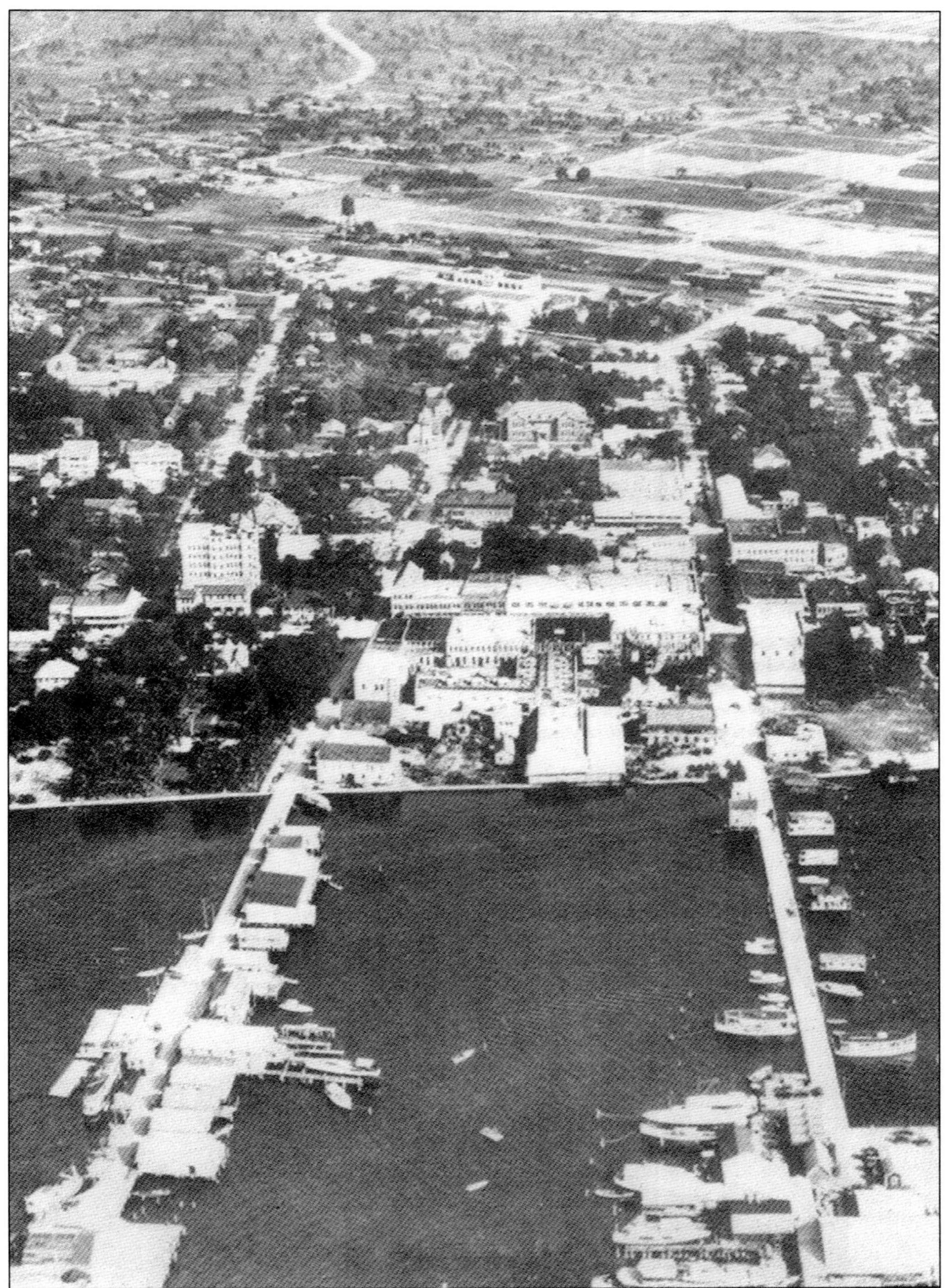

This aerial view (c. 1927) of Fort Myers depicts a busy waterfront. In the center background, near a water tower, the careful observer can spot the recently completed Peck Street station of the Coast Line described in the previous photograph. (Fort Myers Historical Museum.)

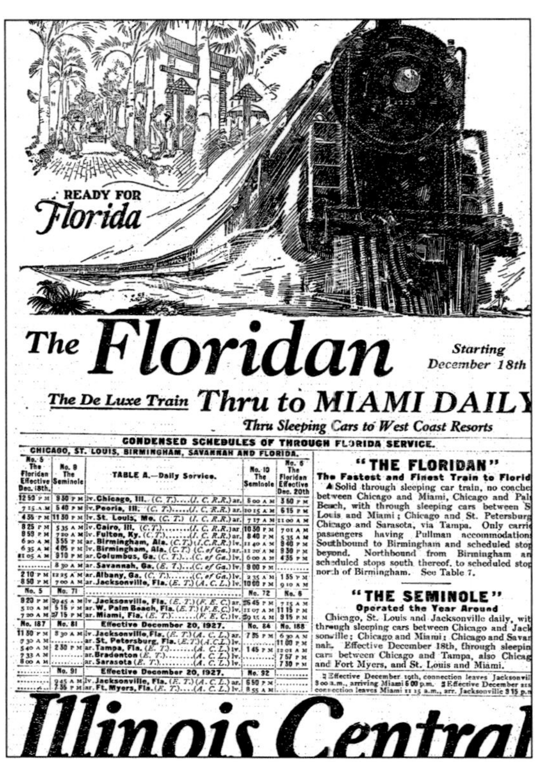

CHICAGO, ST. LOUIS, BIRMINGHAM, SAVANNAH AND FLORIDA.

No. 5 The Floridan Effective Dec. 18th.	No. 9 The Seminole	TABLE A.—Daily Service.	No. 10 The Seminole	No. 6 The Floridan Effective Dec. 20th
12 50 P M	9 30 P M	lv. Chicago, Ill. (C. T.)....(I. C. R.R.) ar.	8 00 A M	3 50 P M
7 15 A M	5 40 P M	lv. Peoria, Ill. (C. T.)....(I. C. R.R.) ar.	10 15 A M	6 15 P M
4 55 P M	11 30 P M	lv. St. Louis, Mo. (C. T.) (I. C. R.R.) ar.	7 17 A M	11 00 A M
8 25 P M	5 35 A M	lv. Cairo, Ill. (C. T.).......(I. C. R.R.) ar.	10 50 P M	7 01 A M
8 59 P M	7 20 A M	lv. Fulton, Ky. (C. T.).......(I. C. R.R.) ar.	8 40 P M	5 35 A M
6 20 A M	3 55 P M	ar. Birmingham, Ala. (C. T.) (I. C. R.R.) lv.	11 40 A M	9 40 P M
6 35 A M	4 05 P M	lv. Birmingham, Ala. (C. T.) (C. of Ga.) ar.	11 20 A M	9 30 P M
11 05 A M	9 10 P M	ar. Columbus, Ga. (C. T.)...(C. of Ga.) lv.	6 00 A M	4 35 P M
....	8 30 A M	ar. Savannah, Ga. (E. T.)...(C. of Ga.) lv.	9 00 P M	....
2 10 P M	12 25 A M	ar. Albany, Ga. (C. T.).......(C. of Ga.) lv.	2 35 A M	1 55 P M
8 50 P M	7 00 A M	ar. Jacksonville, Fla. (E. T.) (A. C. L.) lv.	10 00 P M	9 10 A M
No. 5	No. 71	....	No. 72	No. 6
9 20 P M	9 45 A M	lv. Jacksonville, Fla. (E. T.) (F. E. C.) ar.	6 45 P M	7 15 A M
5 10 A M	5 15 P M	ar. W. Palm Beach, Fla. (E. T.) (F. E. C.) lv.	11 07 A M	11 15 P M
7 20 A M	7 15 P M	ar. Miami, Fla. (E. T.).......(F. E. C.) lv.	9 15 A M	9 15 P M
No. 187	No. 81	Effective December 20, 1927.	No. 84	No. 188
11 30 P M	8 30 A M	lv. Jacksonville, Fla. (E. T.) (A. C. L.) ar.	7 35 P M	6 30 A M
7 30 A M	....	ar. St. Petersburg, Fla. (E. T.) (A. C. L.) lv.	....	11 00 P M
5 40 A M	2 30 P M	ar. Tampa, Fla. (E. T.).......(A. C. L.) lv.	1 45 P M	12 01 A M
7 33 A M	....	ar. Bradenton (E. T.).......(A. C. L.) lv.	....	7 57 P M
8 00 A M	....	ar. Sarasota (E. T.).........(A. C. L.) lv.	....	7 30 P M
....	No. 91	Effective December 20, 1927.	No. 92	....
....	9 45 A M	lv. Jacksonville, Fla. (E. T.) (A. C. L.) ar.	6 50 P M	....
....	7 35 P M	ar. Ft. Myers, Fla. (E. T.)...(A. C. L.) lv.	8 55 A M	....

There was a time when one could take a Coast Line train from Fort Myers to Jacksonville. There, connections could be made with many famous trains, such as "The Floridan" operated by the Illinois Central. This 1927 advertisement also confirms that a through sleeping car from "The Seminole" was brought directly down to the City of Palms.

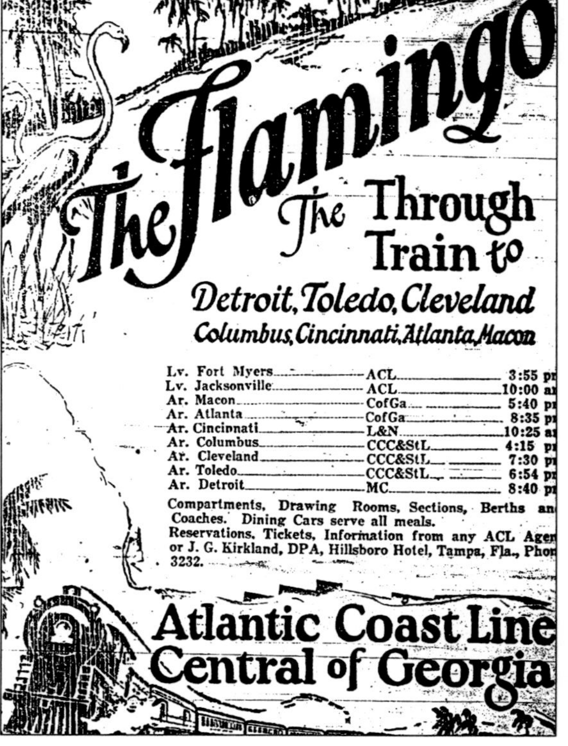

A good part of the day was needed to get from Fort Myers to Jacksonville, which was regarded as the rail nerve center of the Sunshine State. Another famous train that awaited patrons in 1925 was "The Flamingo," which utilized rails of several companies to reach Detroit, Michigan.

Four

THE COLD, HUNGRY, AND NAKED

"Boca Grande has no boom, will have no boom, and does not seek speculative investors."
—land prospectus, Charlotte Harbor & Northern Railroad, 1926

What railroad promoters found attractive about Gasparilla Island was its proximity to Cuba and South American ports. Further, Boca Grande Pass was one of the deepest water inlets in all of Florida, which meant that ships of almost any size and capacity could be accommodated at a railroad pier.

Several railroads were empowered to reach the island, long before it was discovered by society and tourists. Among them were: the Arcadia, Gulf Coast, & Lakeland, the Central Railway & Steamship Company, the Florida West Shore, and the Alafia, Manatee & Gulf Coast Railroad. The firm that won the day however was the Charlotte Harbor & Northern.

About the time future governor Albert Gilchrist was platting the new town of Boca Grande, the pebble phosphate industry was flourishing over in the Peace River Valley. Numerous firms arose to gather the commodity, which was used in the production of fertilizers. Largest of all was the Peace River Pebble Phosphate Company, founded by Joseph Hull. Hull's firm dredged the riverbed and banks for phosphate, and sent it by barge down the Peace River to Charlotte Harbor where it was loaded into ocean-going ships.

It was a labor-intensive operation, and when the Peace River was low in summertime, the phosphate was transported by Florida Southern Railway trains to Long Dock in Punta Gorda, where, again, vessels were stationed.

Among those who invested in Hull's empire was Peter B. Bradley, whose family was identified with the Bradley Fertilizer Works near Boston. In 1899, Bradley helped organize the American Agricultural Chemicals Company. The latter acquired Hull's firm along with other mines in the famed "Bone Valley" (above Arcadia) where some of the world's richest deposits of phosphate existed. What Bradley really desired, however, was a direct rail line from the phosphate mines to a deep water port.

Chartered in 1897, the Alafia, Manatee and Gulf Coast Railroad had the authority to construct a rail line from Plant City down to Charlotte Harbor. A right-of-way had been surveyed on

Gasparilla Island, and laborers had actually performed some grading. But a financial winner the Alafia road was not, and its charter was secured by Bradley's American Agricultural Chemicals Company. In 1905 the Alafia firm was renamed the Charlotte Harbor & Northern Railroad. Bradley then engaged a Tampa attorney to perfect a route on Gasparilla Island, an assignment that lead to meeting Albert Gilchrist, who had land for sale. The Boca Grande Land Company was later formed, which helped supply land for tracks, a phosphate dock, and a railroad-owned hotel that became known as the Gasparilla Inn.

Building the railroad now got down to business. The steamboat *Mistletoe* soon arrived at Boca Grande, and L.M. Fouts, a former executive of the Santa Fe Railroad, got off the vessel along with a civil engineer, surveying party, and 60 laborers. Fouts, himself, became general manager of the new railroad.

The Charlotte Harbor & Northern was to run from Gasparilla Island to Arcadia, some 49 miles away. Irish, Italian, and Greek laborers were hired for the project, who worked 12-hour days at $1 an hour. Seventy-pound (to the yard) steel rail was utilized on the new line, which could ably withstand the heavy phosphate cars.

Many water inlets were encountered along the "Boca Grande Route," and no less than 90 trestles (totaling 17,240 feet) had to be constructed. The Peace River Bridge near Arcadia was nearly one mile long. Longer still was the one over the Myakka River, which required a drawspan. Over 2 miles of trestlework plus two separate drawbridges were needed at Gasparilla Sound and Pass. The drawbridges themselves were built by the Virginia Iron Works.

Construction proceeded on both the island proper and the mainland. In July 1907 they met, and on the first day of August the Charlotte Harbor & Northern was declared open for business between Boca Grande and Arcadia. Company repair shops were established at the latter point, where a connection was made with the Atlantic Coast Line Railroad (successor to the Florida Southern). Within a month of opening, contracts were let to extend the railroad north of Arcadia to the phosphate mines located near Mulberry.

A 3,000-foot phosphate dock was constructed at South Boca Grande. At first cranes loaded the phosphate into ships, but in time a conveyor belt system was installed. An electric power plant had to be built to supply energy for the apparatus, and it was of such design to supply electrical power for the rest of Gasparilla Island—an arrangement that lasted for may decades. A small depot was also built at the dock area, allowing patrons to detrain here and board a private yacht to nearby Useppa Island.

A wood frame station existed at Park and Fourth Streets in Boca Grande proper that in 1909 was replaced with a superb edifice conceived in the Mediterranean Revival style. At the northern end of the island, at Gasparilla, another Charlotte Harbor & Northern depot was built together with two fish houses. Later the railroad installed here 16 small rental homes for the fisherfolk of Peacon Cove.

By 1917, the Charlotte Harbor & Northern possessed 11 steam locomotives, 217 freight cars, 15 passenger coaches, and 56 pieces of work equipment. The company also operated a plant at Hull which creosoted railroad ties. Another railroad venture, the Florida Townsite Company, sold land.

And of the moniker "Cold, Hungry, and Naked?" It evolved after Peter Bradley's younger brother, Robert, took control of the railroad company. His cost-cutting measures and hard-nosed personality alienated workers, who in turn coined the nickname.

In 1926, the Charlotte Harbor & Northern was leased to the Seaboard Air Line Railway. Later, the Seaboard purchased the firm and for many decades its Boca Grande Division was a vital link to the Bone Valley phosphate mines of Central Florida.

Peter B. Bradley, president of the American Agricultural Chemicals Company, had the Charlotte Harbor & Northern built to expedite the movement of phosphate from mines to a deep water port. His railroad terminated at South Boca Grande on Gasparilla Island where phosphate—a key ingredient of fertilizers—was loaded into ocean-going ships and sent around the world. (National Cyclopedia of American Biography.)

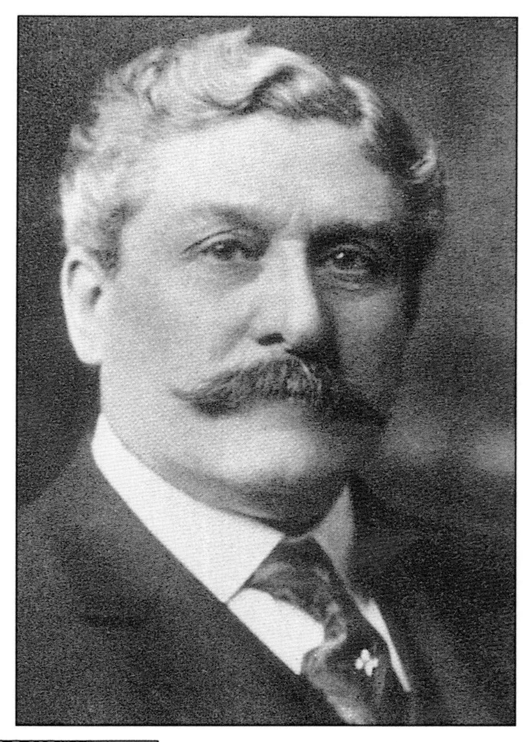

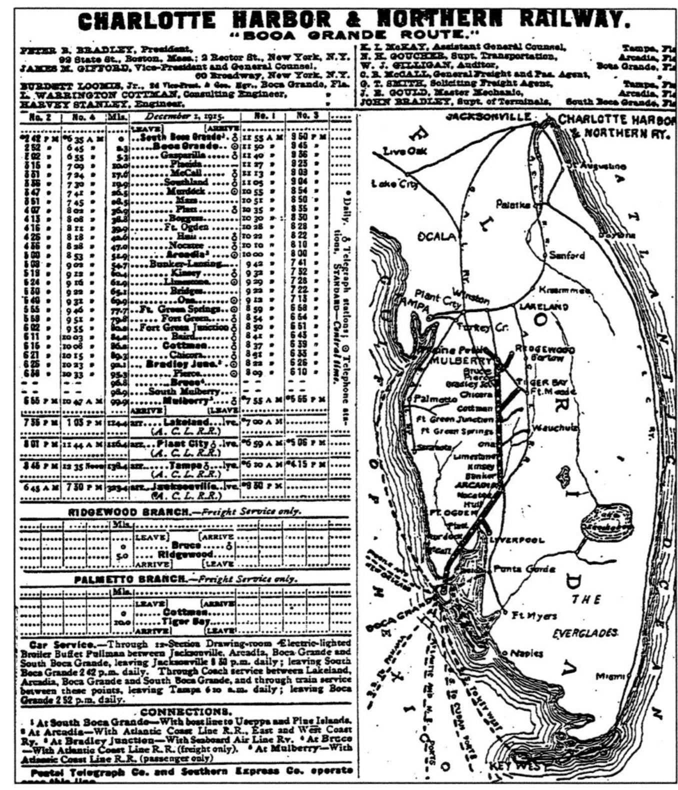

CHARLOTTE HARBOR & NORTHERN RAILWAY.
"BOCA GRANDE ROUTE."

PETER B. BRADLEY, President, 99 State St., Boston, Mass.; 2 Rector St., New York, N.Y.
JAMES M. GIFFORD, Vice-President and General Counsel, 60 Broadway, New York, N.Y.
BURDETT LOOMIS, Jr., 2d Vice-Pres. & Gen. Mgr., Boca Grande, Fla.
L. WARRINGTON COTTMAN, Consulting Engineer, "
HARVEY STANLEY, Engineer, "
K. I. McKAY, Assistant General Counsel, Tampa, Fla.
N. H. GOUCHER, Supt. Transportation, Arcadia, Fla.
W. J. GILLIGAN, Auditor, Boca Grande, Fla.
C. R. McCALL, General Freight and Pas. Agent, "
G. T. SMITH, Soliciting Freight Agent, Tampa, Fla.
J. E. GOULD, Master Mechanic, Arcadia, Fla.
JOHN BRADLEY, Supt. of Terminals, South Boca Grande, Fla.

No. 2	No. 4	Mls.	December 1, 1915.	No. 1	No. 3
			LEAVE] [ARRIVE		
*2 42 P M	*6 35 A M	0	South Boca Grande[1] δ	11 55 A M	9 50 P M
2 52 "	6 45 "	2.3	Boca Grande ⊙	11 50 "	9 45 "
3 02 "	6 55 "	5.3	Gasparilla δ	11 40 "	9 36 "
3 15 "	7 09 "	10.0	Placida	11 27 "	9 25 "
3 31 "	7 24 "	17.6	McCall δ	11 13 "	9 03 "
3 36 "	7 30 "	19.9	Southland δ	11 05 "	9 04 "
3 47 "	7 41 "	26.5	Murdock ⊙	10 55 "	8 54 "
3 51 "	7 45 "	28.5	Mars	10 51 "	8 50 "
4 07 "	8 02 "	36.9	Platt δ	10 35 "	8 35 "
4 13 "	8 08 "	38.8	Boggess	10 30 "	8 30 "
4 16 "	8 11 "	39.9	Ft. Ogden	10 28 "	8 28 "
4 26 "	8 18 "	42.6	Hull δ	10 22 "	8 22 "
4 36 "	8 28 "	47.0	Nocatee δ	10 10 "	8 10 "
5 00 "	8 53 "	52.9	Arcadia[2] ⊙	10 00 "	8 00 "
5 08 "	9 02 "	54.7	Bunker-Lansing	9 42 "	7 41 "
5 19 "	9 12 "	60.4	Kinsey δ	9 32 "	7 32 "
5 24 "	9 16 "	62.9	Limestone ⊙	9 29 "	7 28 "
5 30 "	9 22 "	65.1	Bridges	9 22 "	7 22 "
5 40 "	9 31 "	69.9	Ona ⊙	9 12 "	7 13 "
5 55 "	9 46 "	77.7	Ft. Green Springs ⊙	8 59 "	6 58 "
5 59 "	9 51 "	79.8	Fort Green δ	8 54 "	6 54 "
6 02 "	9 55 "	80.8	Fort Green Junction δ	8 50 "	6 51 "
6 11 "	10 03 "	84.8	Baird δ	8 41 "	6 43 "
6 16 "	10 08 "	86.8	Cottman δ	8 37 "	6 39 "
6 21 "	10 15 "	89.3	Chicora δ	8 31 "	6 33 "
6 25 "	10 23 "	92.1	Bradley Junc.[3] ⊙	8 22 "	6 26 "
6 38 "	10 33 "	95.3	Pierce ⊙	8 09 "	6 10 "
--	--	96.8	Bruce[4]	--	--
--	--	98.9	South Mulberry	--	--
6 55 P M	10 47 A M	99.9	Mulberry[5] δ	*7 55 A M	*5 55 P M
			ARRIVE] [LEAVE		
7 55 P M	1 05 P M	124.4	arr. Lakeland lve. (A. C. L. R.R.)	*7 00 A M	
8 01 P M	11 44 A M	126.4	arr. Plant City δ lve. (A. C. L. R.R.)	*6 59 A M	*5 06 P M
8 45 P M	12 35 Noon	138.4	arr. Tampa δ lve. (A. C. L. R.R.)	*6 10 A M	*4 15 P M
6 45 A M	7 30 P M	323.4	arr. Jacksonville lve. (A. C. L. R.R.)	*8 50 P M	

* Daily. δ Telegraph stations; ⊙ Telephone stations. STANDARD—Central time.

RIDGEWOOD BRANCH.—*Freight Service only.*

Mls.		
	LEAVE]	[ARRIVE
0	Bruce δ	
5.0	Ridgewood	
	ARRIVE]	[LEAVE

PALMETTO BRANCH.—*Freight Service only.*

Mls.		
	LEAVE]	[ARRIVE
0	Cottman	
10.0	Tiger Bay	
	ARRIVE]	[LEAVE

Car Service.—Through 12-Section Drawing-room Electric-lighted Broiler Buffet Pullman between Jacksonville, Arcadia, Boca Grande and South Boca Grande, leaving Jacksonville 8 50 p.m. daily; leaving South Boca Grande 2 42 p.m. daily. Through Coach service between Lakeland, Arcadia, Boca Grande and South Boca Grande, and through train service between these points, leaving Tampa 6 10 a.m. daily; leaving Boca Grande 2 52 p.m. daily.

CONNECTIONS.

[1] At South Boca Grande—With boat line to Useppa and Pine Islands. [2] At Arcadia—With Atlantic Coast Line R.R., East and West Coast Ry. [3] At Bradley Junction—With Seaboard Air Line Ry. [4] At Bruce—With Atlantic Coast Line R.R. (freight only). [5] At Mulberry—With Atlantic Coast Line R.R. (passenger only)

Postal Telegraph Co. and Southern Express Co. operate over this line.

Nicknamed the "Boca Grande Route," the CH&N was initially built from Arcadia south to Gasparilla Island. As the phosphate industry moved north of the Arcadia so did the railroad, and in time the track reached Pierce and Mulberry. Passenger trains were also run over the line, and the railroad operated the Gasparilla Inn. Unlike the railroad, the latter survives.

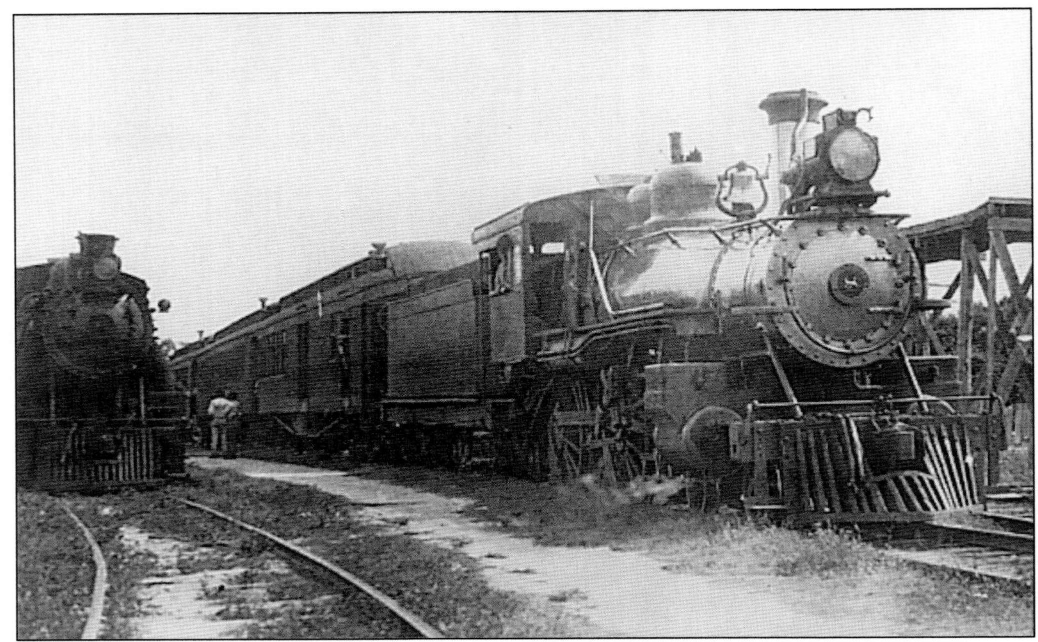

Built by Baldwin in 1913, engine No. 8 was the only locomotive of its kind on the Charlotte Harbor & Northern roster. In this 1924 scene, she heads a local passenger train out of Arcadia where company shops were located. Later, the "Eight-Wheeler" became engine No. 103 on the Seaboard Air Line Railway. In 1933, it was sold to Dowling & Camp Lumber. (Railway & Locomotive Historical Society.)

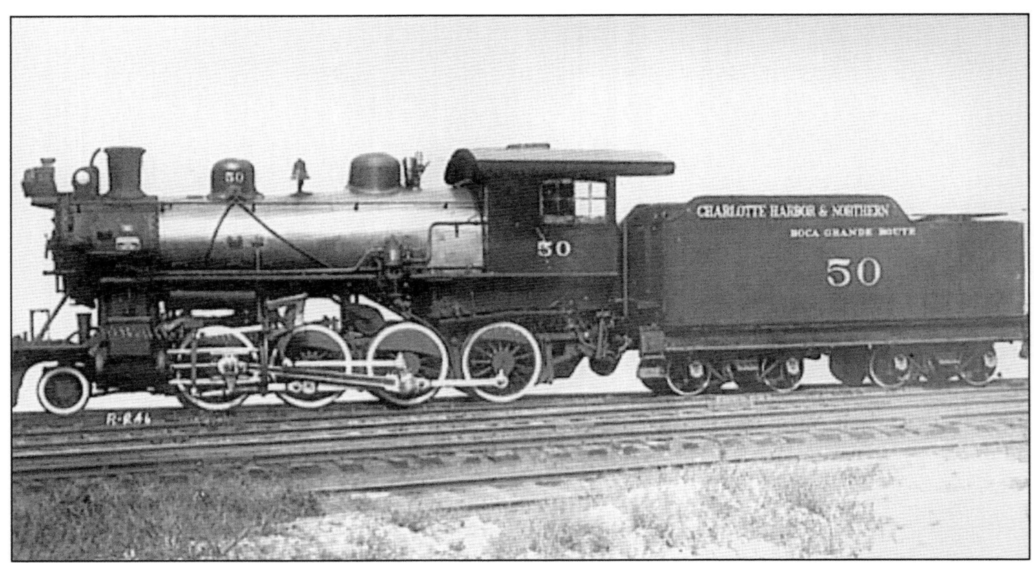

Engine No. 50 was built by Alco in 1913 and burned coal. It had a 2-8-0 wheel arrangement and was nicknamed a "Consolidation" (two pilot wheels and eight driving wheels). After the Charlotte Harbor & Northern was acquired by the Seaboard Air Line Railway, it became the latter's engine No. 927. In 1949 it was scrapped, about the time the South Florida Division of the Seaboard was dieselized. (Railway & Locomotive Historical Society.)

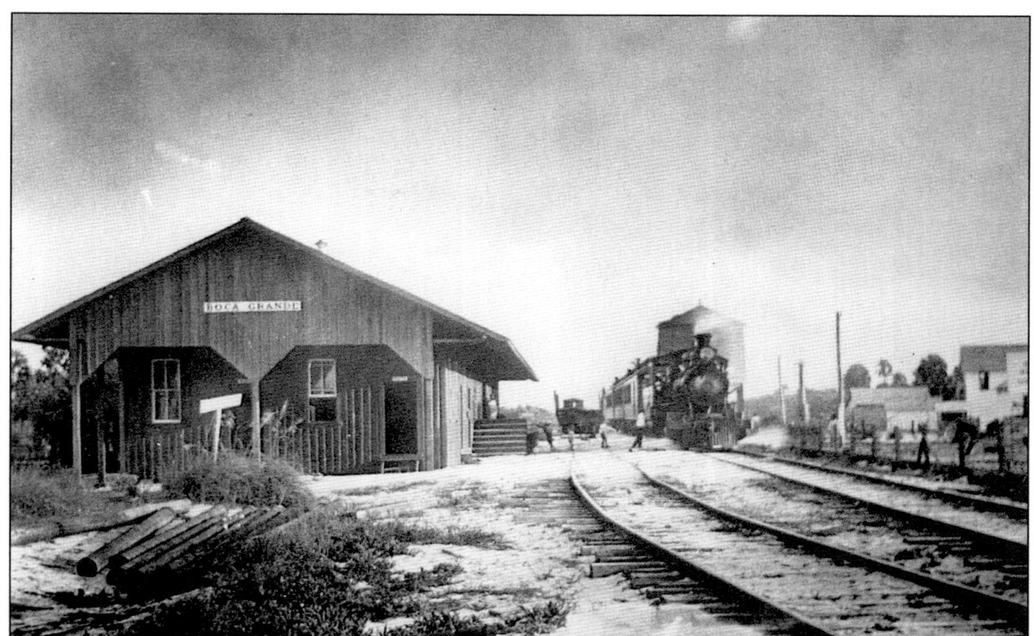

To the delight of the kids standing on a siding track, a passenger train arrives at Boca Grande, c. 1907. This was the first station structure at this location. Looming over the train is a huge wooden water tank, from which engine tenders were filled. It was at South Boca Grande, however, that the actual loading of phosphate into ships took place. (Florida State Archives.)

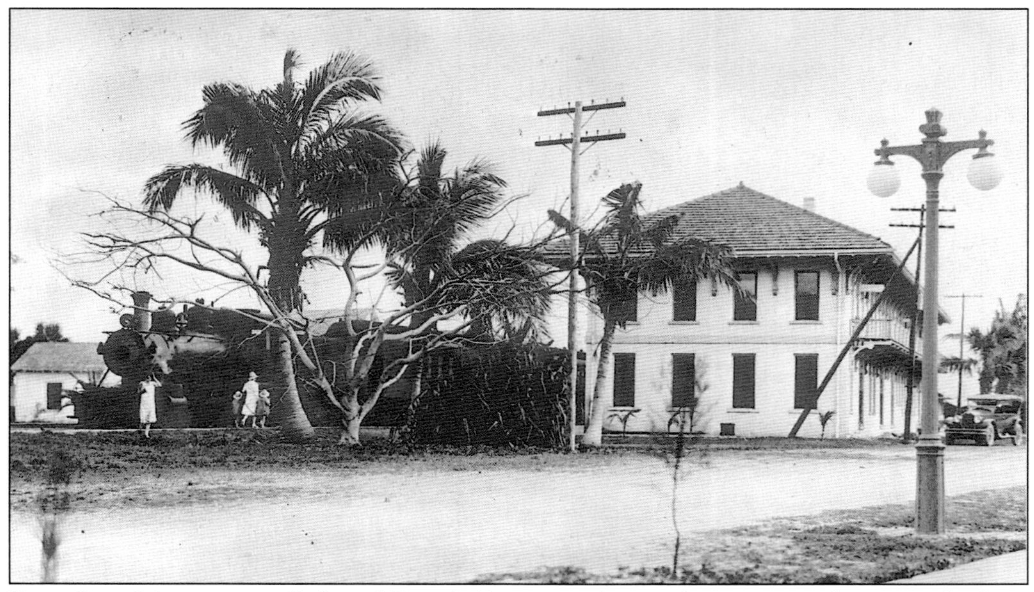

Boca Grande's station at Park and Fourth Streets, replacing the one seen above, was built in the Mediterranean Revival style in two stages. A 12-bay southern section was opened about 1910, and a 9-bay northern section in 1913. The first floor contained waiting rooms, restrooms, ticketing and baggage facilities, and company headquarters occupied the second floor. (Florida State Archives.)

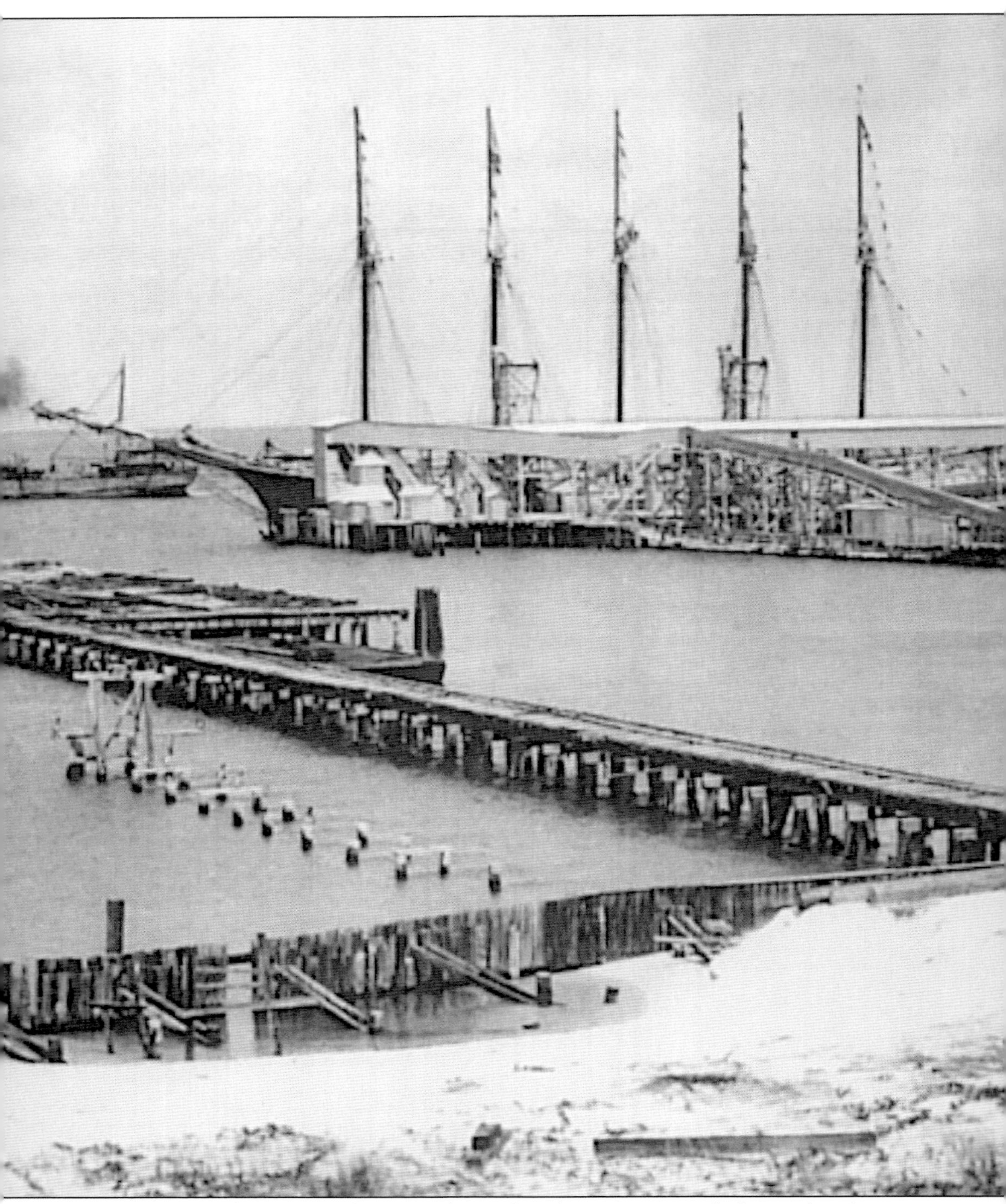

A five-mast schooner—perhaps 400 feet in length—waits patiently for its phosphate cargo at South Boca Grande—nicknamed "South Dock." Loading operations began here using a crane, but in 1911 a belt conveyor system was placed into service. Other docks on the railroad's property accommodated manifests of coal, lumber, vegetables, and citrus. The tank cars seen in the

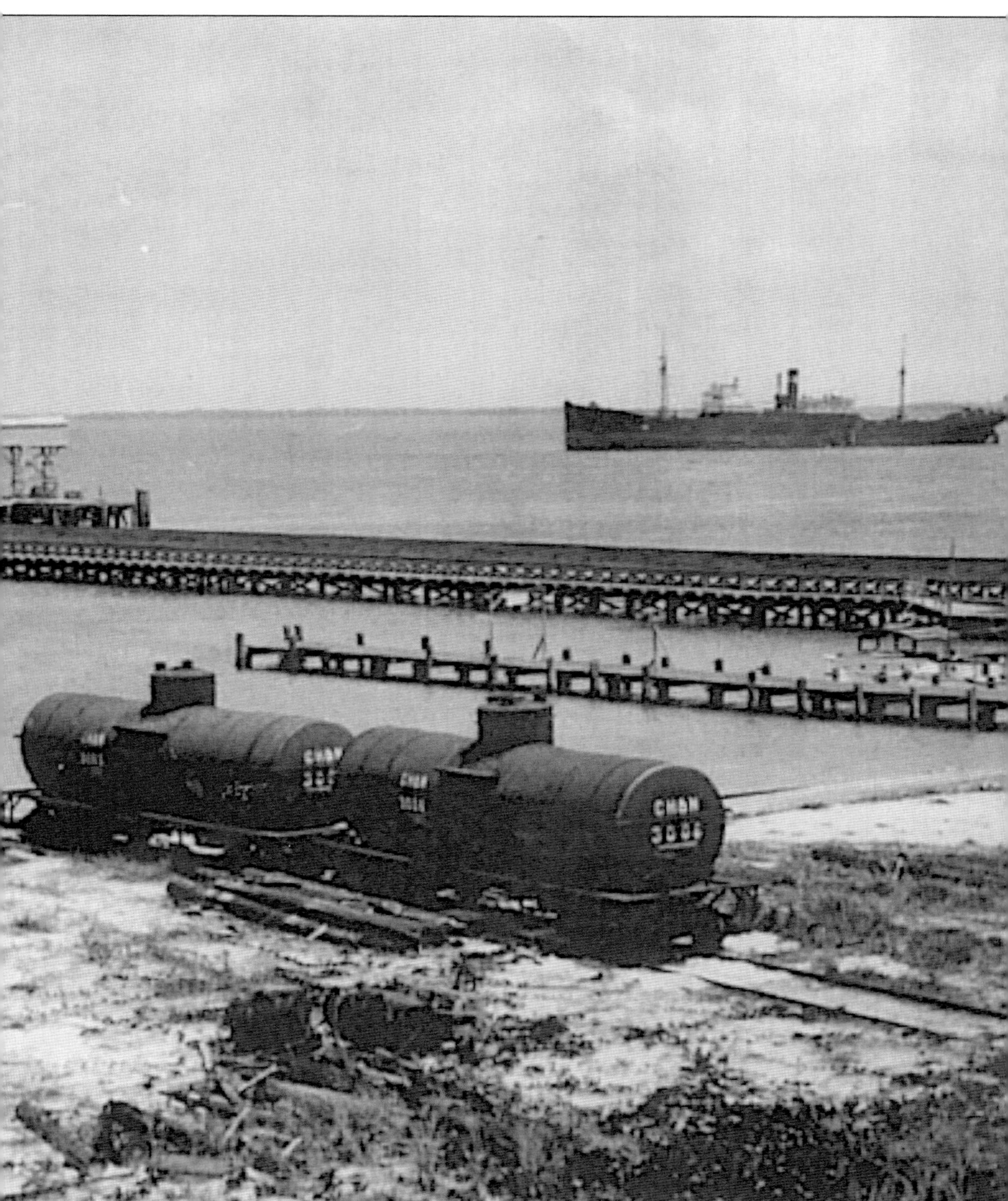

foreground contain water, which was needed by thirsty crews and steam boilers alike. This wonderful image, taken in 1920, is only part of a 6-foot long, 180-degree panoramic view of the waterfront. Not visible are four steam freighters, which also await South Dock. (Charlotte Harbor Area Historical Society.)

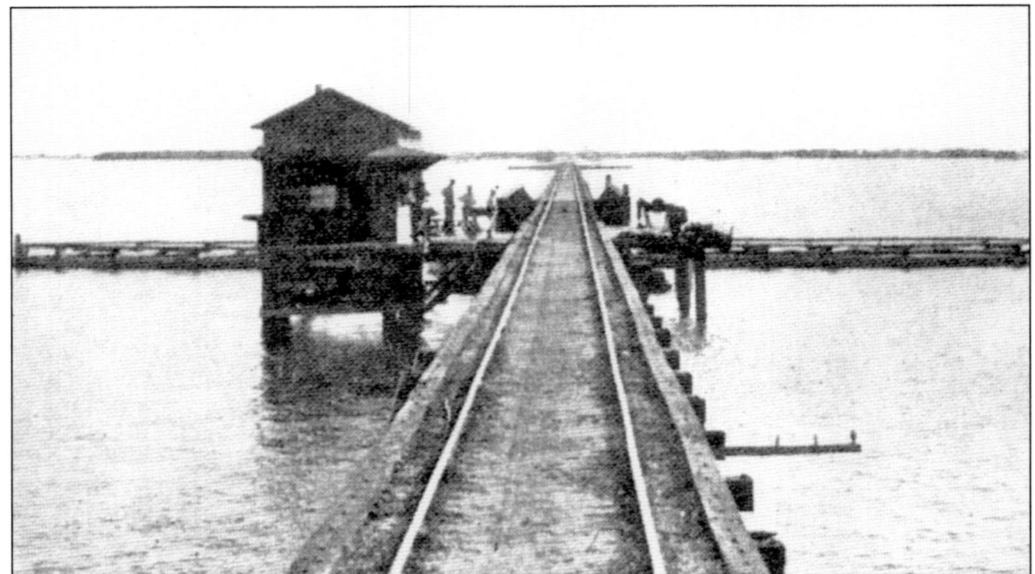

Trestlework carried the Charlotte Harbor & Northern track from mainland to island. Because the waters of Gasparilla Pass and Sound were navigable, the railroad had to install no less than two drawbridges in the area. The bridge tender's cabin of the northernmost structure is seen here. The remains of bridges and trestlework are still in evidence, and often arouse the curiosity of first-time visitors. (Florida State Archives.)

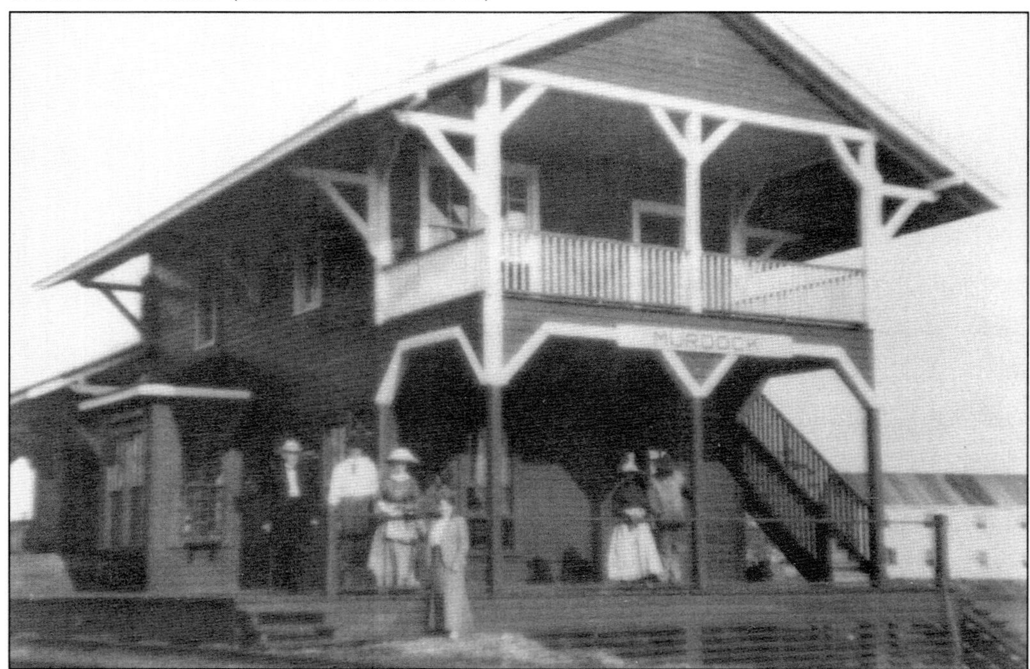

A bunkhouse for Irish track workers once stood at Murdock, together with a loading dock for a nearby turpentine still. In time, Chicago promoter John Murdock developed the area and sold lots. This attractive station once stood near the intersection of modern-day Highways 41 and 776. (Charlotte Harbor Area Historical Society.)

Southland depot stood on the east bank of the Myakka River. A Boston real estate developer, Joel Bean, acquired the locale in 1923 and had it re-platted as El Jo-be-an. During that era, trains of the Charlotte Harbor & Northern carried mail in canvas sacks. When trains did not stop, the sack was retrieved from the apparatus seen here. (Charlotte Harbor Area Historical Society.)

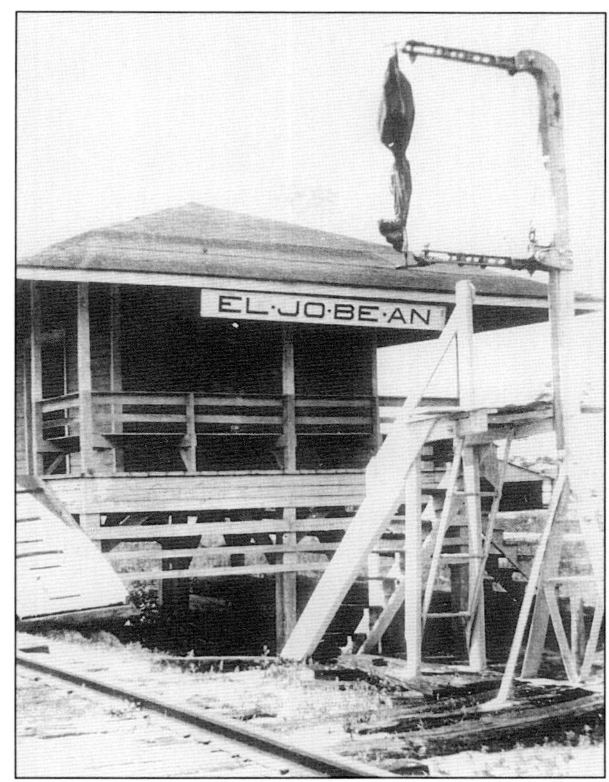

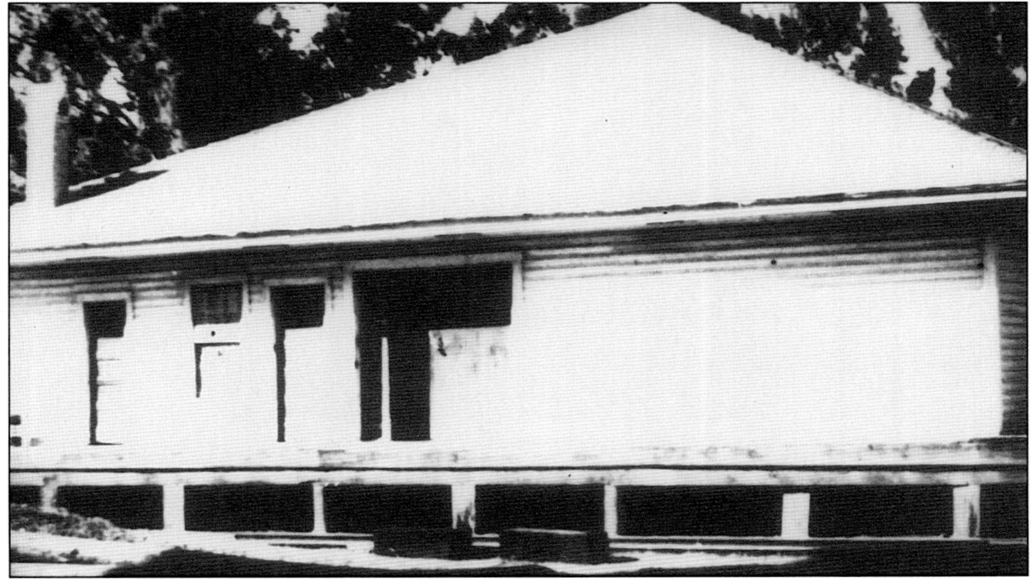

This wood frame building was the depot at South Boca Grande. Whereas most passengers utilized the big station at Park and Fourth Streets at Boca Grande, some 2 miles to the north, workers at the port commuted to this depot by train and trolley. Passengers destined for Useppa Island also got off here then boarded a private yacht.

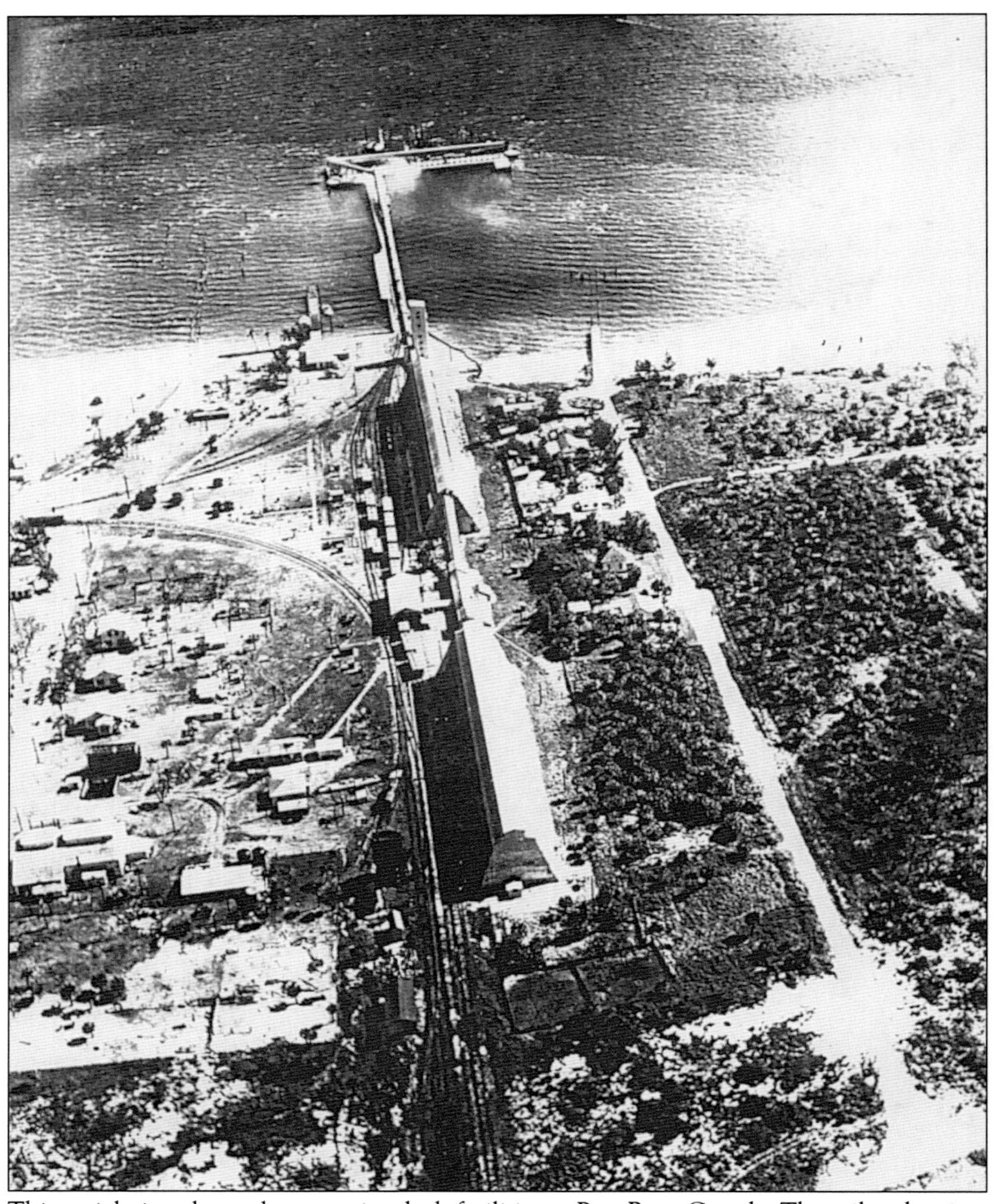

This aerial view shows the extensive dock facilities at Port Boca Grande. The railroad arrives at center left and splits into two directions: eastward to the dock, and west to the phosphate warehouses, where rail cars were unloaded. In realty this triangulation of rails—called a wye—permitted engines to be turned around. Port Boca Grande became redundant when the railroad built modern facilities for phosphate loading on Tampa Bay. The last phosphate ship was loaded September 30, 1979, and not long afterwards the railroad was removed all the way to Arcadia. (Harmon Photo & Video.)

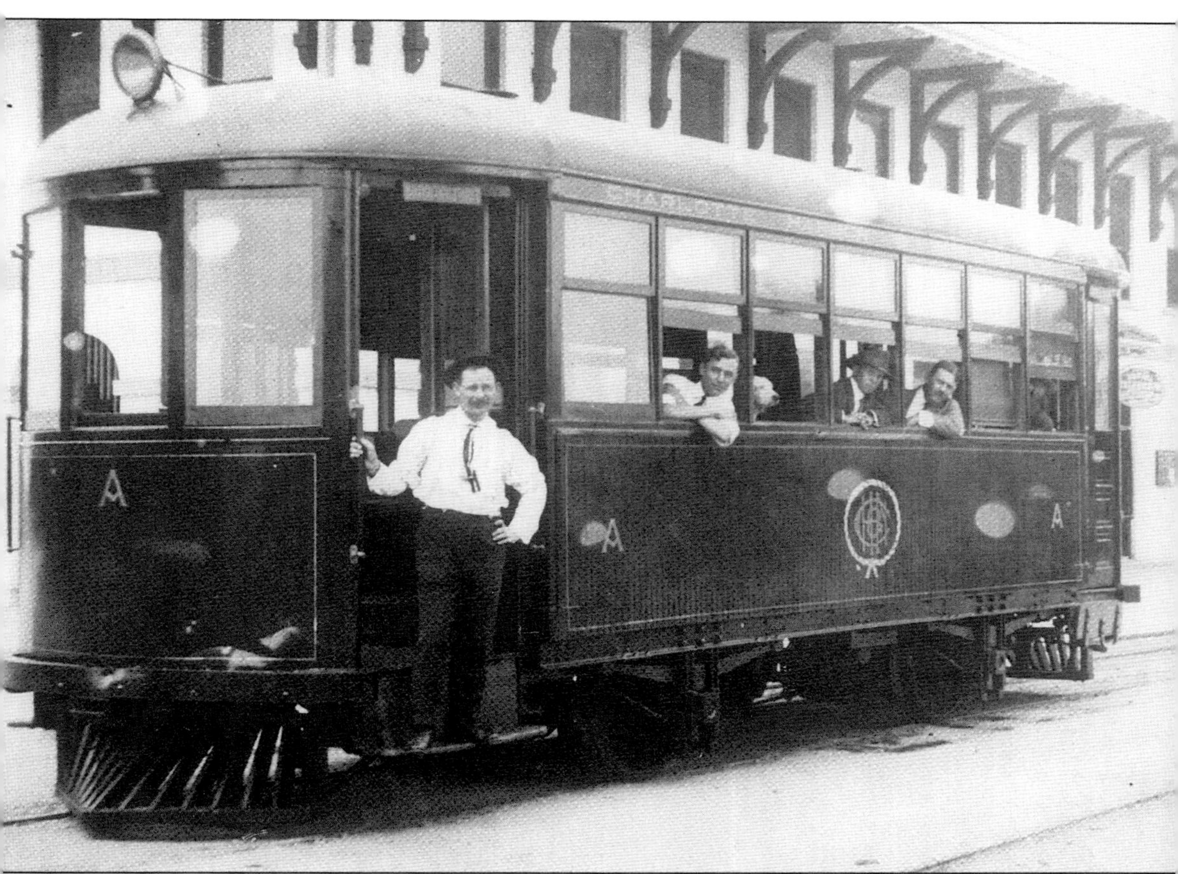

Although trolley cars might seem for the present generation articles for museums, they were in fact a unique chapter in American transportation history. They arrived during the vigorous manhood of steam engines and lasted until the country became hopelessly infatuated with the automobile. The one on Gasparilla Island was owned by the Charlotte Harbor & Northern and was operated for the benefit of passengers and workers needing a lift between Boca Grande station (seen here) and South Dock. It was powered by storage batteries that were re-charged each night at the powerhouse. The motorman—who operated the controls—also served as conductor. Fares were collected, but not from a certain passenger seen in this wonderful setting. (Florida State Archives.)

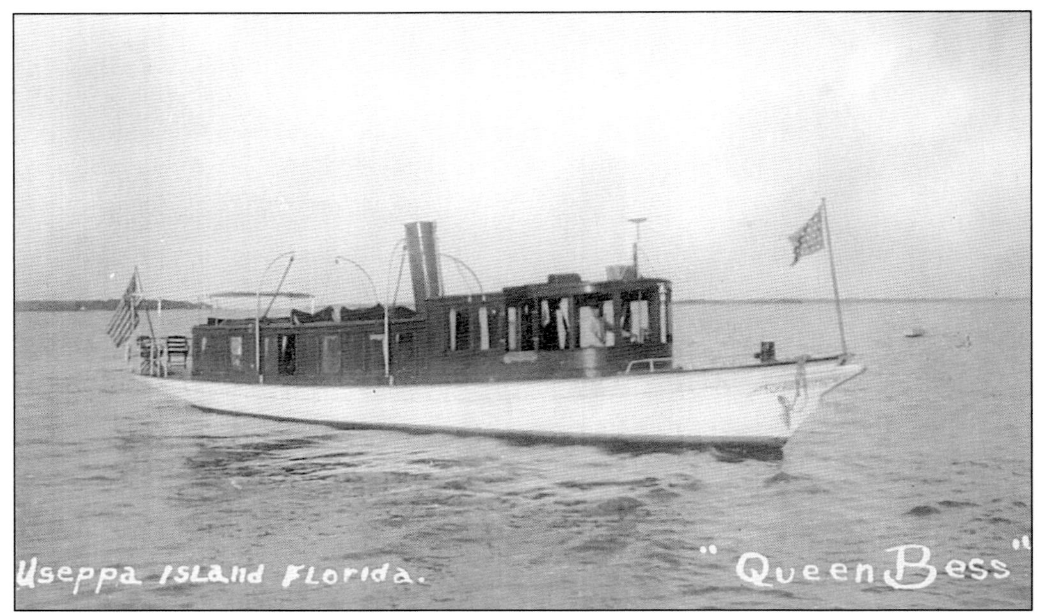

Not all passengers of the Charlotte Harbor & Northern, or its successor the Seaboard Air Line, stayed at Boca Grande. Some preferred the beauty and solitude of nearby Useppa Island. To reach it, patrons got off the train at South Boca Grande, then boarded a private yacht, like *Queen Bess*, for the 30-minute journey. (Charlotte Harbor Area Historical Society.)

CHARLOTTE HARBOR & NORTHERN RY.

"BOCA GRANDE ROUTE"

TIME TABLE NO. 16

IN EFFECT DECEMBER 1st 1915

FOR THE INFORMATION OF THE PUBLIC

SUBJECT TO CHANGE WITHOUT NOTICE.

QUICK SERVICE TO AND FROM ALL POINTS

SOUTHBOUND DAILY Leave	SOUTHBOUND DAILY Leave	STATIONS ATLANTIC COAST LINE	NORTHBOUND DAILY Arrive	NORTHBOUND DAILY Arrive
9 30 P M		JACKSONVILLE	6 45 A M	6 30 P M
7 00 A M		LAKELAND	7 25 P M	11 3[illegible] A M
6 10 A M	4 15 P M	TAMPA	8 45 P M	12 3[illegible] P M
7 22 A M	5 2[illegible] P M	WINSTON	7 20 P M	11 1[illegible] A M
1 A M	3 P M	BOCA GRANDE ROUTE	2 P M	4 A M
s 7 55	s 5 55	L. MULBERRY T..A	s 6 55	s 10 47
s 8 03	s 6 10	PIERCE TT	s 6 38	s 10 33
s 8 22	s 6 26	BRADLEY JUNCTION TT	s 6 30	s 10 22
s 8 31	s 6 33	CHICORA T	s 6 21	s 10 15
f 8 37	f 6 39	COTTMAN T	f 6 16	f 10 08
f 8 41	f 6 43	BAIRD T	f 6 11	f 10 03
f 8 50	f 6 51	FORT GREEN JUNCTION T	f 6 02	f 9 55
f 8 54	f 6 54	FORT GREEN T	f 5 59	f 9 51
s 8 59	s 6 58	FORT GREEN SPRINGS TT	s 5 55	s 9 46
f 9 07	f 7 08	VANDOLAH TT	f 5 45	f 9 36
s 9 12	s 7 13	ONA TT	s 5 40	s 9 31
f 9 22	f 7 22	BRIDGES	f 5 30	f 9 22
s 9 29	s 7 28	LIMESTONE TT	s 5 24	s 9 16
f 9 32	f 7 32	KINSEY T	f 5 19	f 9 12
f 9 42	f 7 41	BUNKER-LANSING	f 5 09	f 9 02
s 9 55	s 7 52	A. ARCADIA TT..L	s 5 00	s 8 50
s 10 00	s 8 00	L. ARCADIA A	s 4 55	s 8 46
f 10 10	f 8 10	NOCATEE T	f 4 36	f 8 28
s 10 22	s 8 22	HULL T	s 4 28	s 8 18
f 10 28	f 8 28	FORT OGDEN	f 4 16	f 8 11
f 10 30	f 8 30	BOGGESS	f 4 13	f 8 08
f 10 35	f 8 35	PLATT T	f 4 07	f 8 02
f 10 51	f 8 50	MARS	f 3 51	f 7 47
s 10 55	s 8 54	MURDOCK TT	s 3 47	s 7 41
f 11 05	f 9 01	SOUTHLAND T	f 3 36	f 7 30
s 11 13	s 9 08	McCALL T	s 3 31	s 7 24
f 11 27	f 9 23	PLACIDA	f 3 15	f 7 08
s 11 40	s 9 36	GASPARILLA T	s 3 02	s [illegible] 55
s 11 50	s 9 45	BOCA GRANDE TT	s 2 52	s [illegible] 45
s 11 55	s 9 50	SOUTH BOCA GRANDE T	s 2 42	s [illegible] 35
Ar. A. M.	Ar. P. M.	Freight Trains Will Not Carry Passengers	Lv. P. M.	Lv. A. M.

SHIP YOUR FREIGHT VIA C. H. & N. RAILWAY

Reference Marks Denote: S—Stop. F—Flag-Stop T—Telegraph. TT—Telephone.

SAFE Y FIRST -- ATTRACTIVE SERVICE

Information not obtainable from Agents will be cheerfully furnished by the undersigned.

BURDETT LOOMIS, JR., 2nd V-Pres. & Gen. M'g'r., Boca Grande, Florida

N. H. GOUCHER, Supt. Transportation, Arcadia, Florida

C. B. McCALL, G. F. & Pass. Agent, Boca Grande, Florida

In 1915, four daily passenger trains ran over the Charlotte Harbor & Northern, as this public timetable reveals. Connections were made with the Atlantic Coast Line. A Pullman car was introduced between Jacksonville and Boca Grande in 1911. Later, the Seaboard Air Line Railway ran direct Pullman service from New York City to Gasparilla Island, which lasted through the 1958–59 winter season. (Railway & Locomotive Historical Society.)

Five

FROM HIGHLANDS TO LOWLANDS

"The country traversed by the Haines City Branch includes an extensive area of rich soil adapted to the growing in one season of several crops of early vegetables. The line also extends through the most extensive tract of cypress timber standing in the country."

—Annual Report, Atlantic Coast Line Railroad, 1928

In the fall of 1910, the Atlantic Coast Line started constructing a new branch from Haines City to Lake Hare near Sebring. This 47-mile taproot, which became known as the Haines City Branch, served the citrus and vegetable growers of the Scenic Highlands region and opened in June 1912.

Later, amidst the prosperity of 1916, Coast Line directors decided to extend the new branch for another 81 miles to the vegetable and timber resources at Immokalee, in Southwest Florida. At Harrisburg, below Palmdale, the contractor was also directed to build a branch over to Moore Haven, on the western shore of Lake Okeechobee. The mainline was advanced past Harrisburg to Hall City, Ortona, and later halted on the south bank of the Caloosahatchee River near Goodno. Immokalee was not immediately reached owing to capital retrenchments and labor shortages associated with the First World War.

James Moore, a hotel owner from Seattle, founded Moore Haven. Marian Horwitz, its first mayor, persuaded the Coast Line to come to town, and on May 13, 1918, the first passenger train arrived with 20 freight cars and 20 passengers. At that moment no depot existed at Moore Haven, which forced the Coast Line freight agent to operate out of a box car that had been placed on a side track.

Late train arrivals were apparently common on the Moore Haven Branch, as well as unannounced schedule changes, faulty equipment, and derailments. Two trains had nicknames: the Muck City Express and a local mixed called the Hinky Dink. A local quip was that a middle-aged man who got off in Moore Haven on the Hinky Dink had left Haines City as young boy. The editor of the Moore Haven *Times* said that riding on it was like "being with a shy young girl afflicted with the St. Vitus dance."

Not far from Moore Haven was the lake town of Clewiston, which had been conceived by Tampa banker Alonzo Clewis. It, too, craved railroad transportation, and in 1920 the Moore

Haven & Clewiston Railway was chartered. The Coast Line furnished a locomotive and coach for the 14-mile firm, and in 1921 the first passenger train arrived at Clewiston. "A happy throng of people from Moore Haven had made a rollicking trip over the rough roadbed in order to attend a barbecue and baseball game which were part of the festivities." The Coast Line leased the little line in 1925 and purchased it outright in 1944.

The commodity that made Clewiston famous of course was sugar. In 1931, the United States Sugar Corporation acquired Southern Sugar and improved the drainage districts in the Clewiston area, introduced new sugar strains, plus opened a research department. To transport cut cane between fields and mills, the firm also built its own railroad system which boasted over 100 miles of track. Where once 1,500 tons of cane was grinded in a day, the number quickly rose to 45,000 tons.

The Atlantic Coast Line profited handsomely from the Clewiston traffic. A constant parade of chemicals, materials, and supplies were brought to Clewiston, and endless carloads departed with raw and processed sugar, plus sugar by-products. Previously in 1929, during the era of Southern Sugar Company, the Coast Line extended its track past Clewiston for 9 miles to the Miami Canal where a connection was made with the Florida East Coast Railway. The rich mucklands of this region yielded not only cane but wonderful vegetables.

Work began anew on the Haines City Branch mainline, but in an intermittent fashion. Goodno proper was reached in 1919. Then, in October 1920, work resumed towards Sears, Keri, and Felda. Bi-weekly train service to Immokalee commenced on October 16, 1921. About this time, Atlantic Coast Line chairman Henry Walters decided to extend the branch all the way to Everglades City, the southernmost point that the railway system would ever reach. Enormous tracts of timber existed along the way, and the potential traffic was great—as our opening quote relates. By 1927, Coast Line rails had reached the Deep Lake area.

Millionaire Barron G. Collier, founder of Collier County, owned the Deep Lake Hammock where fine grapefruit was grown. His Deep Lake Railroad brought the crop to Everglades City where it was shipped on Collier Line boats. Passengers and freight were also conveyed on the 14-mile rail line, plus logging trains hauled pine and cypress logs to the Collier-owned sawmill at Everglades City.

The Atlantic Coast Line acquired the Deep Lake Railroad from Collier in 1928. Then, a Collier subsidiary (Alexander, Ramsay & Kerr) rebuilt the frail line to Coast Line specifications. In June 1928, the company's first passenger train rolled into Everglades City proper. The Haines City Branch, begun in 1910, was at last complete from highlands to lowlands.

Many stations on the Haines City Branch had colorful names. Harrisburg, for instance, was named for the "Harris Track-Laying Machine," which a Coast Line contractor used; it could install a mile of rail each day. Hall City was the dream of Chicago preacher Dr. George Hall, who wanted to build a university funded by orange grove production. LaBelle businessman and developer Jerome Attanasio hailed from Ortona, Italy, and grew the Carmen grape on land near Ortona station. Richard Sears (of Sears and Roebuck fame) thought Florida pine ideal for his catalog, pre-built homes. Standard Lumber was expanded by his widow and sons, and Sears, Florida, was begun in 1925. A huge sawmill was built, roads and houses appeared, and a 30-room hotel was completed. Unfortunately, the 1926 hurricane struck. Sears was rebuilt, but the nearby forests of pine and cypress were leveled. Later, customers canceled contracts, the 1929 Depression hit, and the game was up in the 1930s.

The aforementioned hurricane of September 1926 destroyed much of South Florida. A great loss of life occurred at Moore Haven, when lake waters were hurled at the town by 150-mile per hour winds. Stories of heroism still abound, including that of Coast Line foreman Percy Silcox, who managed to transport survivors on a railroad handcar. Many of the deceased were brought to Ortona cemetery and were buried in wood boxes furnished by the railroad. Damage to the Coast Line itself was quickly repaired, and service resumed.

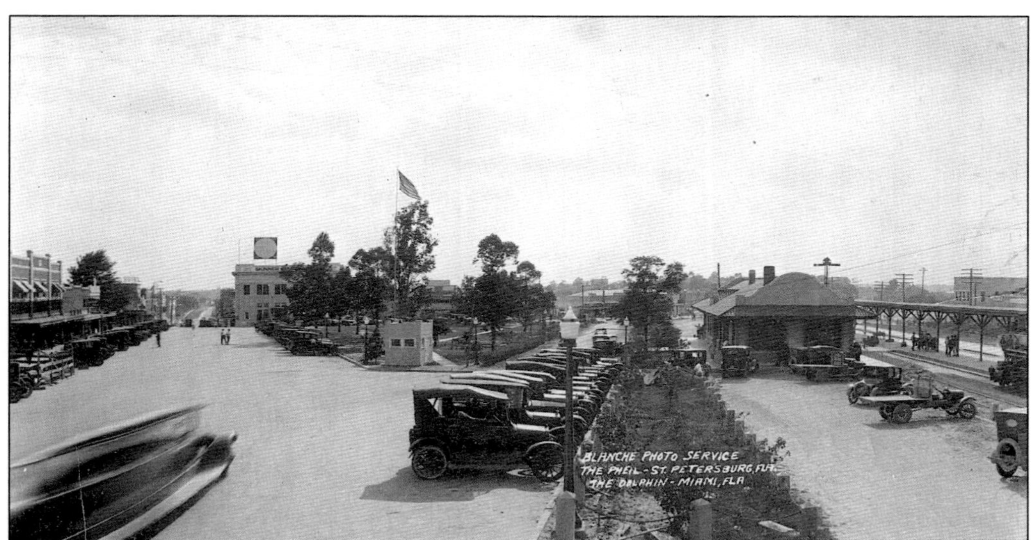

Haines City was located on the Atlantic Coast Line mainline between Jacksonville and Tampa. From its station, seen here in 1925, the Haines City Branch diverged to the Sebring area. But no railroad official ever imagined that one day it would stretch out for 167 miles to Everglades City in Collier County, or reach the Moore Haven and Clewiston area by a branch track from Harrisburg.

ATLANTIC COAST LINE RAILROAD—Continued
Haines City to Everglades

Station	Miles	Station	Miles	Station	Miles
Haines City	0.0	Avon Park	38.5	Goodno	100.4
Prine	3.0	Sebring	46.3	Sears	110.4
Lake Hamilton	5.2	DeSoto City	50.6	Keri	113.7
Leco	5.9	Istopoga	55.1	Felda	118.6
Dundee	6.8	Lake Placid	62.9	Immokalee	126.1
Waverly	9.8	View	67.8	Bunker Hill	129.0
Mountain Lake	11.4	Childs	68.8	Harker	133.2
Lake Wales	15.3	Hicora	73.6	Sunniland	138.6
Highland Park	17.2	Venus	79.5	Miles City	146.4
Babson Park	21.3	Palmdale	88.3	Deep Lake	154.0
Frostproof	27.8	Harrisburg	89.4	Copeland	160.7
Pittsburg	34.5	Hall City	93.1	Carnestown	163.1
Aro	36.6	Ortona	98.0	Everglades	167.1

Harrisburg to Lake Harbor

Station	Miles	Station	Miles	Station	Miles
Harrisburg	0.0	Cobert	17.1	Gunson	25.7
Muckway	9.8	Roumania	18.1	Sugartown	26.8
New Hall	14.3	Benbow	19.7	Highway Spur	27.6
Moore Haven	15.7	Frierson	21.7	Clewiston	30.8
Caspur	16.1	Capar	22.5	Lakeside	34.8
Gram	16.6	Liberty Point	22.7	Lake Harbor	41.0

A list of all stations in the state appeared in the annual reports of the Florida railroad commissioners. This one confirms those that existed in 1939 on the Haines City Branch, and the line to Moore Haven and Clewiston. Not all possessed a depot building.

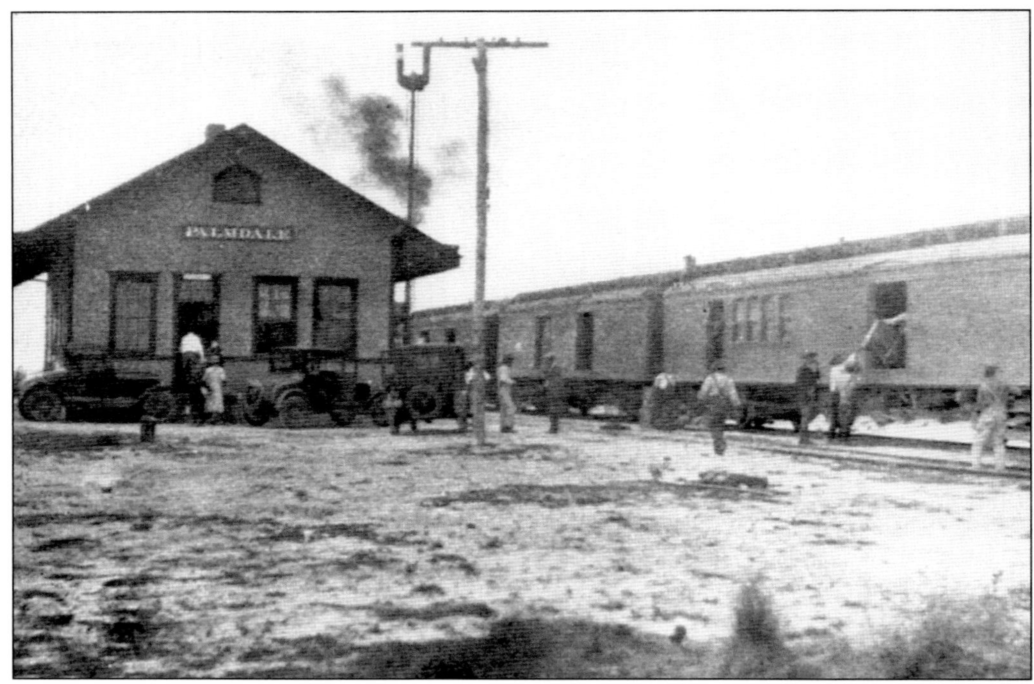

Palmdale was pioneered by the Florida Fruit Farm, and what attracted homesteaders to the area was farming. The lack of good transportation however forced many to move on. A "tent city" arose when the Coast Line arrived in 1917. Later, a coal chute for engines appeared plus a water tower and cattle shutes. Jack Frost, the first station agent, lived in the freight house with his family—and cages of rabbits. Business appears good in this 1929 scene. (Florida State Archives.)

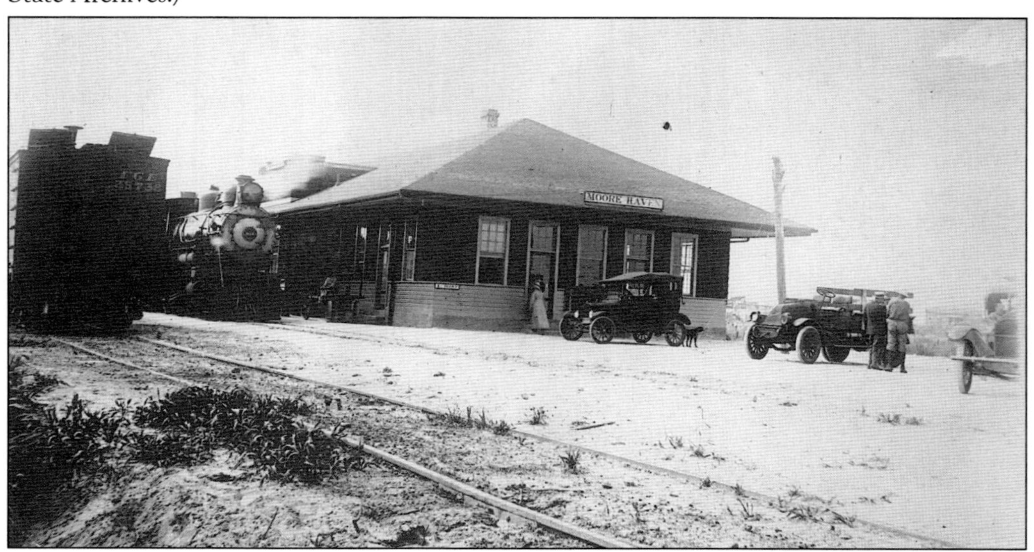

An attractive depot was constructed at Moore Haven, and in this 1920s view a passenger train is ready to leave town. Vegetables were grown in the nearby mucklands and transported to northern markets by rail. The freight car on the left could accept ice through the open roof hatches, thus manifests were kept cool. (Florida State Archives.)

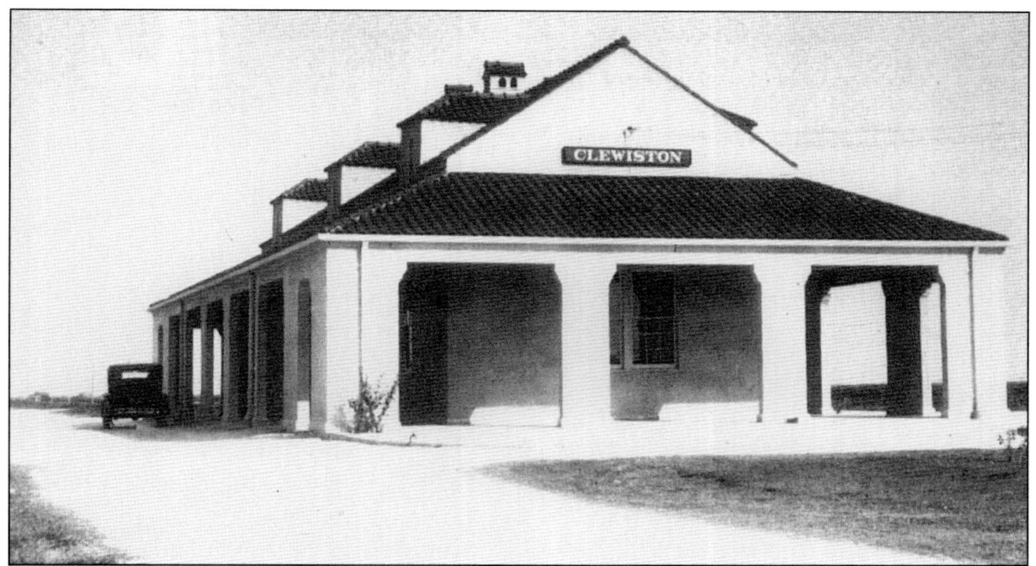

John Nolen, the eminent city designer, conceived Clewiston and likely specified that a substantial depot be built. Atop the roof can be seen a Spanish campinelle, or bell tower. Nolen later designed Venice, Florida. (Florida State Archives.)

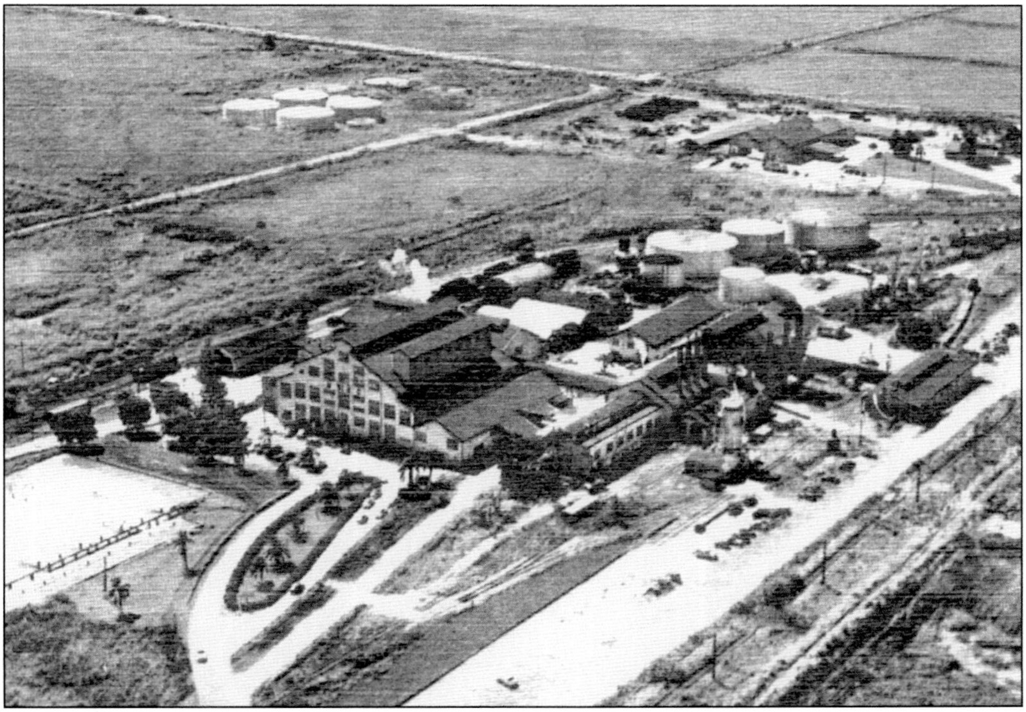

What really interested the Atlantic Coast Line about Clewiston was the United States Sugar Corporation. Countless tons of cut cane went to the millhouse (seen in this postcard view); processed sugar and sugar by-products (like molasses) came out. Most everything came and went by train. So great was the operation that the company built its own internal railroad, replete with engines and cars.

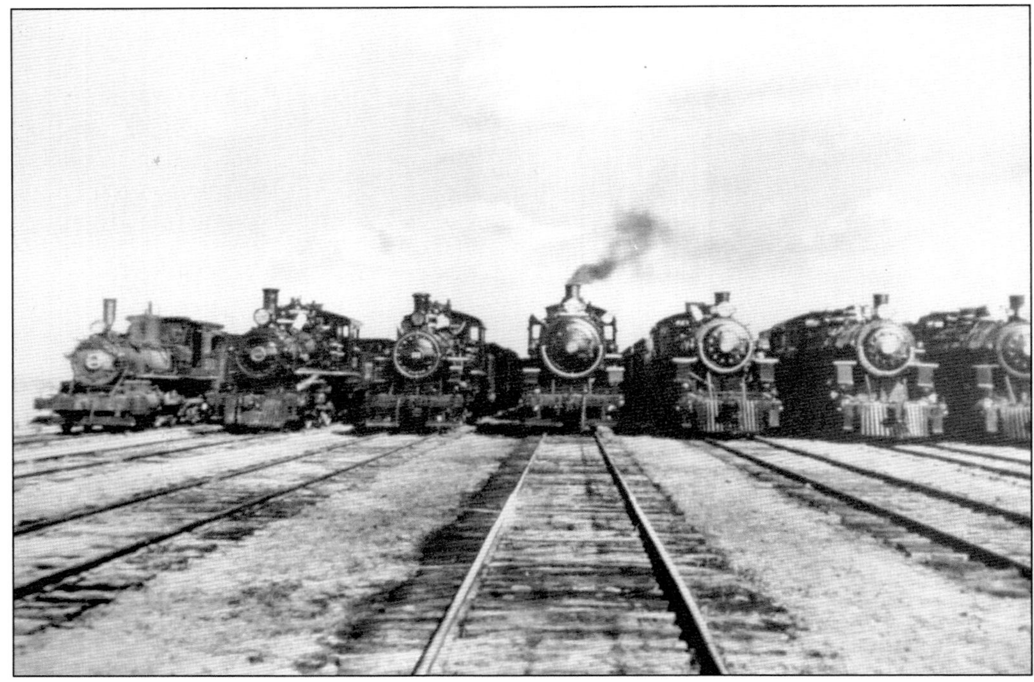

This bevy of steam power belonged not to the Atlantic Coast Line, but to United States Sugar! Operating an internal railroad system proved far more cost efficient. (Railroad Museum of South Florida Collection courtesy of U.S. Sugar.)

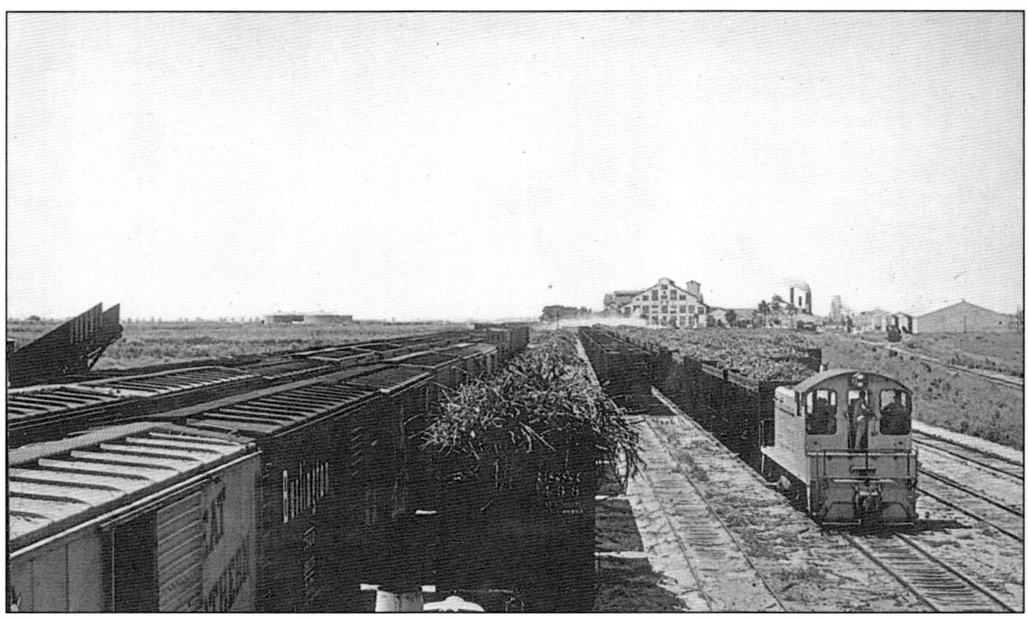

The steam engines seen in the previous photograph were replaced by diesel electric locomotives, like the one seen here in front of the Clewiston mill house. They were far less costly to operate and maintain. And, they required just an engineer—no fireman.

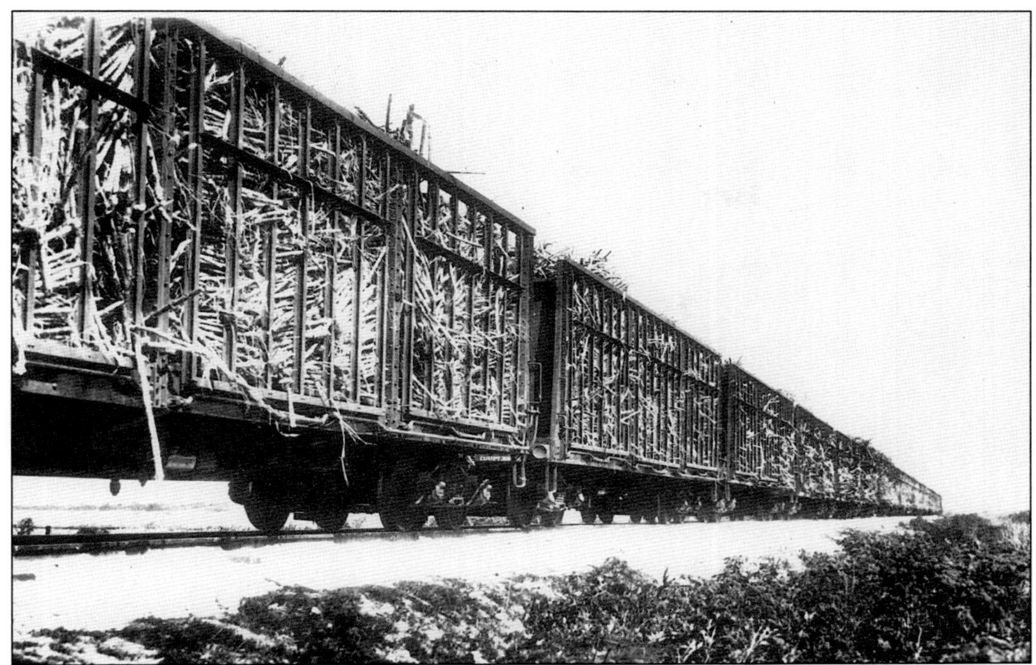

After harvesting, the cut cane is loaded into cars—owned by U.S. Sugar—and transported to the mill house. (Florida State Archives.)

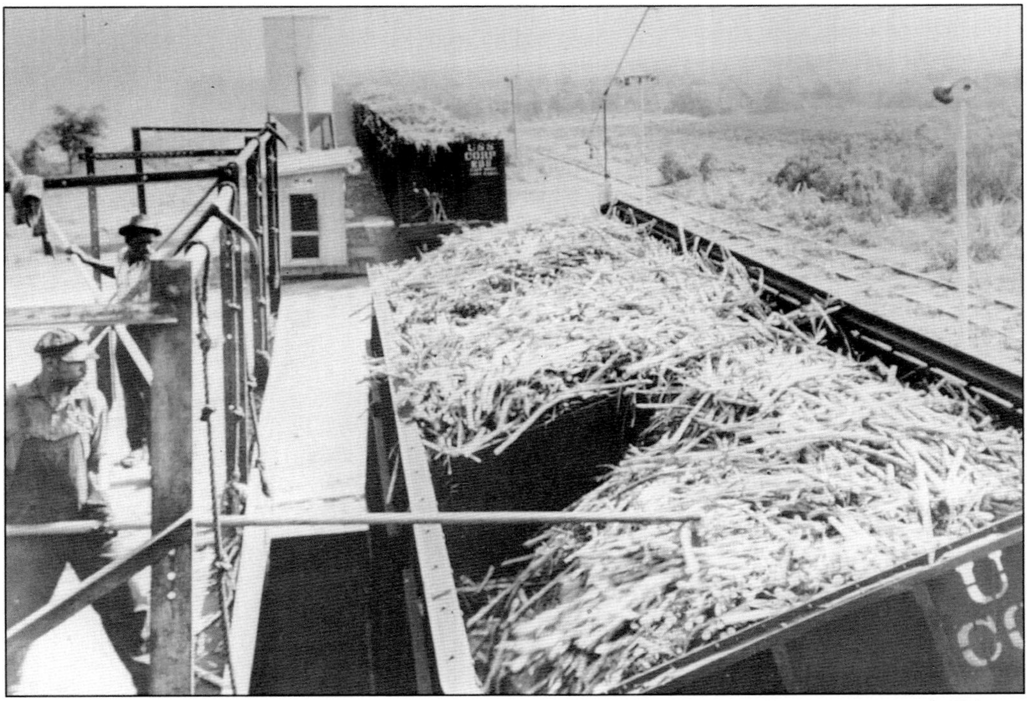

Workers are seen here "raking" cane into a receiving shute, prior to it being processed. Tilting cars help expedite the process. (Railroad Museum of South Florida Collection courtesy of U.S. Sugar Corporation.)

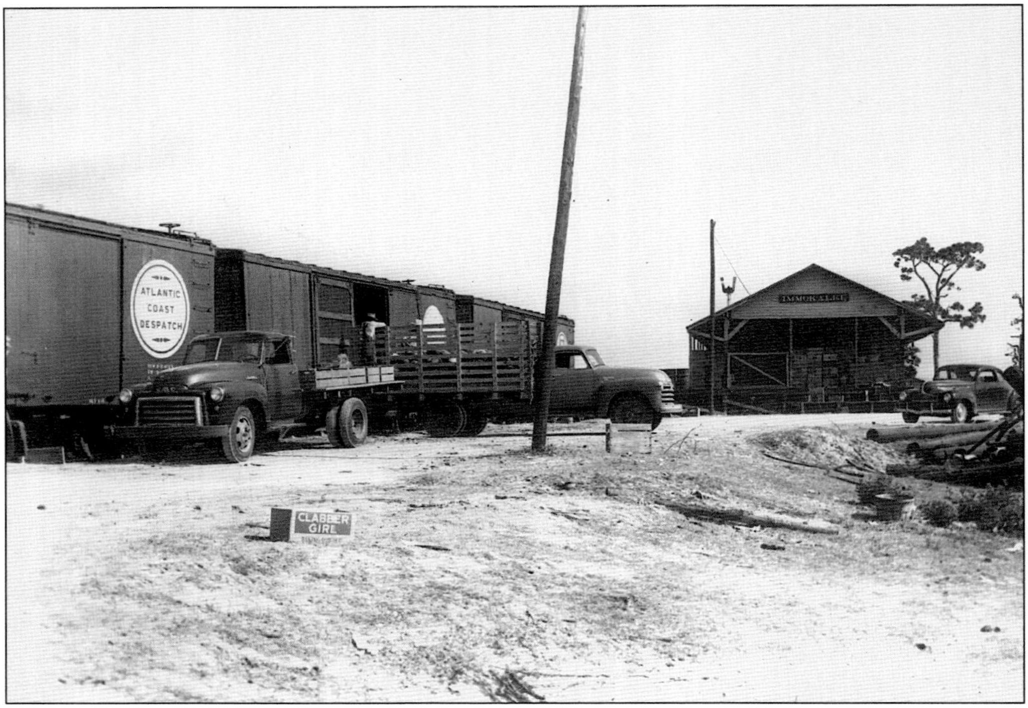

Vegetables, citrus, and timber drove the economy of Immokalee, and much of it moved to market by rail. Here, truck farmers load crates into freight cars that sport ventilated louvers. A fleet of such cars—called the Atlantic Coast Despatch—was first established by the Coast Line in 1887. (Florida State Archives.)

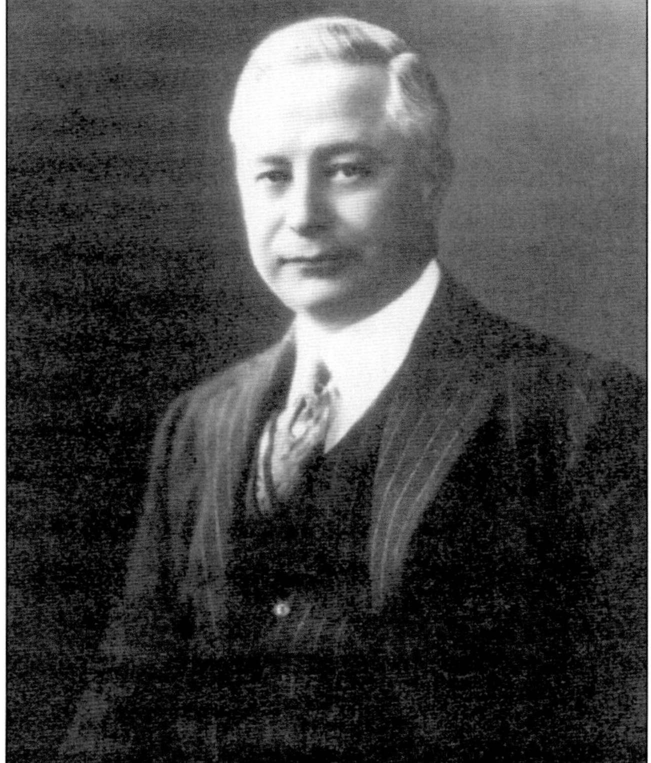

Once the largest private landowner in Florida, Barron Gift Collier made a fortune selling advertising placards for street cars. The Deep Lake Railroad helped comprise the Collier portfolio, which transported grapefruit, vegetables, timber, and passengers from Deep Lake to Everglades. The Coast Line acquired it during the Florida land Boom of the 1920s. (Florida State Archives.)

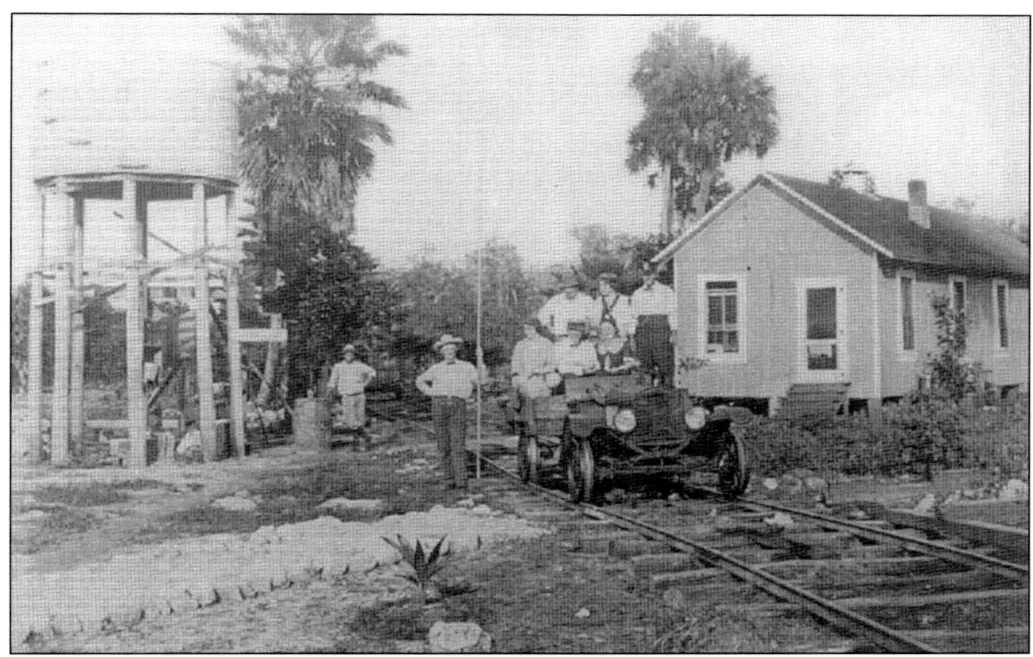

Operations on the Deep Lake Railroad were not glamorous, as this scene at Deep Lake suggests. A Ford gas engine mounted on rail wheels served as the locomotive. Once acquired by the Coast Line, the little line was thoroughly rebuilt and modernized. (Courtesy of the Collier County Museum, Naples, FL.)

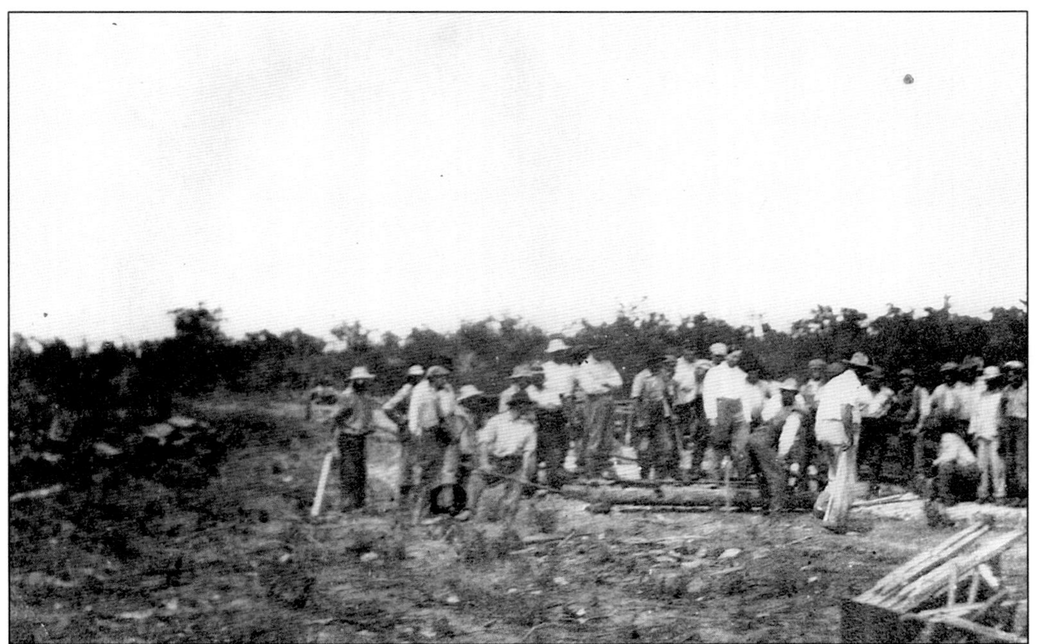

A construction crew is seen here rebuilding the Deep Lake Railroad at Carnestown. The route was graded, and new ties and rails were installed. A construction firm owned by Barron Collier was engaged for the work. (Courtesy of the Collier County Museum, Naples, FL.)

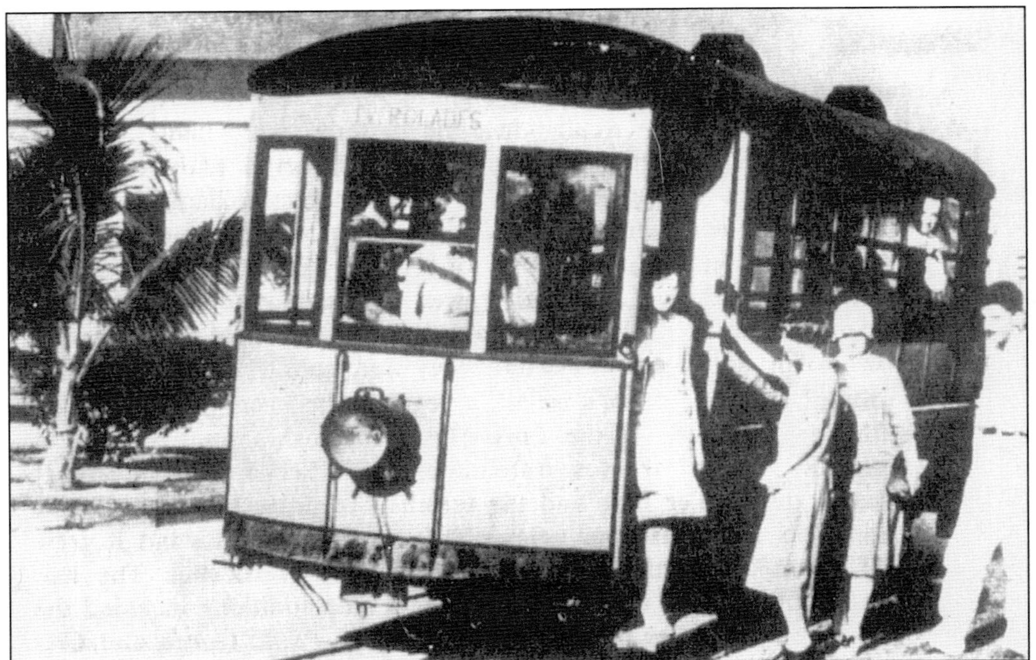

Barron Collier installed a trolley line at Everglades City that shuttled folks from Dupont—the industrial sector of Everglades City—to Carnestown. Battery-powered, its interior sported advertising placards, reminders of how the Collier fortune was first made. (Florida State Archives.)

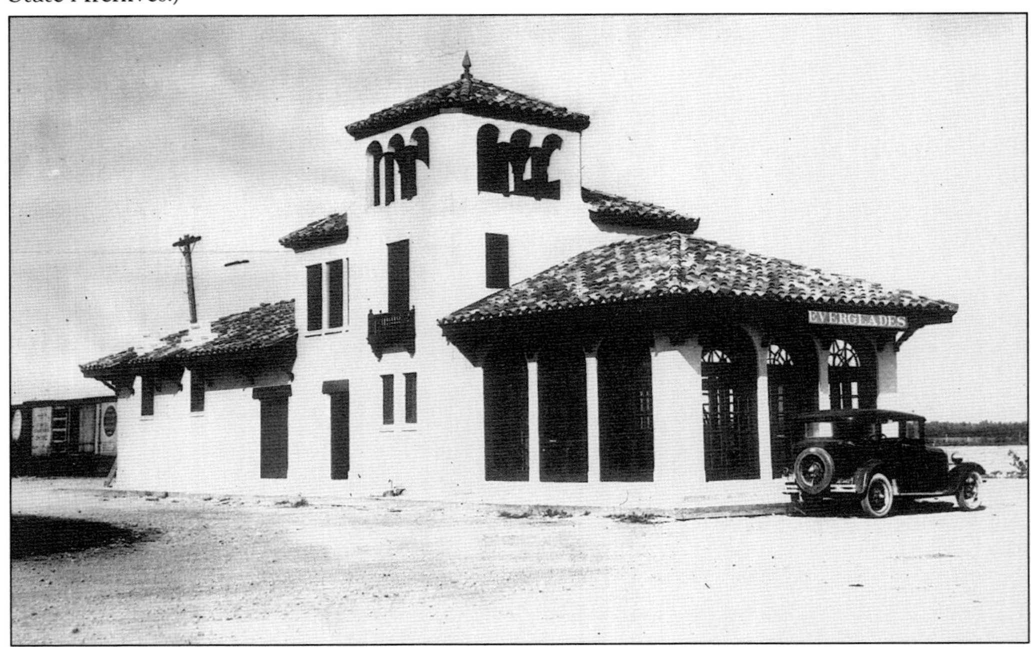

A certain Spanish charm radiates from the Coast Line station at Everglades City, seen here in 1930. To the left of the structure are ventilated box cars of the Atlantic Coast Dispatch, which confirm that vegetables left here for northern markets. (Florida State Archives.)

Six

The Boom!

"For sometime it had become apparent . . . that . . . Florida presented unusual opportunities for development. The Seaboard Air Line Railway, however, was not receiving the share of business originating in the territory for which it was justly entitled."

—President S. Davies Warfield, Seaboard annual report, 1924

The Florida land Boom of the 1920s was fueled by real estate speculation and development. Huge numbers of people migrated to the Sunshine State, and many arrived by train. Freight traffic also dramatically increased as materials and supplies flowed into the state for new hotels, apartments, commercial buildings, and homes.

To meet the demand, Florida's railroads launched a number of expansion and improvement initiatives. Tracks and facilities were upgraded, engines and cars were purchased, new lines were built, and dozens of beautiful stations appeared.

Both the Atlantic Coast Line and Seaboard Air Line railroads unveiled projects in Southwest Florida during the Boom, and when the dust settled in 1927, the rail map of the region stood at its greatest extent. In fact, the variety and frequency of service then offered has never been replicated.

The Coast Line Expands

The Tampa Southern Railroad connected Tampa with Sarasota by way of Palmetto and Bradenton. Rails of this Coast Line subsidiary (incorporated 1917) reached Sarasota on May 17, 1924. Passenger train service commenced in early December, and a platform near the Sarasota freight house on Fruitville Road temporarily accommodated folks until an elegant station was erected the following year at Main Street and School Avenue.

In May 1925, the Tampa Southern received permission from the Interstate Commerce Commission to extend its track for some 39 miles past Sarasota to Southfort, near Fort Ogden, in the Peace River Valley. There, the track merged with the Coast Line's Lakeland-Fort Myers route. An agricultural, timber, and livestock traffic was expected from the new extension, which passed trough East Sarasota, Utopia, Honore, and Sidell. Southfort itself was reached in August 1927.

In reality, the "Fort Ogden Extension" furnished a shortcut for Coast Line trains running between Tampa and the lower Gulf Coast, and in time, Pullman sleepers from several famous trains passed over the extension's track to Fort Myers and Naples.

Not to be forgotten was the Tampa Southern's little railroad "war" during the Boom. For several years the Coast Line wanted to install a spur track at Sarasota to the Payne Terminal facility located at Hog Creek, where a Seaboard track existed. In court, the latter tried to block the former from crossing its track to reach the facility. City fathers, however, welcomed the competition, and on the night of May 5, 1928—under the glare of torches and flares—a Coast Line section crew spiked rails to the terminal.

By using the charter of the Fort Myers Southern Railroad, the Atlantic Coast Line was able to extend its track past Fort Myers to reach Bonita Springs, Naples, and Collier City. Construction commenced in mid-1924 to Estero and Bonita Springs, which opened for service October 1925. Progress resumed into the following year—the rival Seaboard was on its way!—and the first regularly scheduled train arrived at Naples on December 27, 1926. However, the Coast Line was obliged to locate its depot outside the city proper—near today's airport—because the Seaboard had quietly obtained the best right-of-way into the city. Eleven days after the Coast Line began service, the Seaboard's "Orange Blossom Special" eased into Naples proper.

A drawbridge over the Marco River allowed Coast Line rails to reach Collier City—today Marco Island—in June 1927. A small freight facility was built on the island together with a turning wye for locomotives. The line officially opened that October, and for a time islanders had mixed train service to Naples and Fort Myers. Whereas the railroad served passengers and fruit growers, the principal customer on the island was the Doxsee clam cannery, whose products were packed in crates and barrels and sent to northern markets.

The final Coast Line Boom project in Southwest Florida involved the Haines City Branch, covered in Chapter Five. By acquiring Barron Collier's Deep Lake Railroad in Collier County, the company was able to advance its rails to Everglades City, which became the southernmost point of the Atlantic Coast Line system.

The Seaboard Responds

The amount of traffic enjoyed by the Coast Line (and the Florida East Coast) disturbed Seaboard President S. Davies Warfield, as our opening quote suggests. Expansion was the remedy.

On New Year's Day 1926, the Seaboard leased the Charlotte Harbor & Northern Railroad, whose story was explored in Chapter Four. In doing so, the Seaboard secured a deep water terminal at South Boca Grande, and obtained a line that penetrated the lucrative phosphate industry in the famed Bone Valley of Central Florida.

The Venice, Englewood and Southern Railway, conceived by the Seaboard in 1925, was to extend company rails at Venice down to Englewood on Lemon Bay. Rich timber resources existed along the route, and it was rumored that portions of the old Gulf Coast Railroad, a logging line between Venice and Woodmere, would be utilized. After Englewood, the track was to make its way to the Charlotte Harbor & Northern. But as the Boom fizzled, so did the Venice, Englewood and Southern. It was never built.

A bit player in Southwest Florida was the East & West Coast Railway, whose 50-mile route connected Arcadia with Bradenton by way of Verna, Myakka City, and Pine Level. Piney woods dotted its route, which attracted lumber camps, sawmills, and turpentine stills. Logs were conveyed over the line, plus naval stores, grain, feed, and even groceries. Engines and cars were supplied by the Seaboard, which formally leased the little line in 1925. The Seaboard, though, had little use for the firm after leasing the Charlotte Harbor & Northern. Mail ceased to be carried in 1928, the firm drifted into receivership, and most of the line was removed in 1934.

Greatest of all Boom projects in Southwest Florida was the Seaboard's Fort Myers-Naples Extension. To build it, and other projects, President S. Davies Warfield had the Seaboard-All Florida Railway created in 1925. On the West Coast, the subsidiary was authorized to build a line from Fort Ogden to the Estero River by way of Fort Myers. Branches to LaBelle and Punta Rassa were sanctioned from the City of Palms. The charter of the Naples, Seaboard & Gulf Railway (another Seaboard subsidiary) would advance the extension from the Estero River for another 20 miles to Naples. Once the Interstate Commerce Commission nodded approval, a $25 million bond issue was floated to help pay for the Florida projects.

Foley Brothers of St. Paul, Minnesota—one of the country's largest railroad contractors—built most of the Fort Myers-Naples Extension. In January 1926, company officials arrived in Fort Myers and began evaluating the line's biggest engineering challenge: bridging the Caloosahatchee River. They remained in town for groundbreaking ceremonies on February 8, then oversaw the first grading work at Billy's Creek.

The extension itself started at Hull, a way station on the Charlotte Harbor & Northern near Fort Ogden. The single track then crossed the Coast Line's Lakeland-Fort Myers route and proceeded straight as an arrow to Fort Myers. Several locales were noted on the engineering plan, such as Longview, Shell Creek, Saline, Tuckers, Gilchrist, Tamiami Shores, and Salvista. At Gilchrist, the Seaboard again crossed the Coast Line track en route to Fort Myers.

By driving test pilings, subcontractors determined that the Caloosahatchee River bed had a soft bottom. Ultimately, 60-foot pilings from Mississippi were brought in for the big bridge project. The structure itself ended up being 4,271 feet long with a drawspan of 160 feet.

Over $1 million was spent by Foley Brothers on machinery and equipment. Steam and gas locomotives for instance had to be purchased to move construction trains about, plus a Roberts Track-Laying machine was acquired to expedite tie and rail installation. Drag lines and steam shovels dealt with the muck and swampland that was encountered along the route.

Laborers for the project were housed at several construction camps along the extension; the one at Michigan Avenue in Fort Myers accommodated 100 workers. Overall, about 500 men were employed for the work and Foley's monthly payroll ran about $70,000.

The Seaboard demanded free land in Fort Myers for its right-of-way and terminal facilities. To help fund the purchases and create goodwill, a contingent of business and civic leaders formed the Fort Myers Seaboard Committee. Over 700 citizens were recruited who signed a pledge card to make Fort Myers a two-railroad city. Their trumpet call? "The surest way to kill Fort Myers in its present stage of growth is to keep the Seaboard out."

Several Fort Myers landowners, perhaps friendly to the Coast Line, at first refused to sell parcels to the Seaboard, which disturbed President Warfield. He told one newspaper reporter: "I was disappointed to learn that those who own property essential to Seaboard's entrance to Fort Myers should still feel that individual interests are paramount to those of this city and the west coast of Florida." Once the railroad filed condemnation suits, the "holdouts" gave in.

The Seaboard erected a beautiful passenger station at Fort Myers on East River Drive and Palm Beach Boulevard. On Michigan Avenue, a substantial freight house was built as well as a coal shute, water tower, and a 14-track switching yard. On November 10, 1926, the first Seaboard freight train arrived in the city.

The extension itself continued in a southerly direction—in direct view of the Coast Line!—to Mullock Creek, Estero, and the Estero River. Another contractor, John S. Jones, advanced Seaboard rails over the Imperial River (on a lift drawbridge) to Bonita Springs and Vanderbilt. Rails reached Naples proper in early December 1926.

It was Warfield's dream to make Naples the "Miami" of the lower Gulf Coast, and to that end the company purchased some 2,500 acres of land in the greater Naples area. The city itself was extolled in the company's 1925 annual report as "a most attractive place with beautiful beaches, the latitude approximately that of Miami, and one of the best situated winter resorts on the West Coast. The territory to be served is developing, and in addition to citrus fruits, early vegetables and canning industries, there are large timber areas that will later afford substantial tonage."

A station befitting Naples' future importance was constructed on Fifth Avenue South. Architect L. Philips Clarke of West Palm Beach drew the plans, which resembled the Seaboard edifice at Deerfield Beach. Sidings, yard tracks, a water tower, and a turning wye for engines were also part of the Naples complex.

Another Warfield dream was to convert the old cattle dock at Punta Rassa into a deepwater marine terminal—where today's causeway to Sanibel Island begins. But the 8-mile Punta Rassa Branch from South Fort Myers ended up serving growers and truck farmers. The line meandered along today's Gladiolus Drive through Lakes Park, and partly followed Summerlin Road to reach "Truckland" at McGregor Boulevard. Packing houses were eventually erected by the railroad at Biggar (Summerlin and Gladiolus), at San Carlos (Pine Ridge Road and San Carlos Boulevard), Cottage Point (Summerlin and John Morris Road), and at Truckland.

The Seaboard's 30-mile branch to LaBelle stemmed from Fort Myers proper and served Buckingham, Alva, Floweree, and Fort Denaud. A lift drawbridge carried rails over the Orange River at East Fort Myers. Farm products and livestock were carried over the line, but the biggest commodities were citrus and timber. In early March 1927, the first Seaboard train arrived at LaBelle. The branch officially opened the following month, and a one point a wooden palace car—*Caloosahatchee*—helped from the local mixed train.

A Gala Celebration

The Fort Myers-Naples Extension was opened in grand style by President Warfield, who invited some 600 of the Seaboard's nearest and dearest to the event including Governor John Martin. These "Captains of Industry" (as Warfield called them) came from 90 cities and 18 states, and for several days, beginning on January 7, 1927, they were wined and dined on five separate sections of the famed "Orange Blossom Special."

The Warfield entourage stopped at many points along the Fort Myers-Naples Extension, and thousands greeted the Blossom sections. At Fort Ogden, school children sang "Welcome Mr. Warfield" to the tune of "How Do You Do" as the trains pulled in. At Estero, citizens presented Warfield with a special edition of the local newspaper. At nearby Bonita Springs, another welcoming committee was at the ready, and upon the platform were more displays of locally grown fruits and vegetables.

Movie men from several national news organizations recorded the Blossom's arrival at Naples. A calvacade of cars—preceded by bands—took Warfield and his guests to the Naples Hotel for a luncheon. Later, a tour was given of the beach area and the beautiful Bay of Naples.

The trains returned to Fort Myers where a gala reception was staged at the Royal Palm Hotel. Gifts were presented to Warfield, who then addressed the gathering. Late that night the entourage left for the East Coast and even more festivities. The Seaboard's Fort Myers-Naples Extension—the last big Boom project in Southwest Florida—was now officially open.

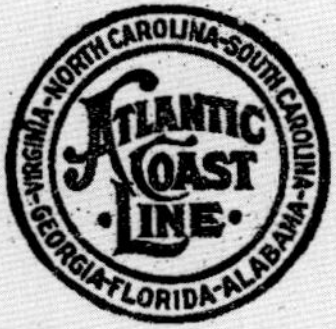

FLORIDA FASTER

VIA THE

"Palmetto Limited"—No. 83-82

3 1-2 Hours Faster to Central and East and West Coast Florida
5 5-6 Hours Faster to the Scenic Highlands (The Ridge)

DAILY SCHEDULE

7 10 P M	lve.	**NEW YORK** (Penna. Station)	(Penna. R.R.)	arr.	12 30 P M
9 23 P M	lve.	**WEST PHILADELPHIA**	"	arr.	10 23 A M
11 26 P M	lve.	**BALTIMORE**	"	arr.	8 18 A M
a12 45 A M	lve.	**WASHINGTON**	(Rich., Fred. & Pot.)	arr.	7 00 A M
3 55 A M	lve.	**RICHMOND**	(Atlantic Coast Line)	arr.	3 45 A M
2 40 P M	arr.	**CHARLESTON**	"	arr.	4 20 P M
5 55 P M	arr.	**SAVANNAH**	"	arr.	1 10 P M
10 00 P M	arr.	**JACKSONVILLE**	"	lve.	9 05 A M
b4 55 A M	arr.	**HAINES CITY**	"	lve.	a12 10 A M
6 41 A M	arr.	**MOUNTAIN LAKE**	"	lve.	9 37 P M
6 50 A M	arr.	**LAKE WALES** (Highland Park)	"	lve.	9 29 P M
7 17 A M	arr.	**FROSTPROOF**	"	lve.	9 03 P M
7 41 A M	arr.	**AVON PARK**	"	lve.	8 45 P M
8 00 A M	arr.	**SEBRING**	"	lve.	8 30 P M
8 37 A M	arr.	**LAKE PLACID** (Lake Stearns)	"	lve.	7 55 P M
10 15 A M	arr.	**MOORE HAVEN**	"	lve.	6 25 P M
c5 37 A M	arr.	**LAKELAND**	"	lve.	a11 20 P M
11 15 A M	arr.	**FORT MYERS**	"	lve.	4 20 P M
7 00 A M	arr.	**TAMPA**	"	lve.	10 00 P M
9 48 A M	arr.	**SARASOTA**	"	lve.	7 30 P M
7 45 A M	arr.	**ST. PETERSBURG**	"	lve.	9 00 P M
6 20 A M	arr.	**WEST PALM BEACH**	(Fla. East Coast)	lve.	11 30 P M
8 30 A M	arr.	**MIAMI**	"	lve.	9 30 P M

(*a*) Sleeper available at 10 00 p.m.; (*b*) Sleeper available until 6 15 a.m.; (*c*) Sleeper available until 7 00 a.m.

EQUIPMENT

Dining Car.......New York and Jacksonville.
10-Section, 2 Compartment, 1 Drawing-room.......New York and St. Petersburg.
12-Section, 1 Drawing-room.......New York and Miami.
12-Section, 1 Drawing-room.......New York and Miami.
12-Section, 1 Drawing-room.......New York and Sarasota. (Extend to Fort Myers December 18, 1927.)
10-Section, 2 Compartment, 1 Drawing-room.......New York and Lake Placid.
12-Section, 1 Drawing-room.......New York and St. Petersburg.
12-Section, 1 Drawing-room.......Washington and St. Petersburg.
12-Section, 1 Drawing-room.......Washington to Miami. (Temporarily discontinued.)
12-Section, 1 Drawing-room.......Jacksonville and Orlando.
12-Section, 1 Drawing-room.......Jacksonville and Fort Myers.
12-Section, 1 Drawing-room.......Jacksonville and Sebring.
12-Section, 1 Drawing-room.......Jacksonville and Sarasota.
Coaches.......All Points.

A FAST PULLMAN DINING CAR AND COACH TRAIN FOR FLORIDA AND THE SOUTH AFTER A COMPLETE DAY IN NEW YORK—AND OVER "THE SEA-LEVEL DOUBLE-TRACK ROUTE TO FLORIDA."

ATLANTIC COAST LINE

The Standard Railroad of the South

Crack trains like the "Palmetto Limited" ran during the Florida land Boom of the 1920s. Whereas Southwest Florida was removed from the Coast Line's main route between Tampa and Richmond, the company still sent coaches and Pullman sleepers to the region (via connecting trains) as this 1927 ad reveals.

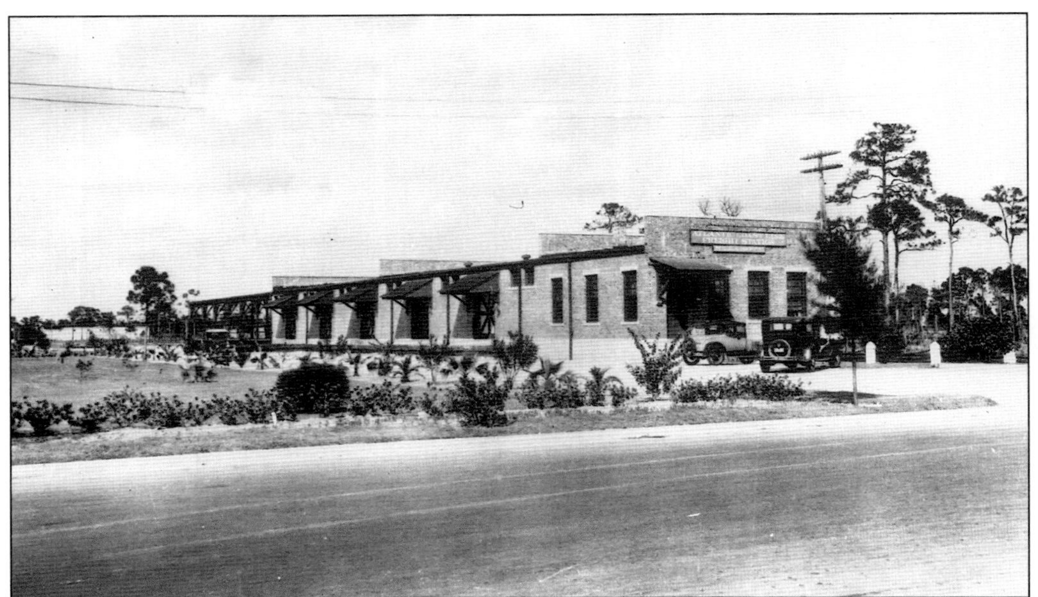

All 2,000 shares of Tampa Southern Railroad stock were owned by the Atlantic Coast Line. Incorporated in 1917, it was not until 1924 did rails actually reach Sarasota. A substantial brick freight house (seen here) was erected at 2227 Fruitville Road. (Historical Resources, Sarasota County Government.)

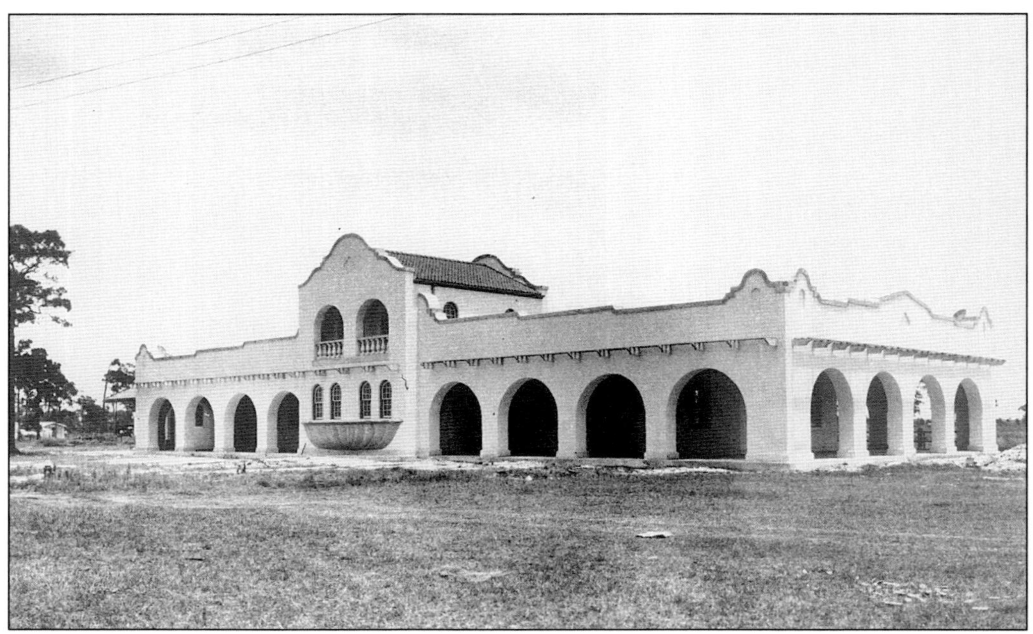

Coast Line architect Alpheus M. Griffin conceived Sarasota's elegant station at Main Street and School Avenue. Built of masonry and hollow clay tile, the Spanish mission-style structure had waiting rooms and bathrooms for both white and black patrons. It opened October 1, 1925, and cost $100,000. Seaboard Coast Line trains used it until May 1, 1971. After a series of owners, it was demolished in January 1986. (Historical Resources, Sarasota County Government.)

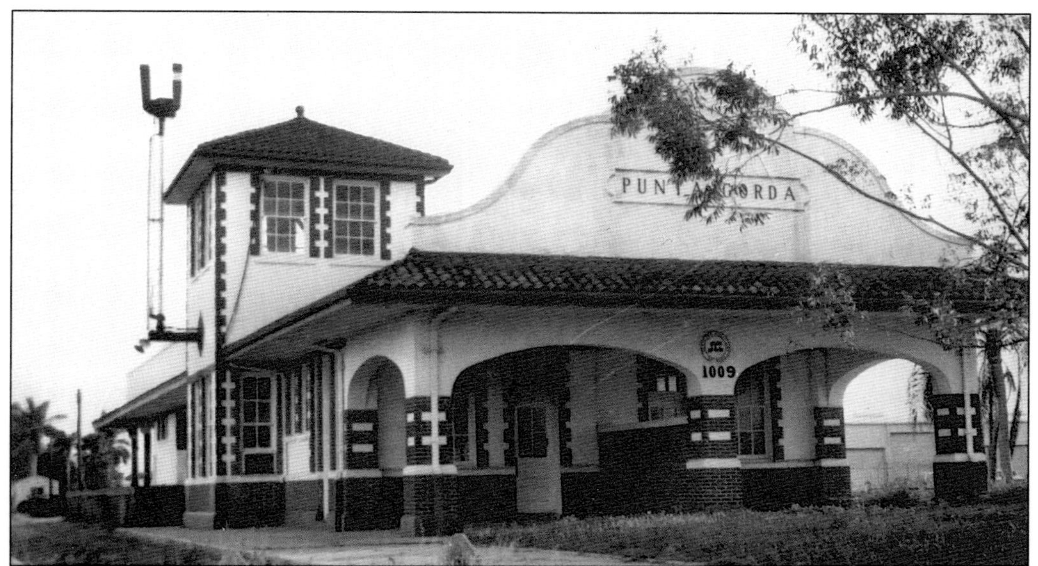

Many significant stations were erected by the Coast Line during the Florida land Boom years. The one at Punta Gorda was built at Taylor Street in 1928. It closed in 1971 and was purchased by industrialist Fred Babcock, who donated it in 1996 to the "Old Punta Gorda" history foundation. An antique mall now operates inside. (Florida State Archives.)

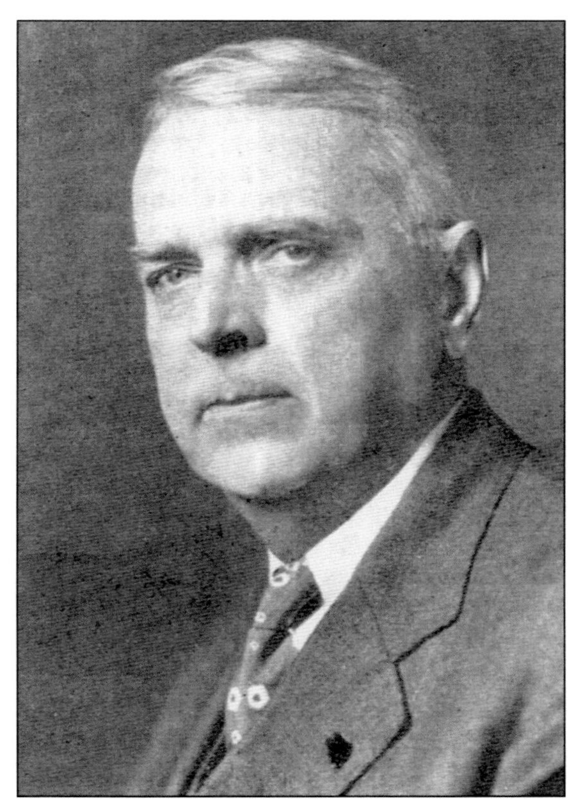

Frank C. Alderman Sr., a prominent Fort Myers lawyer and banker, got the Fort Myers Southern Railroad organized together with tycoon Barron Collier. By using its charter, the Atlantic Coast Line was able to extend its route south of Fort Myers to Bonita, Naples, and Collier City (Marco Island). (Fort Myers Historical Museum.)

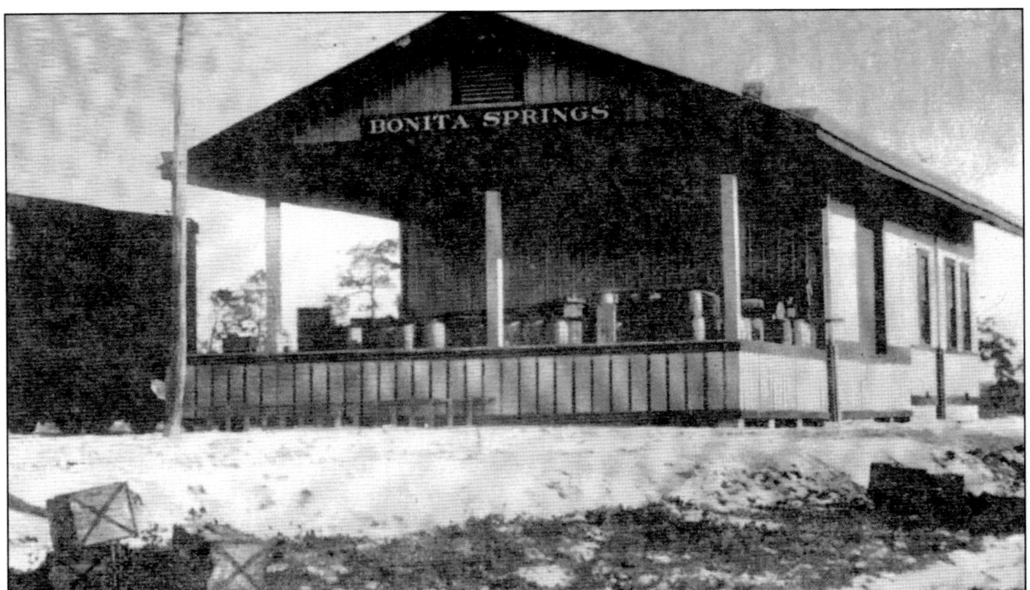

Bonita Springs was one of several depots along the Coast Line route between Fort Myers and Collier City. The line, though, was not all built at once. A wye track was installed at Bonita Springs which allowed engines to be turned. In fact, for many years engines arriving from Fort Myers were turned on the wye, then they backed down—with train—to Naples where no wye existed. (Florida State Archives.)

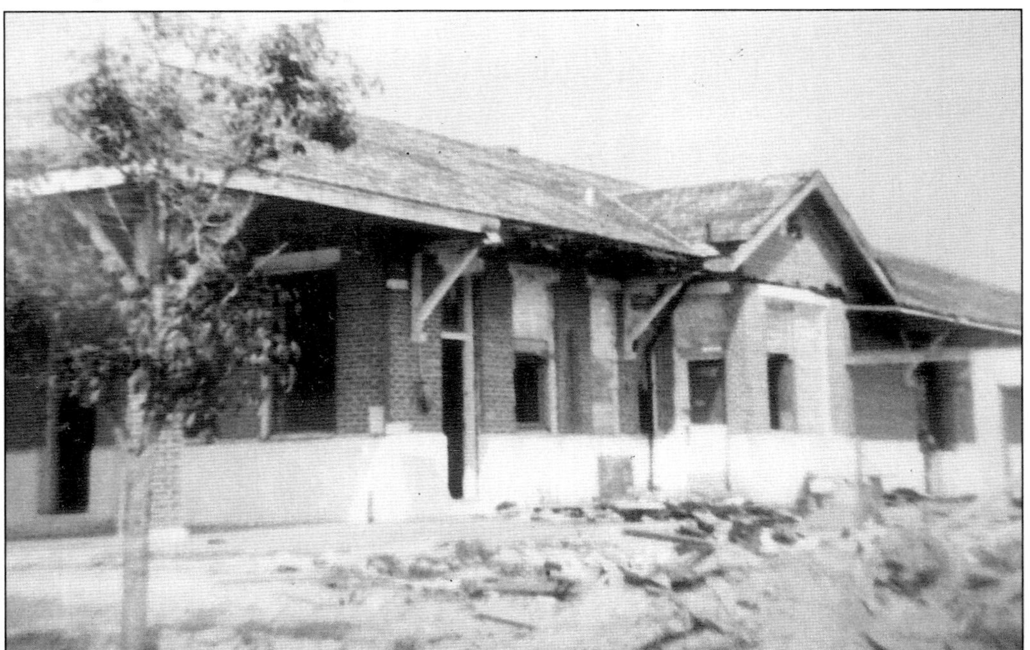

On Airport Road in Naples stood the attractive depot of the Atlantic Coast Line Railroad. However, after the company purchased the old Seaboard route from Bonita to Naples in the 1940s, the brick structure (near today's airport) became redundant and fell into disrepair, as this image confirms. It was later demolished. (Railroad Museum of South Florida Collection.)

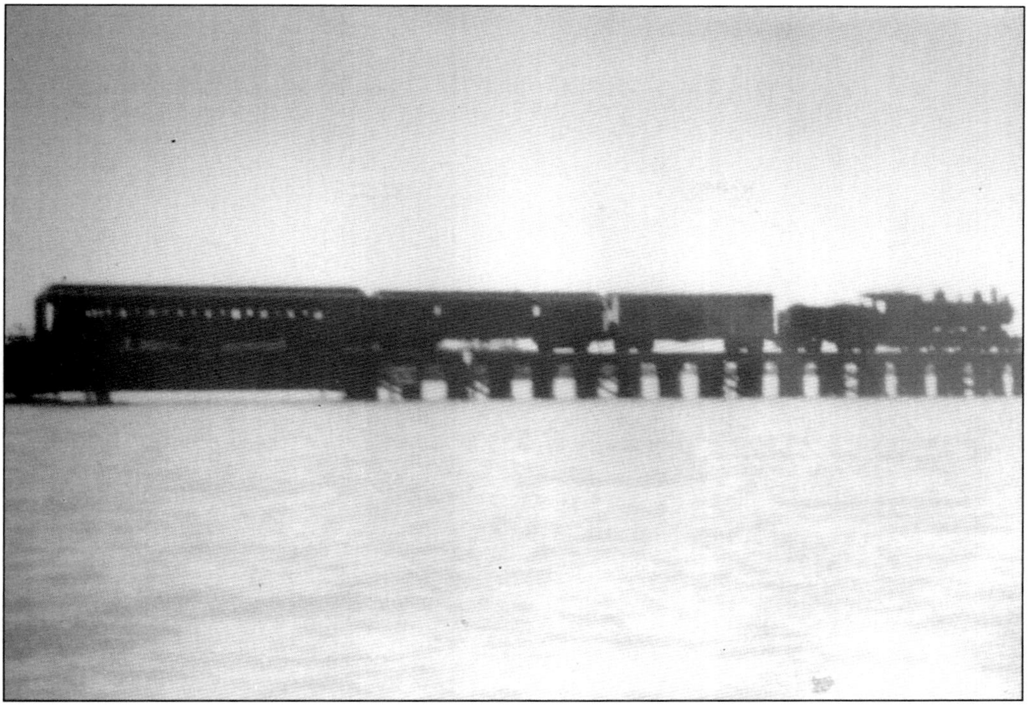

Both freight and passenger cars comprise a mixed train, and in this Coast Line view one is easing across the Marco River drawbridge. The trip from Collier City to Fort Myers was slow—a little over three hours—for the "mixed" stopped everywhere in search of business. (Collier County Historical Society courtesy Railroad Museum of South Florida Collection.)

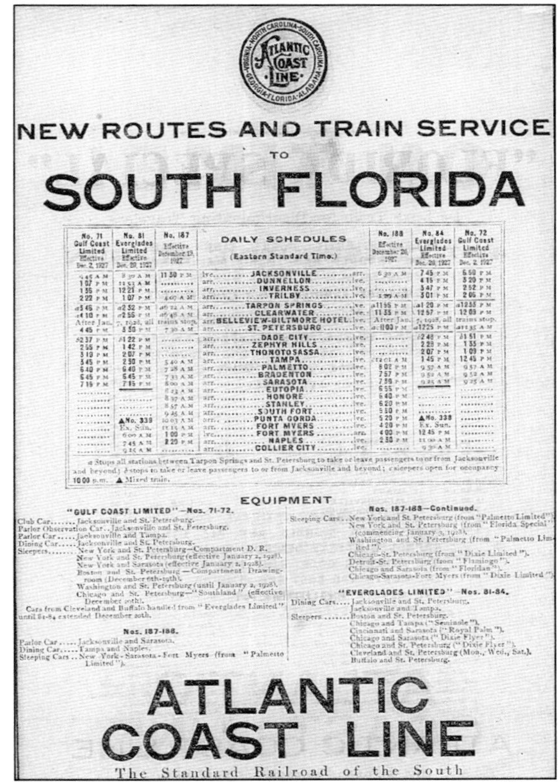

VIRGINIA · NORTH CAROLINA · SOUTH CAROLINA · GEORGIA · FLORIDA · ALABAMA · ATLANTIC COAST LINE

NEW ROUTES AND TRAIN SERVICE

TO

SOUTH FLORIDA

No. 71 Gulf Coast Limited Effective Dec. 2, 1927	No. 81 Everglades Limited Effective Dec. 20, 1927	No. 187 Effective December 19, 1927	DAILY SCHEDULES (Eastern Standard Time.)	No. 188 Effective December 20, 1927	No. 84 Everglades Limited Effective Dec. 20, 1927	No. 72 Gulf Coast Limited Effective Dec. 2, 1927
9 45 A M	8 30 A M	11 50 P M	lve. .... JACKSONVILLE .... arr.	6 30 A M	7 45 P M	6 50 P M
1 07 P M	11 53 A M	....	arr. .... DUNNELLON .... lve.	....	4 15 P M	3 20 P M
1 36 P M	12 21 P M	....	arr. .... INVERNESS .... lve.	....	3 47 P M	2 52 P M
2 22 P M	1 07 P M	4 07 A M	arr. .... TRILBY .... lve.	[illegible] A M	3 01 P M	2 06 P M
a5 46 P M	a2 52 P M	a6 22 A M	arr. .... TARPON SPRINGS .... lve.	a11 55 P M	a1 20 P M	a12 35 P M
a4 10 P M	a2 56 P M	a6 48 A M	arr. .... CLEARWATER .... lve.	11 35 P M	12 57 P M	12 09 P M
After Jan.	7, 1928, all	trains stop.	arr. BELLEVIEW-BILTMORE HOTEL. lve.	After Jan.	7, 1928, all	trains stop.
4 45 P M	3 50 P M	7 30 A M	arr. .... ST. PETERSBURG .... lve.	a11 00 P M	a12 25 P M	a11 35 A M
b2 37 P M	b1 22 P M	....	arr. .... DADE CITY .... lve.	....	b2 48 P M	b1 51 P M
2 55 P M	1 42 P M	....	arr. .... ZEPHYR HILLS .... lve.	....	2 28 P M	1 35 P M
3 19 P M	2 07 P M	....	arr. .... THONOTOSASSA .... lve.	....	2 07 P M	1 09 P M
3 45 P M	2 30 P M	5 40 A M	arr. .... TAMPA .... lve.	c12 01 A M	1 45 P M	12 45 P M
6 40 P M	6 40 P M	7 28 A M	arr. .... PALMETTO .... lve.	8 02 P M	9 57 A M	9 57 A M
6 45 P M	6 45 P M	7 33 A M	arr. .... BRADENTON .... lve.	7 57 P M	9 52 A M	9 52 A M
7 15 P M	7 15 P M	8 00 A M	arr. .... SARASOTA .... lve.	7 39 P M	9 25 A M	9 25 A M
....		8 23 A M	arr. .... EUTOPIA .... lve.	6 55 P M		....
....	....	8 37 A M	arr. .... HONORE .... lve.	6 40 P M	....	....
....	....	8 57 A M	arr. .... STANLEY .... lve.	6 20 P M	....	....
....	....	9 25 A M	arr. .... SOUTH FORT .... lve.	5 50 P M	....	....
....	▲No. 339	10 03 A M	arr. .... PUNTA GORDA .... lve.	5 20 P M	▲No. 338	....
....	Ex. Sun.	11 15 A M	arr. .... FORT MYERS .... lve.	4 20 P M	Ex. Sun.	....
....	6 00 A M	1 00 P M	lve. .... FORT MYERS .... arr.	4 00 P M	12 45 P M	....
....	7 45 A M	2 20 P M	arr. .... NAPLES .... lve.	2 30 P M	11 00 A M	....
....	9 25 A M	....	arr. .... COLLIER CITY .... lve.	....	9 30 A M	....

a Stops all stations between Tarpon Springs and St. Petersburg to take or leave passengers to or from Jacksonville and beyond; b stops to take or leave passengers to or from Jacksonville and beyond; c sleepers open for occupancy 10 00 p.m. ▲ Mixed train.

EQUIPMENT

"GULF COAST LIMITED"—Nos. 71-72.

Club Car....... Jacksonville and St. Petersburg.
Parlor Observation Car.. Jacksonville and St. Petersburg.
Parlor Car..... Jacksonville and Tampa.
Dining Car..... Jacksonville and St. Petersburg.
Sleepers........ New York and St. Petersburg—Compartment D. R.
New York and St. Petersburg (effective January 2, 1928).
New York and Sarasota (effective January 2, 1928).
Boston and St. Petersburg—Compartment Drawing-room (December 6th-19th).
Washington and St. Petersburg (until January 2, 1928).
Chicago and St. Petersburg—"Southland" (effective December 20th).
Cars from Cleveland and Buffalo handled from "Everglades Limited" until 81-84 extended December 20th.

Nos. 187-188.

Parlor Car..... Jacksonville and Sarasota.
Dining Car..... Tampa and Naples.
Sleeping Cars.. New York-Sarasota-Fort Myers (from "Palmetto Limited").

Nos. 187-188—Continued.

Sleeping Cars... New York and St. Petersburg (from "Palmetto Limited").
New York and St. Petersburg (from "Florida Special") (commencing January 3, 1928).
Washington and St. Petersburg (from "Palmetto Limited").
Chicago-St. Petersburg (from "Dixie Limited").
Detroit-St. Petersburg (from "Flamingo").
Chicago and Sarasota (from "Floridan").
Chicago-Sarasota-Fort Myers (from "Dixie Limited").

"EVERGLADES LIMITED"—Nos. 81-84.

Dining Cars.... Jacksonville and St. Petersburg.
Jacksonville and Tampa.
Sleepers........ Boston and St. Petersburg.
Chicago and Tampa ("Seminole").
Cincinnati and Sarasota ("Royal Palm").
Chicago and Sarasota ("Dixie Flyer").
Chicago and St. Petersburg ("Dixie Flyer").
Cleveland and St. Petersburg (Mon., Wed., Sat.).
Buffalo and St. Petersburg.

ATLANTIC COAST LINE

The Standard Railroad of the South

This timetable ad was issued in 1927, the year in which the Coast Line reached Collier City. The darkened triangle alongside the schedule for trains 338 and 339 indicate that only "mixed train" service was offered between Collier City and Fort Myers. The schedule also reflects train numbers 187 and 188, which used the Coast Line's recently completed Fort Ogden Extension between Sarasota and Southfort.

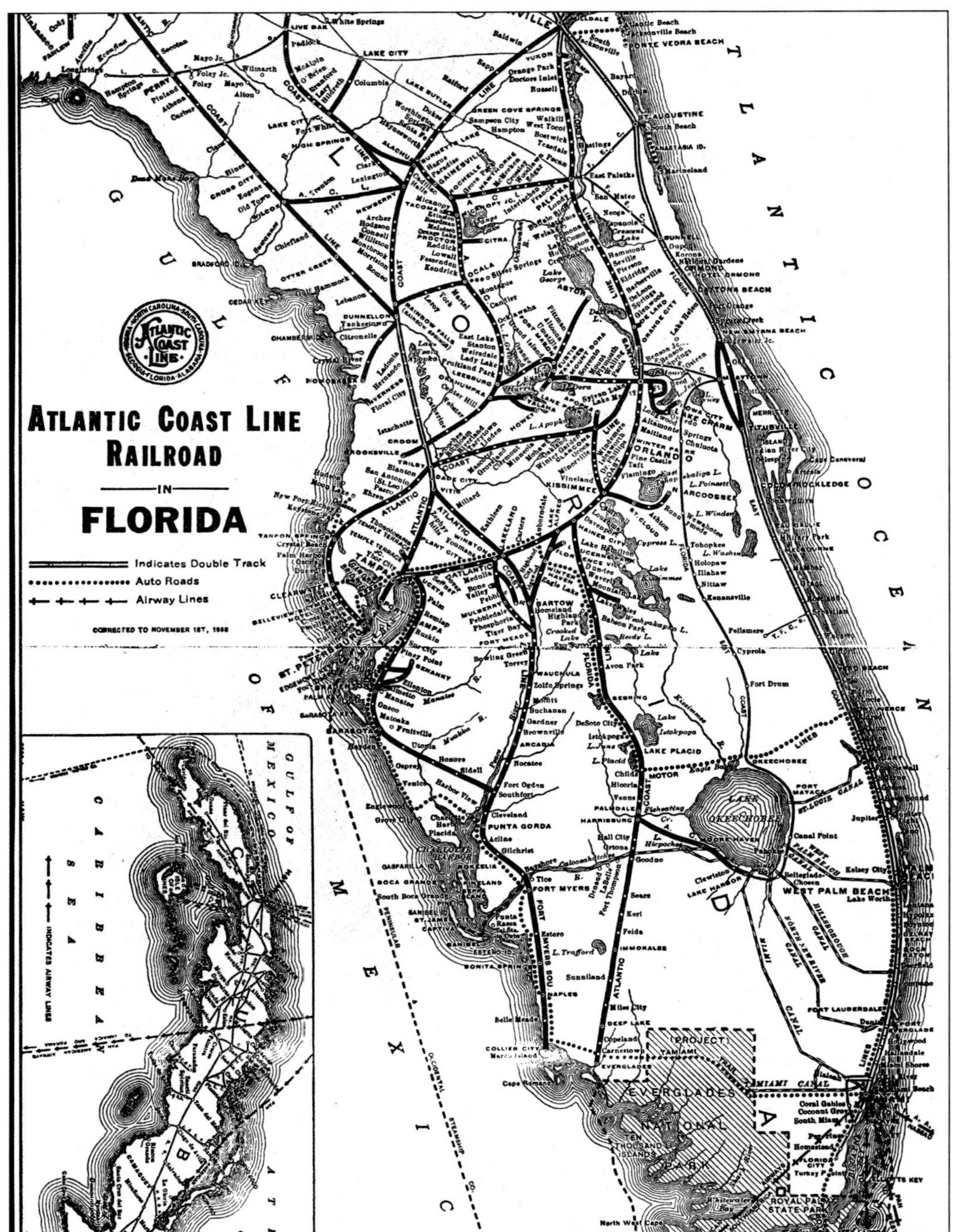

This corporate map of the Atlantic Coast Line illustrates how extensive its operations were in the Sunshine State. During Boom years, the firm completed three strategic lines in Southwest Florida: Sarasota to Southfort, Fort Myers to Collier City, and Deep Lake to Everglades City. All are visible. Not visible are lines belonging to rival Seaboard Airline Railway. By intentionally omitting them, the public would conclude that no other carrier served this part of the world.

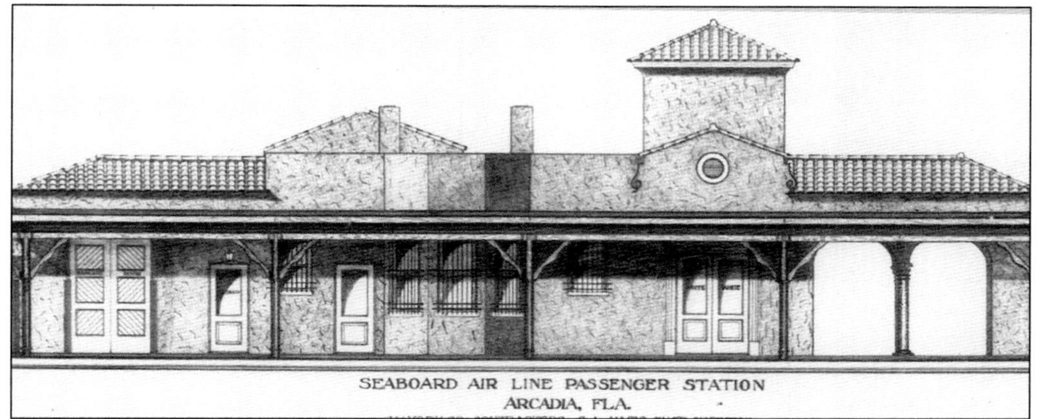

Many new stations appeared in Florida during the Boom years. The Seaboard erected a new passenger depot at Arcadia during the era near the Peace River on the old road to Bradenton. It no longer stands, but the drawing seen here suggests it had a Mediterranean Revival style. (Howard Melton.)

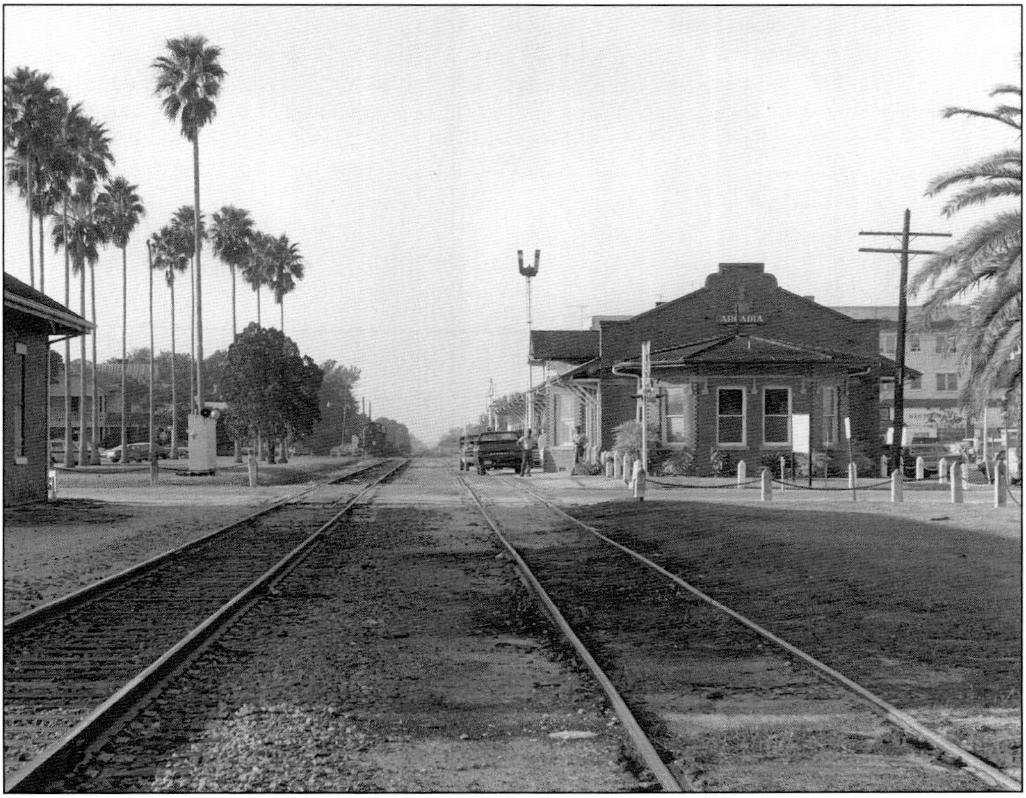

Arcadia was also served by the Atlantic Coast Line Railroad which erected a substantial brick station in 1911 to replace an earlier one of wood. The noted railroad photographer Fred Clark Jr. composed this peaceful image of it in November 1974. The building still stands and is today beautifully restored.

East and West Coast Railway

"MYAKKA RIVER ROUTE"

TIME TABLE No. 4

In Effect Nov. 14th, 1915 For Information of the Public

SUBJECT TO CHANGE WITHOUT NOTICE

Quick Freight & Passenger Service To & From All Points

Eastward 4 PASS'GR Sunday Only	Eastward 2 MIXED Daily Ex. Sun	Telegraph & Telephone	STATIONS (Between BRADENTOWN and ARCADIA)		Distance from Bradentown	Westward 1 MIXED Daily Ex. Sun	Westward 3 PASS'GR Sunday Only
P. M.	P. M.					A. M.	A. M.
3 30	1 50	TT	Lv........BRADENTOWN........	Ar	0.0	s10 00	s10 00
s3 33	s1 57		........BRADENTOWN JCT		1.0	s9 53	s9 57
s3 35	s2 00	TT	Ar ....MANATEE........	Lv	1.3	9 50	9 55
f3 37	f2 05		Lv	Ar		s9 45	s9 53
s3 39	s2 08		........S. A. L. .CT.........			s9 42	s9 51
f3 43	f2 14		........EAST MANATEE........		3.2	f9 32	f9 47
......	......		........BRADEN RIVER........				
f3 49	f2 24		........ALSACE........		5.1	f9 22	f9 41
f4 09	f2 42	T	........LORRAINE........		11.7	f9 02	f9 21
f4 38	f3 02	T	........ST. CLAIRE........		21.4	f8 42	f8 52
f4 48	f3 17		........PARMELEE........		24.5	f8 32	f8 42
s4 58	s3 32	TT	........MYAKKA CITY........		28.5	s8 20	s8 32
......	......		........MYAKKA RIVER........				
s5 01	s3 42	T	........EAST MYAKKA........		29.4	s8 15	s8 29
f5 18	f4 00		........PARKTON........		35.2	f7 55	f8 12
s5 34	s4 20	TT	........PINE LEVEL........		40.6	s7 33	s7 56
......	......		........HORSE CREEK........				
f5 40	f4 30		........TRYON........		42.4	f7 25	f7 50
s5 45	s4 35		........NOCATEE JCT..(K L.CO.)x		44.1	s7 17	s7 45
f5 50	f4 42	T	........BELGIUM........		47.0	f7 10	f7 40
......	......		........PEACE RIVER........				
s5 54	s4 47	T	......C. H. & N. CROSSING........		49.6	s7 05	s7 36
s6 00	s4 50	TT	Ar........ARCADIA........	Lv	50.3	7 00	7 30
P. M.	P. M.					A. M.	

A Direct Way Through the Heart of South Florida

SAFETY FIRST——Prompt Service——COURTESY

The Seaboard formerly leased the East & West Coast Railway during the Boom years, though a relationship developed between the two many years before. Timetables contain useful information, and this one of 1915 indicates that the only dedicated passenger train the company ran was on Sundays; otherwise, you took the "mixed."

It is not known where these couples posed on the East & West Coast Railway, or why, nor have their names come to light. Readers with information are asked to come forward. (Howard Melton.)

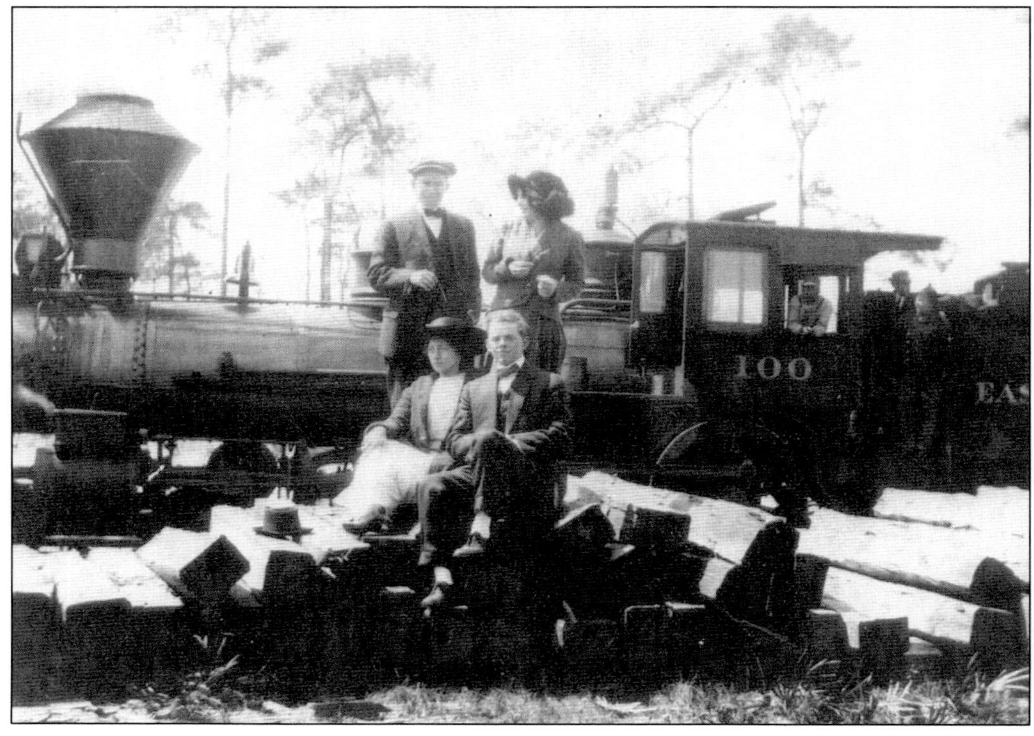

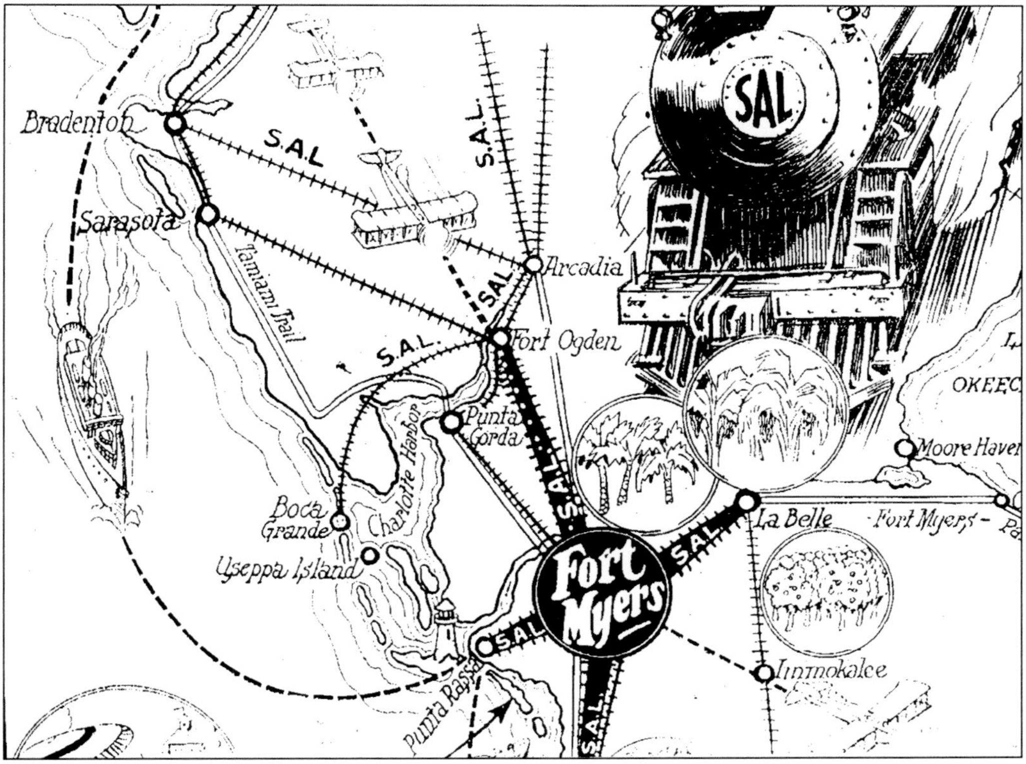

The message in this ad was unmistakable: the Seaboard Air Line was coming to Fort Myers. The unlabeled tracks belong to rival Atlantic Coast Line, whose territory the new extension pierced.

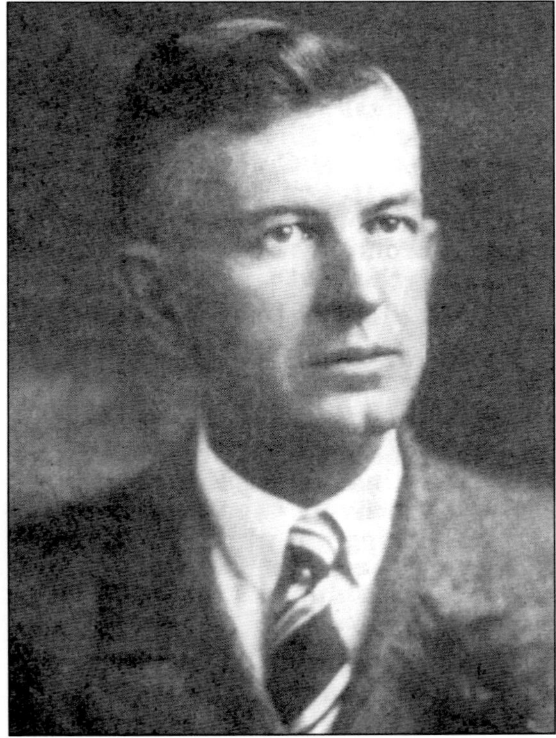

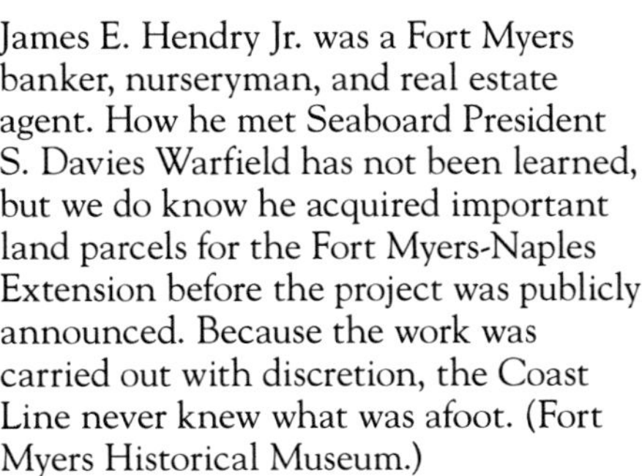

James E. Hendry Jr. was a Fort Myers banker, nurseryman, and real estate agent. How he met Seaboard President S. Davies Warfield has not been learned, but we do know he acquired important land parcels for the Fort Myers-Naples Extension before the project was publicly announced. Because the work was carried out with discretion, the Coast Line never knew what was afoot. (Fort Myers Historical Museum.)

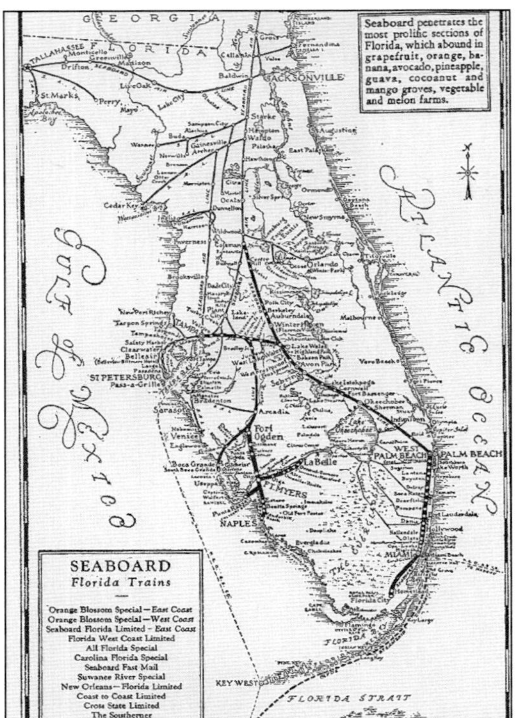

The thick black lines on this map depict two Seaboard extension projects: the one between Fort Myers and Naples, and the one from West Palm Beach to Miami. Both works were authorized under the Seaboard All-Florida Railway charter. The map was part of a commemorative booklet issued by the Seaboard just after both lines opened in early January 1927.

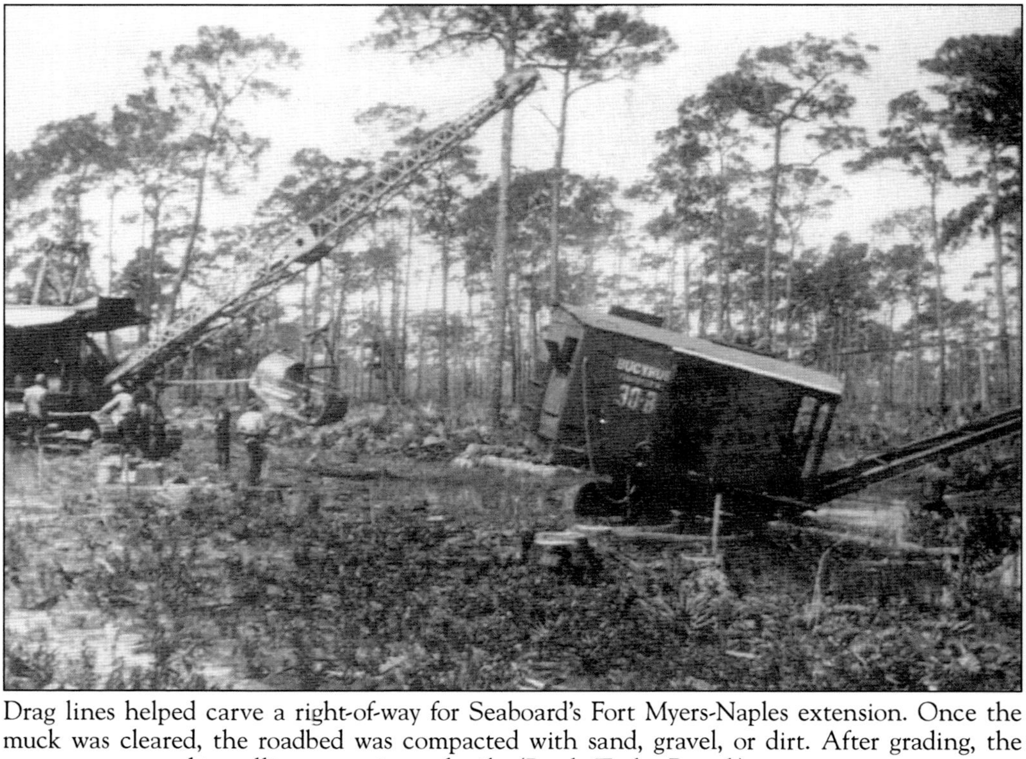

Drag lines helped carve a right-of-way for Seaboard's Fort Myers-Naples extension. Once the muck was cleared, the roadbed was compacted with sand, gravel, or dirt. After grading, the contractor started installing cross ties and rails. (Prudy Taylor Board.)

Construction crews on the Fort Myers-Naples extension occasionally encountered critters. This 11-foot specimen contested the railroad's invasion, and lost. (Prudy Taylor Board.)

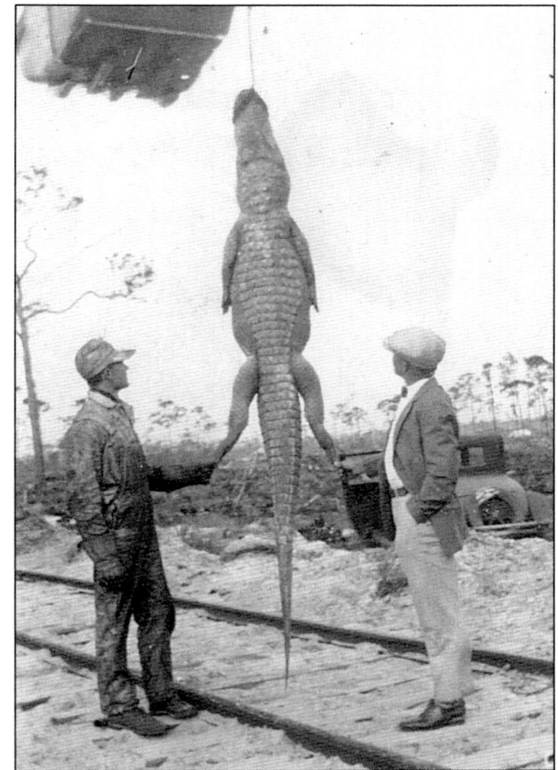

A "runabout" was needed as rail construction went forward on the Fort Myers-Naples extension. With a few cables one was hoisted on or off a flat car as needed. The derrick itself—self-propelled—climbed aboard the flat cars too, using a portable ramp. (Prudy Taylor Board.)

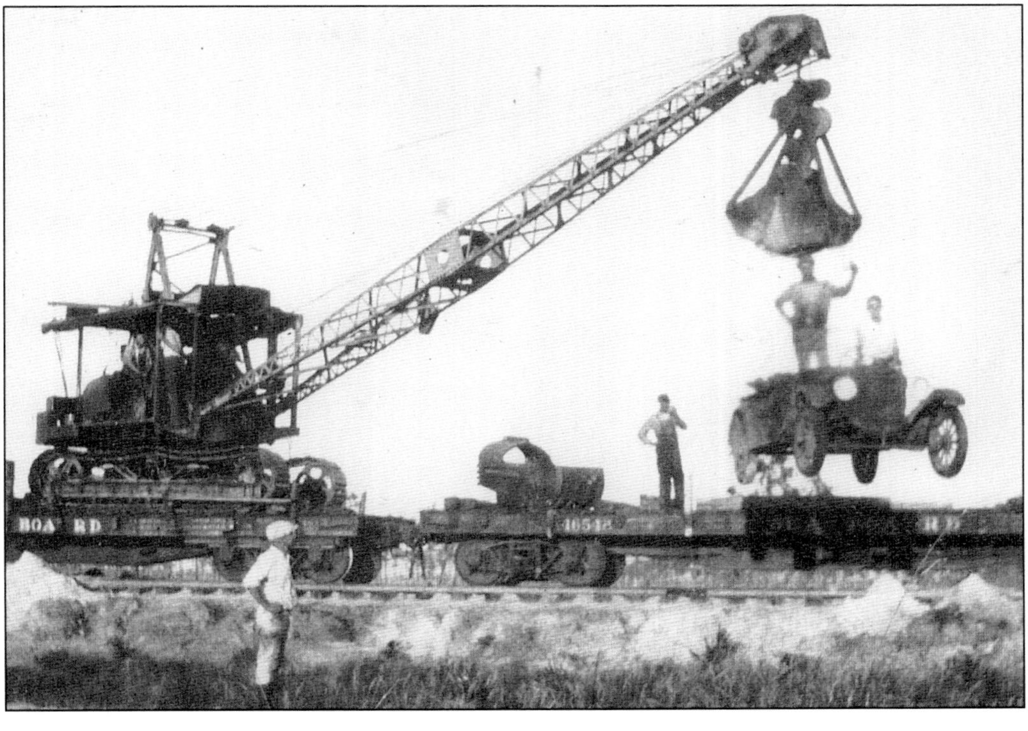

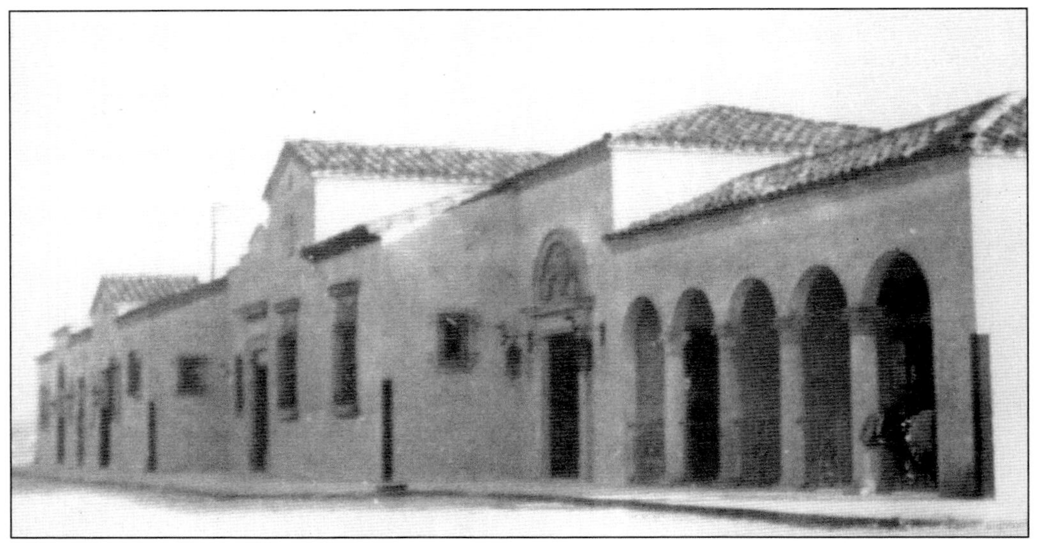

The Seaboard's passenger station at Fort Myers was located on East Riverside Drive and cost $75,000. The building itself was 200 feet long while the train shed measured over 500 feet. Inside, walls and ceilings were finished in mottled cream stucco with ivory trim. Architects Wiley & Clarke of West Palm Beach drew the plans. (Railroad Museum of South Florida Collection.)

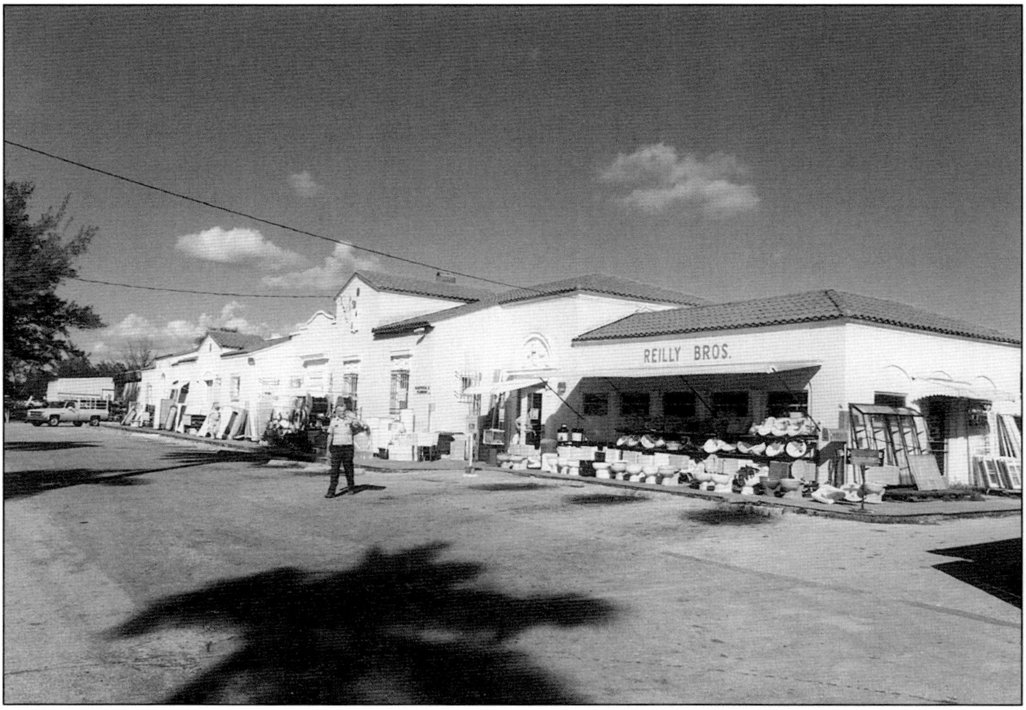

In 1952, the Seaboard exited the Fort Myers area. The station building was sold as well as the freight house on Michigan Avenue. Both survive. Whereas each have been modified through the decades, they still retain their Spanish mission flavor. A building supplies firm, Reilly Brothers, occupies the passenger station. (Photo by Mike Mulligan.)

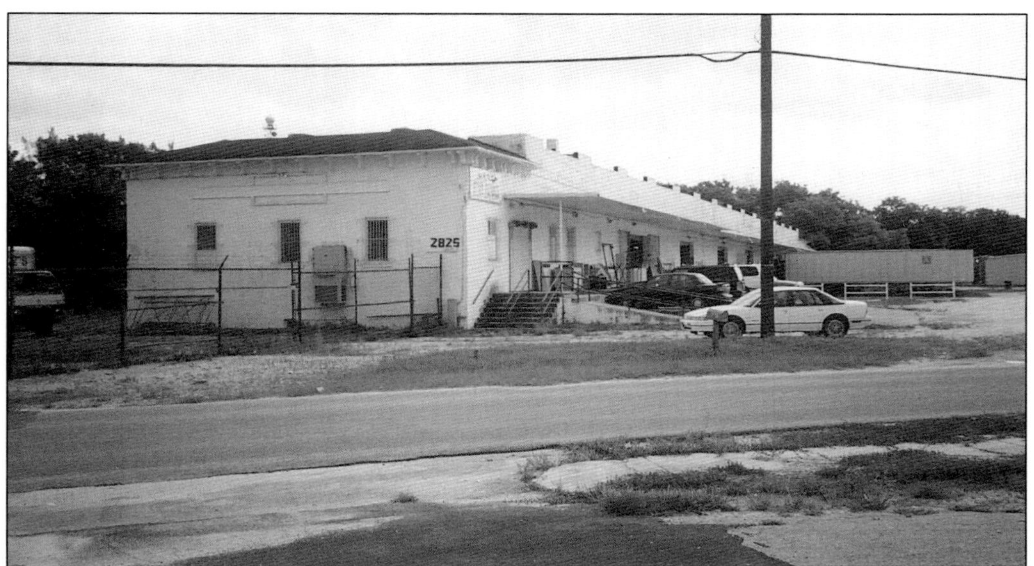

The Seaboard's freight house at Fort Myers cost $66,000 and had over 7,000 square feet of space. Platforms and ramps also existed at the Michigan Avenue facility; rail yards were next door. Today, the structure is occupied by Gully's Discount Store Fixtures.

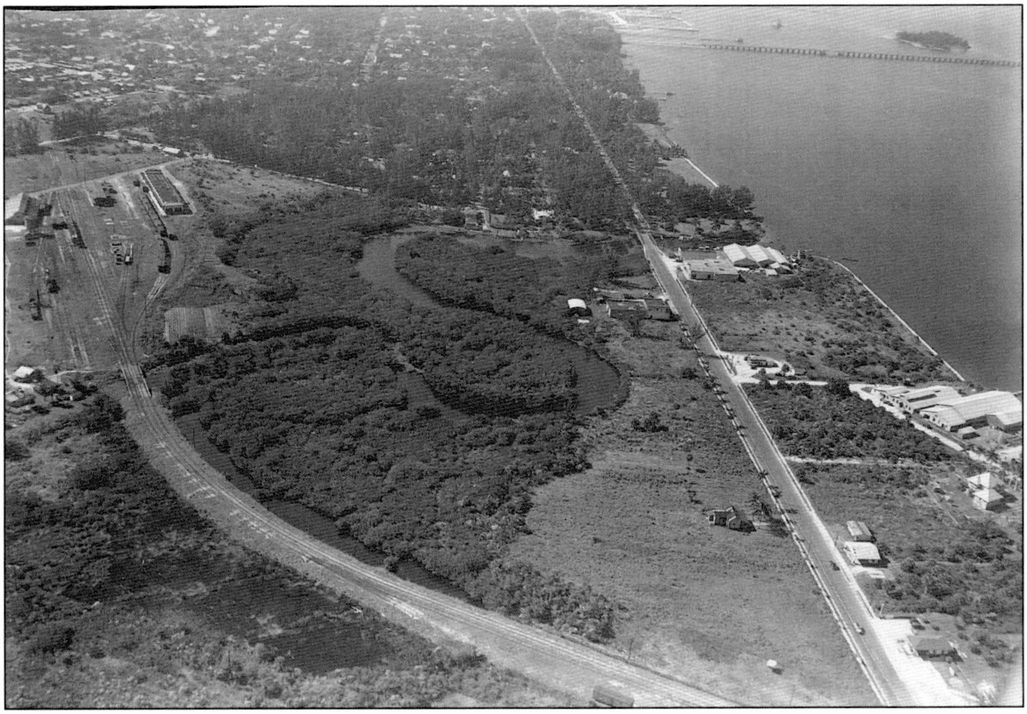

By closely inspecting the upper left side of this aerial photograph, the reader will see the Seaboard's terminal facilities at Fort Myers. To the right of yard tracks is the company's big freight house facing Michigan Avenue (seen in the previous photo). Paralleling the Caloosahatchee River is Palm Beach Boulevard. Billy's Creek snakes its way between the Boulevard and the north end of the yard tracks. (Harmon Photo & Video.)

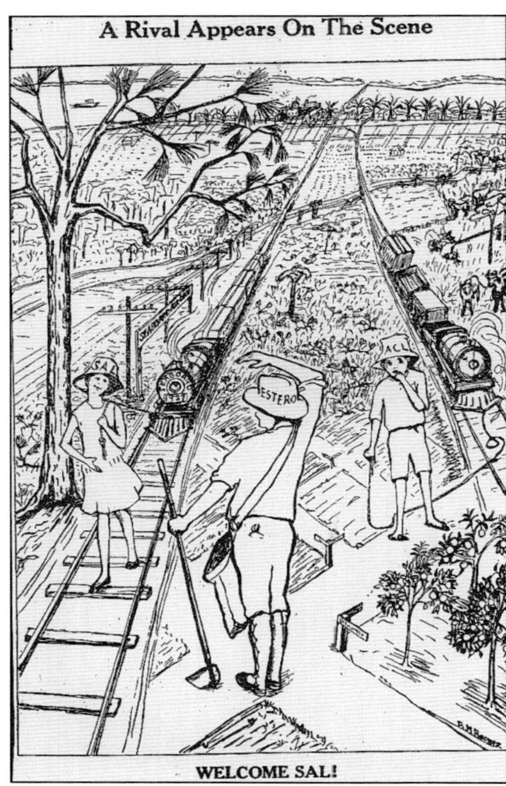

The Fort Myers-Naples Extension passed through tiny Estero. In this cartoon, an Estero citizen (see hat) is waving to an arriving Seaboard train pulled by "SAL," and ignores—on the opposite track—the Atlantic Coast Line which first served the hamlet.

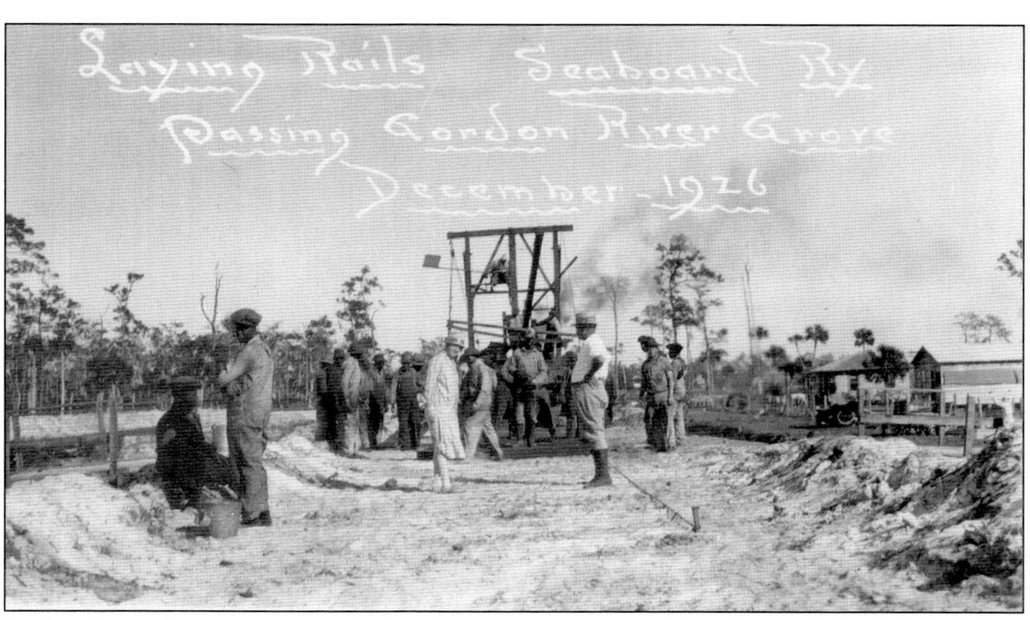

In this December 1926 scene, workers ease crossties and rails into position at Gordon River Groves in Naples. A stringline and stake, seen in the right foreground, helps guide the Roberts Track Laying machine which looms above workers. Previously the contractor has graded and smoothed the right-of-way. (Courtesy of the Collier County Museum, Naples, FL.)

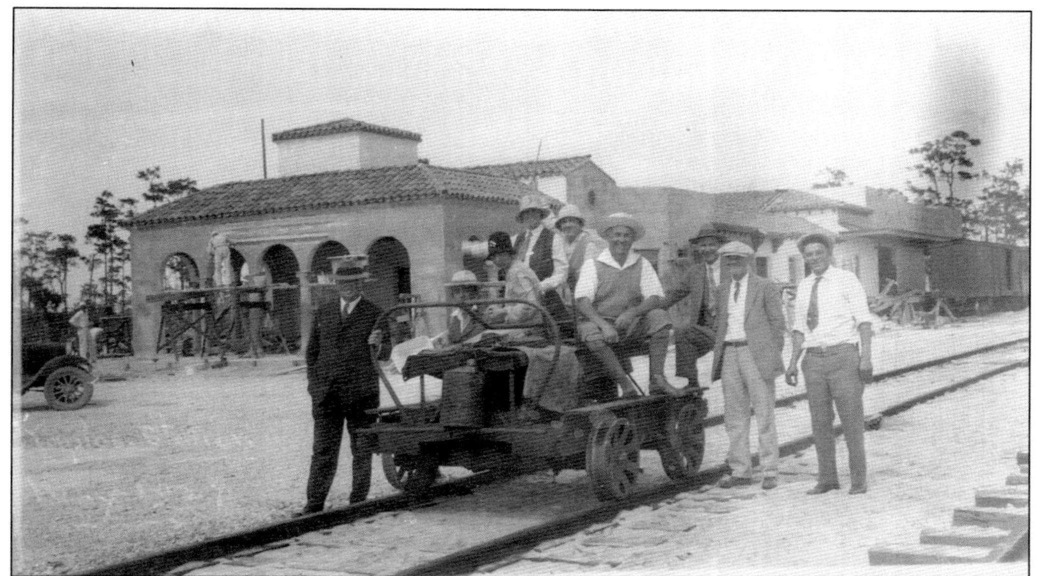

Employees of the Naples Company pose on a motorized section car that transports track workers up and down the line. Behind the party, a mason trowels the signboard of the new Naples depot. Freight was received at the opposite end of the building, where a lone box car rests. (Courtesy of the Collier County Museum, Naples, FL.)

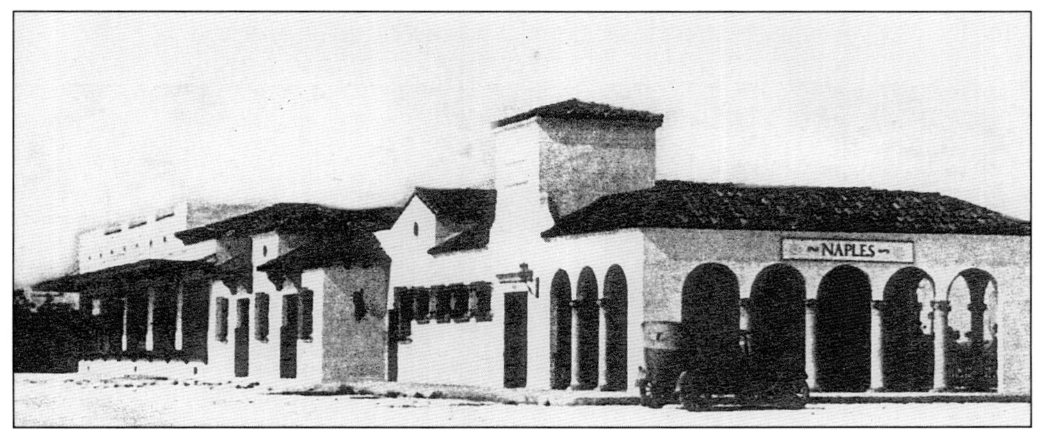

Ideally located at Fifth Avenue South at Tenth Street, the Seaboard station at Naples was conceived in the Mediterranean Revival style with a three-sided open arcade, five semi-circular arches, and four Corinthian columns. Trains no longer come and go, but the building has been beautifully restored and serves as a community arts center and railroad museum.

THE OPENING

of the Miami Extension

EAST COAST OF FLORIDA

AND THE

Fort Ogden-Fort Myers-Naples Extension

WEST COAST

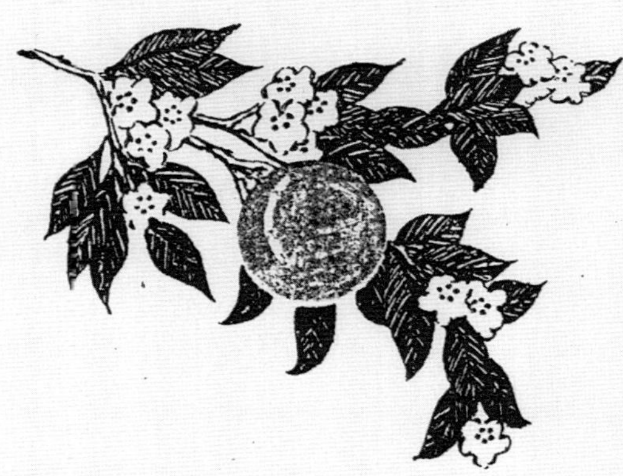

Seaboard Air Line Railway System

ORANGE BLOSSOM SPECIAL

(PRESIDENT'S SPECIAL)

1927

Celebrations marked the completion of Seaboard's Fort Myers-Naples Extension. Beginning on January 7, 1927, President S. Davies Warfield toured some 600 guests over the line using multiple sections of the famed Orange Blossom Special. A brochure was distributed to guests (cover seen here) that described the project and regions served. After touring Southwest Florida, the Specials departed for the East Coast where another Seaboard extension was opened. In all, some 21 cities and points were visited.

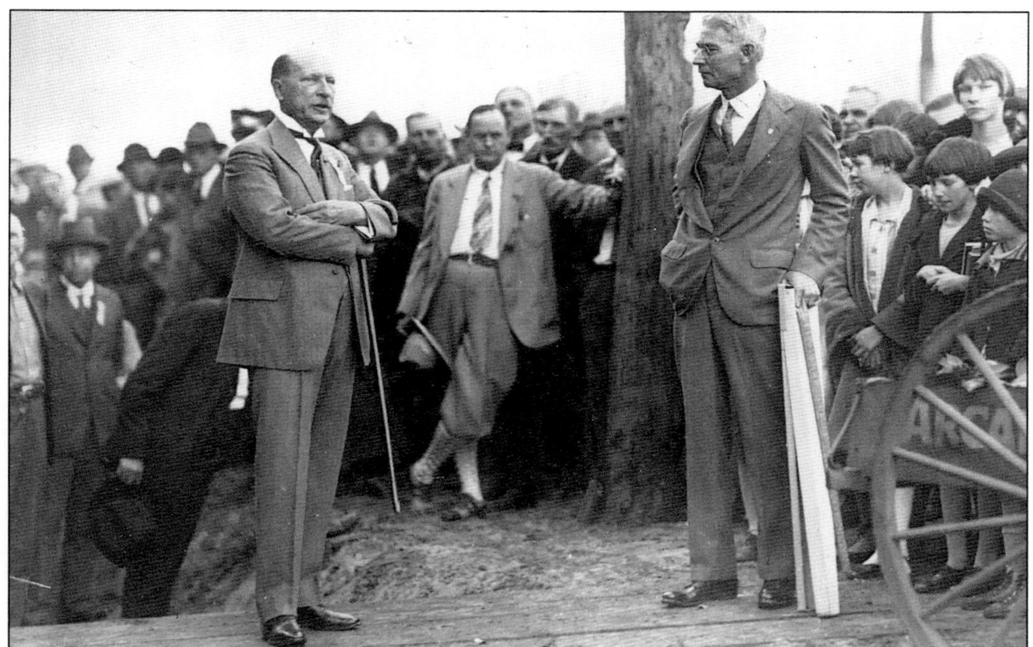

When Warfield descended his private car at Arcadia on the morning of January 7, 1927, he saw an astonishing sight: 2,000 citizens were on hand to greet the chairman. Chamber of Commerce secretary L.F. Eigle (near kids) has just presented Warfield with a cane, "to protect [him] against any interest that might in some way try to injure [him]." Most of Warfield's guests missed the outpouring, though—they were asleep in Pullman berths. (Florida State Archives.)

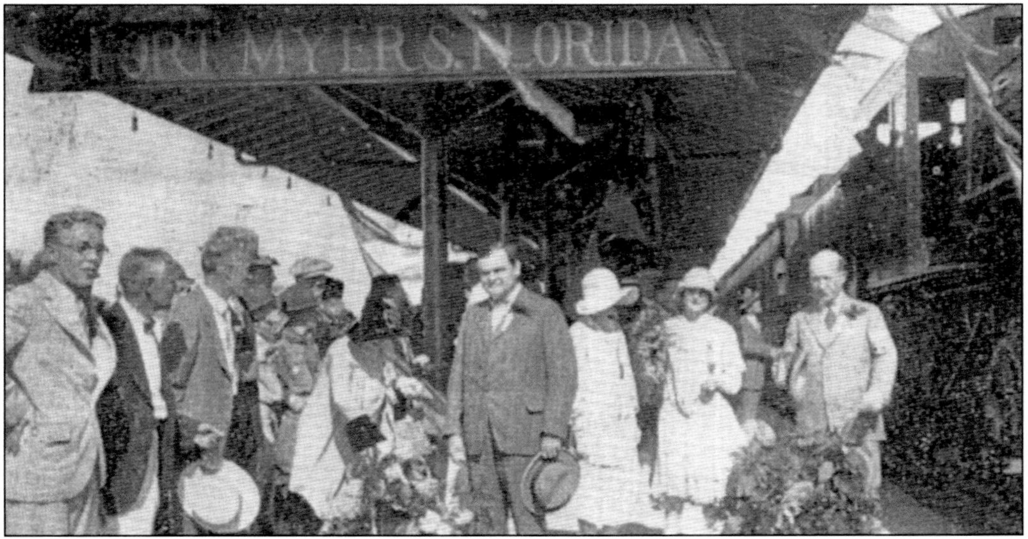

The Orange Blossom Special arrived in Fort Myers later that morning where a huge reception was staged. Warfield (far right) has just appeared on the station platform with Governor John Martin, who stands facing the camera with hat in hand. Motorcars toured guests around the City of Palms, but not before the bachelor chairman was photographed in the lead locomotive with Miss Southwest Florida.

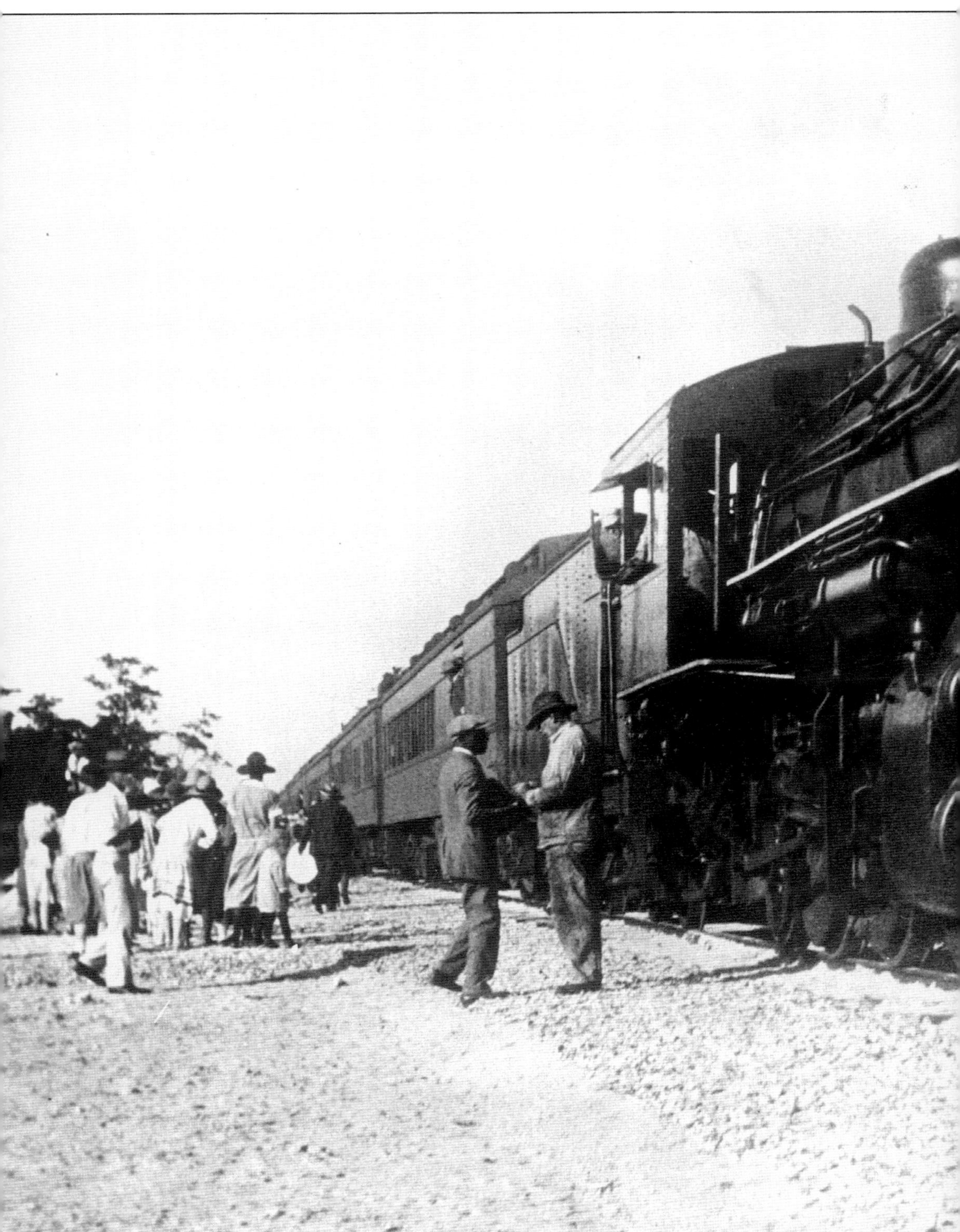

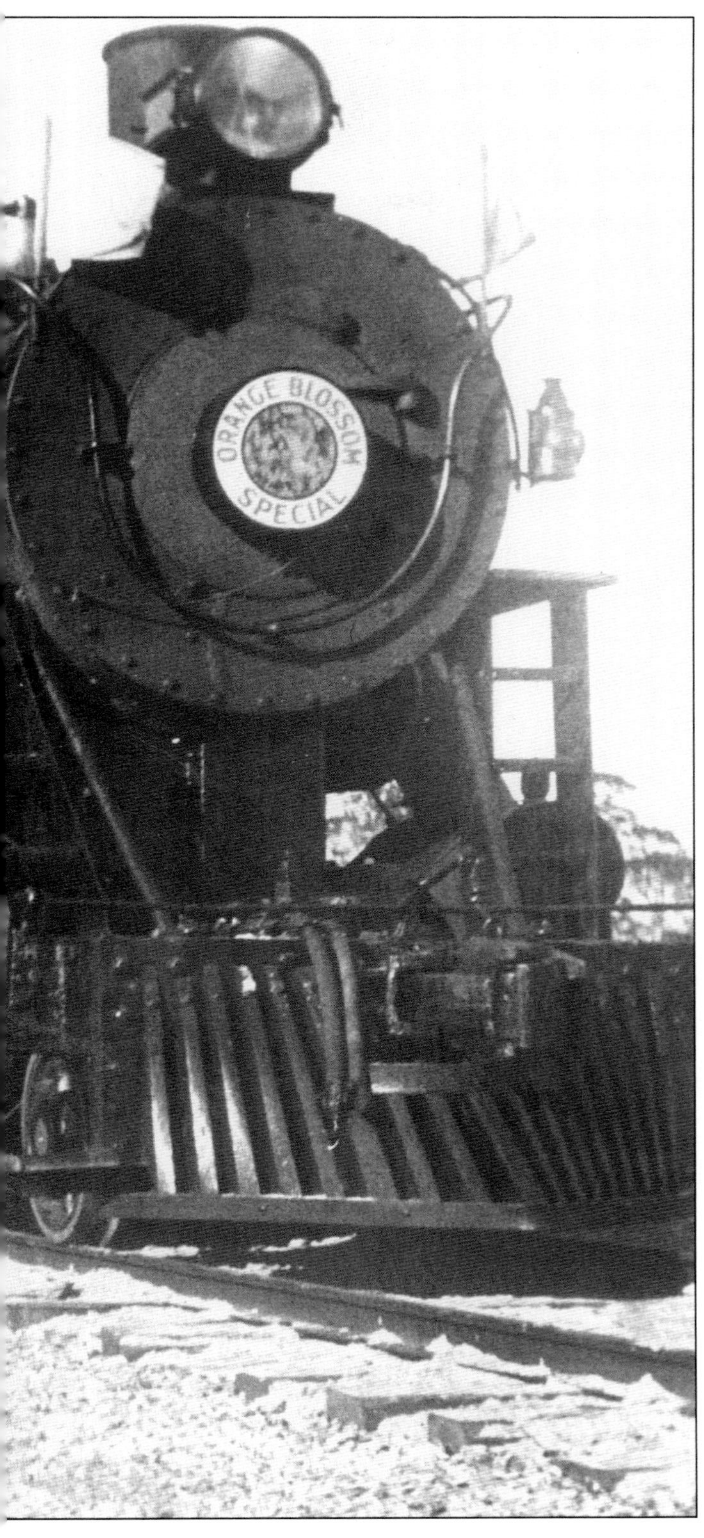

As five sections of the Orange Blossom Special eased into Naples, thunderous cheers went up from the crowd. Bands played and flags were waved. Hundreds of gaily decorated motorcars brought the Warfield entourage to the Naples Hotel for lunch, then took them sightseeing. Cameramen of the Pathe News Service recorded the event, which later appeared in moviehouses all across America. (Guests had been warned of this, and Seaboard officials asked that they "look pleasant.") In this wonderful photograph by Robert Fohl Sr., the lead locomotive pants under balmy Florida skies. The Naples station was not yet completed, nor—says legend—was the wye track for turning locomotives. Thus, all five Blossom sections had to be ignominiously backed up to Fort Myers that day in order that trains could be turned around. (Railway & Locomotive Historical Society.)

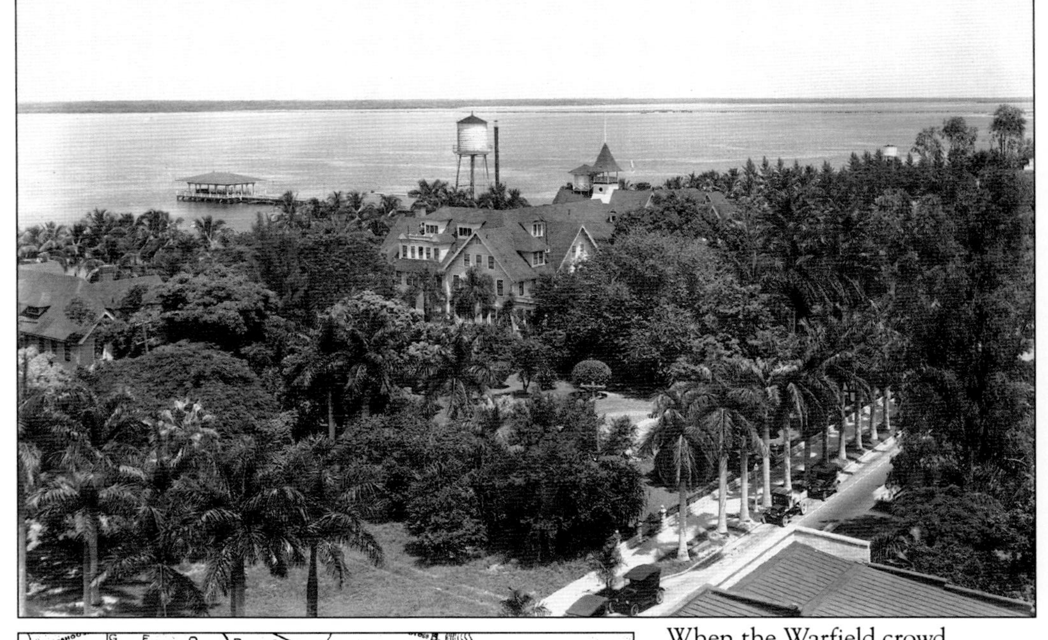

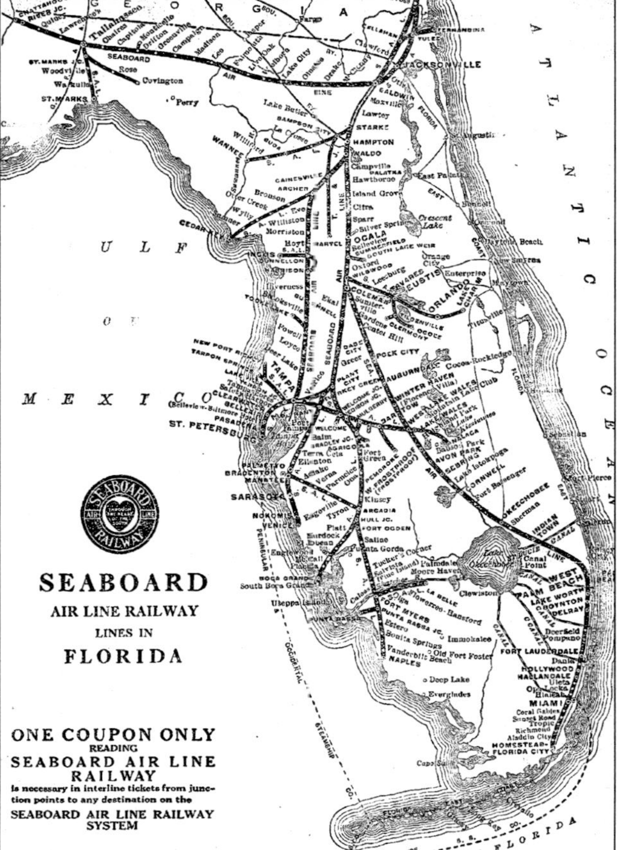

When the Warfield crowd returned to Fort Myers they were shuttled to the Royal Palm Hotel for ceremonies and dinner. Royal palms in fact lined the hotel's entranceway on Palm Beach Boulevard, and in the distance is the Seaboard's long drawbridge over the Caloosahatchee River. Prominent civic and business leaders feted Warfield, and after the party the trains departed for Miami and more festivities. (Fort Myers Historical Museum.)

The Seaboard routes in Florida are depicted in this 1927 map, including the recently completed Fort Myers-Naples Extension. That year the railroad map of Southwest Florida reached its greatest extent. Almost every town or city had a rail connection, or was very close to one.

Seven

The Pursuit of Business

"Your company believes that a great industrial expansion period lies ahead for the South."
—Annual Report, Atlantic Coast Line Railroad, 1943

The Atlantic Coast Line and Seaboard Air Line railroads competed for the transportation business of Southwest Florida for nearly 70 years. Passengers provided valuable revenues for each firm, but the serious money was made in the movement of freight. To obtain it, business had to be pursued.

At one time, this region of Florida yielded vast amounts of forest products. Logging companies harvested the timber—often using their own private railroad—whereupon the traffic was shipped over Coast Line or Seaboard rails. Manasota Land & Timber, for instance, operated near Venice, while J. Ray Arnold Company penetrated timber stands near Laurel. McWilliams Lumber built a huge sawmill complex at Slater in North Fort Myers, reputedly the largest in Florida, and logged most of Northern and Western Lee County. Dowling & Camp, which succeeded McWilliams in 1929, stripped enormous quantities of old-growth pine from eastern Lee County during the 1930s and 1940s, and in the process established logging camps at Hickey Creek. No less than 10 locomotives comprised the D & C roster, and its rail line connected with both the Coast Line and Seaboard firms.

Roux Crate & Lumber acquired huge timber rights in Charlotte County during the 1930s. Yellow Pine was harvested, which was fashioned into tunnel supports for mines in South America and South Africa. Roux, too, operated its own internal railroad which connected with the Seaboard. Cummer & Sons penetrated timber stands near Immokalee that were owned by the Barron Collier family. Jones Lumber operated at Jerome, while Copeland became homebase for Lee Tidewater Cypress. Vestiges of these old logging railroads can still be detected, and hopefully one day a book will appear chronicling their unique and colorful operations.

Both the Seaboard and Coast Line dealt with explosive growth during the Roaring Twenties, but the decade which held so much ended on a sour note. The stock market crashed, a national depression loomed, and railroads everywhere hunkered down to survive.

S. Davies Warfield, Seaboard's dynamic leader whose faith in Florida was unshakable, died in 1927. That year Seaboard reported a mere $31,576 of net income on revenues of $61.7 million. The company's Boom projects had proved costly, plus the railroad was facing heightened competition—as was the Coast Line—from automobiles, trucks, buses, boat lines, and airplanes. Economies were quickly instituted by both companies. Expenses were slashed, and poorly patronized passenger trains were canceled. But the measures, at least for the Seaboard, were not enough. In 1930, the company slipped into receivership where it remained until 1946. On June 7, 1931, passenger train service on its Fort Myers-Naples Extension was reduced to a mixed (freight and passenger) train operating just three days a week. Two years later, even this vanished. Most of the company's East & West Coast Railway subsidiary (Arcadia to Bradenton) was ripped up in 1933, a casualty of the Depression.

The Atlantic Coast Line escaped bankruptcy for it was better capitalized and more conservatively run. Nevertheless, it was forced to skip dividends, lower wages, and dismiss valuable personnel. Not a single new engine or passenger car was purchased from 1926 until 1938. Revenues in 1929 were $72.3 million, and net income amounted to $9.3 million. Three years later a loss of $6.6 million was sustained on revenues of $37.2 million. The Depression impacted every form of traffic. Agricultural prices were depressed and market demand for Florida-grown products was small. Refrigerated ships even appeared that robbed the railroads of citrus shipments.

To regain passenger traffic, both railroad companies went on the offensive. Air-conditioning was installed in coaches, fares were cut, new trains were added, and schedules were speeded up. Streamlined cars and fast diesel engines were also ordered—two areas in which the Seaboard excelled. Company-printed booklets and pamphlets appeared touting Florida's attractions, climate, and accommodations. To the delight of railroad executives, the trucking industry became regulated under the Motor Carrier Act of 1935, which was administered by the Interstate Commerce Commission.

Business started to improve as the 1940s approached. Then, traffic increased in earnest as the nation faced wartime challenges. Military installations could be found all over Florida, and many received supplies, materials, and munitions by rail.

At the start of World War II, Florida possessed 5,331 miles of railroads. The Coast Line operated 1,983; the Seaboard claimed 1,680. The single biggest commodity moved by both firms were products of mines—phosphate, sand, gravel, minerals, etc. Later, as the submarine menace took hold, the railroads transported endless trains of petroleum and phosphate. Foodstuffs increased, too. Cuban sugar, once landed in Florida, departed for American markets by rail and increased during the war by 233%; bananas rose by 419%. Seaboard revenues jumped to $110.2 million in 1942 (versus $64.6 million the year before) while a 70% increase in revenues was experienced on the Coast Line. Service personnel were shuttled about on trains, and the number of men and women in uniform that were transported eclipsed that of tourists.

In 1942, in an effort to cut expenses, the Seaboard abandoned parts of its Fort Myers-Naples Extension, which was a mere 15 years old. A 27-mile section between Punta Rassa Junction (South Fort Myers) and Naples was scrapped and almost 2 miles were lopped off the Punta Rassa Branch from Truckland to San Carlos. Thirteen miles also vanished on the LaBelle Subdivision between Alva and LaBelle, including the LaBelle uptown spur. The cost of maintaining these lines was prohibitive, and the traffic insignificant. In 1943, the Seaboard finally showed a profit of $15.7 million after all obligations (except bond interest) were paid. The same report also noted that $1.2 million was charged off regarding the recent abandonment of the old Naples, Seaboard & Gulf Railroad between the Estero River and Naples proper.

Meanwhile, revenues on the Coast Line hit a new high in 1942 ($153.6 million) and for the first time the company's tax bill ($51.2 million) became the largest single expense item of doing business. Stockholders were told the following year that the spectacular earnings of late "were affected by factors which will not be present in the postwar period. The volume of traffic will decrease and competition of other transportation agencies will increase."

News concerning Southwest Florida appeared in the Coast Line's 1944 annual report. The company's spur tracks that serviced the Caloosahatchee River waterfront in Fort Myers had been removed, plus a new entrance into Naples proper had been achieved by purchasing the recently abandoned Seaboard mainline between Bonita, Vanderbilt, and Naples. A connecting track was installed at Bonita to reach Seaboard rails, whereupon the old Seaboard line into Naples proper was rebuilt. Even the Seaboard station at Naples was acquired. Later, the Coast Line removed its own rails—some 23 miles—between Bonita Springs and Marco Island, including the drawbridge over Big Marco Pass.

During the 1940s and 1950s the Coast Line derived a considerable traffic along the Immokalee Branch. Packing houses appeared and a great variety of products were grown, such as tomatoes, watermelons, cucumbers, squash, okra, peppers, beans, eggplant, cabbage, peas, green beans, cantaloupes, sweet potatoes, strawberries, and Irish potatoes. Timber also contributed to traffic revenues. Lee Tidewater Cypress became the world's largest producer of cypress lumber during the era. Cypress logs from Collier County left Copeland for Perry, Florida—417 miles away—where they were milled. By October 1956, over 36,000 carloads had been sent in this manner. The May 29, 1954 edition of the *Saturday Evening Post* magazine ran a feature story about the operation entitled "Loggers of the Unknown Swamp." By 1957, though, the last desirable cypress stands had been cut.

Germany surrendered in May 1945 and Japan followed suit 90 days later. In the following year, a new Seaboard Air Line Railroad emerged from the bankruptcy courts, and both it and the Coast Line began adjusting to the postwar economy. Fortunately, many military personnel and manufacturers had discovered the South during the war years, and many stayed or relocated to the region. In 1949, the Coast Line eliminated most of its little used Fort Ogden Extension between Sarasota (Belspur) and Southfort (Fort Ogden).

A Coast Line subsidiary hardly known to the public was the Atlantic Land & Improvement Company. Formed in 1898, its purpose was to operate terminal properties and to acquire, rent, and sell real estate. Eventually it acquired some 250,000 acres of land, and the timber thereon was used for fuel, crossties, trestles, buildings, and box car construction. Many of the tracts were located in Southwest Florida and consisted of pine and palmetto flatwoods, scrub oak, and piney highlands. In 1948, the company established its South Florida Program at LaBelle to manage the properties. Grazing leases were increased, plus the project undertook farming, citrus, and cattle endeavors. In 1960, the land project became known as Alico Land Development Company, then Alico, Inc. in 1974. A controlling interest was later obtained by Ben Hill Griffin Jr., a self-made Florida millionaire, citrus grower, processor, rancher, and banker. Under Griffin's direction, Alico truly prospered. Today, the firm is publicly traded on the NASDAQ exchange, and recently the company supplied a location for Florida Gulf Coast University in Fort Myers.

Whereas both the Seaboard and Coast Line experienced postwar industrial growth along its routes, not all areas of Florida benefited. In 1950, traffic had declined to such a point in Southwest Florida that the Seaboard decided to abandon the last of its Fort Myers-Naples Extension. The company complained to the Interstate Commerce Commission that timber deposits of the region had been depleted, truckers were moving most of the citrus and vegetable harvests, and what was left could easily be moved by the Atlantic Coast Line. Company officials also documented that the Seaboard's physical plant needed rebuilding. Rails on the little-used LaBelle subdivision (Fort Myers to Alva) were now completely worn out, plus the archaic, crank-lift bridge over the Orange River faced major repairs. Worst of all was the decaying condition of the Caloosahatchee River drawbridge at Fort Myers, which needed total replacement.

Area potato and gladiolus growers on the Punta Rassa Branch fought the Seaboard abandonment as did politicians and representatives from the railroad brotherhoods. The commission, however, ultimately sided with the Seaboard for it believed Lee County did not require the services of two trunk railroads. As the Seaboard's 1952 annual report noted: "In view of diminished traffic without prospect for sufficient improvements to justify continued operation, coupled with the immediate need for heavy maintenance . . . your Company sought and obtained authority from the ICC to abandon its line from Hull (Fort Ogden) to Fort Myers and the two extensions Fort Myers to San Carlos and to Alva, a total of 65 miles." Operations were discontinued in November 1952, and the physical removal of the lines commenced at once. In retrospect, the line that Warfield had opened amidst such fanfare in 1927 lasted a mere 25 years. Later, on April 25, 1959, the Seaboard withdrew passenger service to Boca Grande.

The Coast Line inaugurated its popular "Champion" vacation packages (named after Coast Line trains) in 1954. Radio communication was experimented with the following year at Fort Myers. In 1958, because of diminished traffic, the company abandoned part of its Immokalee Branch between Everglades City and Copeland; three years later it removed trackage between Copeland and Sunniland.

Perhaps the biggest news of the decade occurred in 1958 when the Seaboard and Coast Line jointly announced that they were in merger discussions. Whereas the marriage proposal surprised many industry executives and observers, most felt it made perfect sense to combine two healthy, comparable firms that served the same territory.

Both companies went about their business while final approval was sought for the merger. In July 1960 the Coast Line sold its downtown Fort Myers property for municipal purposes and completed a 40-acre yard complex south of town. During that decade, the Coast Line also opened a new headquarters building in Jacksonville, inaugurated piggyback train service, installed the industry's first data processing equipment, and shuttled visitors to the New York World's Fair. The Seaboard was equally busy buying new diesel locomotives, locating new business customers, improving freight and passenger train services, and installing welded rail. Finally on July 1, 1967, the Coast Line and Seaboard railroads became one, and a new chapter in Florida railroad history began.

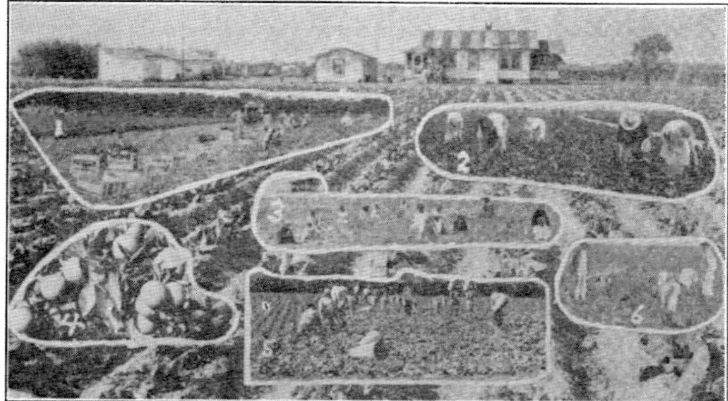

A wide variety of vegetable and fruit crops increases the possibilities for profitable winter farming in Florida. The illustrations show:

(1) Harvesting celery.
(2) Picking bell peppers.
(3) Hired colored labor picking strawberries in December.
(4) Citrus fruits.
(5) Harvesting lettuce.
(6) Gathering snap beans.

A small truck farm home is shown in background.

Thomas A. Edison Says Unlimited Field For Farmers In South

IN A recent interview at his famous winter home at Fort Myers, Florida, Mr. Edison said: "There is an unlimited field for the farmer in the South . . On my field trips through South Florida, I have noticed men clearing land and preparing it for fall. That is working in the right direction." Evidently this noted genius quickly recognized the advantages of Florida, for he has maintained his winter residence there for many years. In fact, it is claimed he lighted his first incandescent light in his experimental work shop at Fort Myers.

TARIFF ON IMPORTED VEGETABLES SHOULD BENEFIT FLORIDA TRUCK FARMERS

Mr. Arthur M. Hyde, Secretary of the U. S. Department of Agriculture, in a recent radio talk stated that the new tariffs will affect approximately $620,000,000 worth of imported agricultural products in both raw and processed forms, based on quantities imported in 1928. Some of the leading commodities that have heretofore been heavily imported are grapefruit, tomatoes, peppers, green peas, string beans, egg-plant, cucumbers and cabbage. Thousands of acres of these and other vegetables and fruits are produced in Florida each year; and there are many locations in that state where climatic and soil conditions combine to offer unsurpassed opportunities for the expansion of these activities to meet the entire demand of the Northern markets in winter.

This Department is in position to assist in the selection of lands and locations suited to practically any phase of agriculture. We have contacts with those who own large and small tracts of desirable farm lands that may be leased by the season, or purchased on terms. Complete data describing opportunities and conditions in specific localities in various districts of Florida, and other states of the Southeast, will be gladly furnished upon request.

"Wealth and fertility unlimited are in Florida soil."—*Arthur Brisbane.*

SEABOARD AIR LINE RAILWAY

J. N. McBRIDE,

General Agricultural and Land Settlement Agent,
202 Liberty Bank Building, Savannah, Ga.

The fertile growing fields of Southwest Florida yielded traffic for both the Seaboard Air Line and Atlantic Coast Line railroads. In this 1931 ad, inventor Thomas Alva Edison, who wintered in Fort Myers, extolls the wonders of Florida farming. Hopefully a party "up North" would read the endorsement and become interested. Whereas both railroads were at the ready with land, the real goal was to bring crops to marketplace over Seaboard or Coast Line rails.

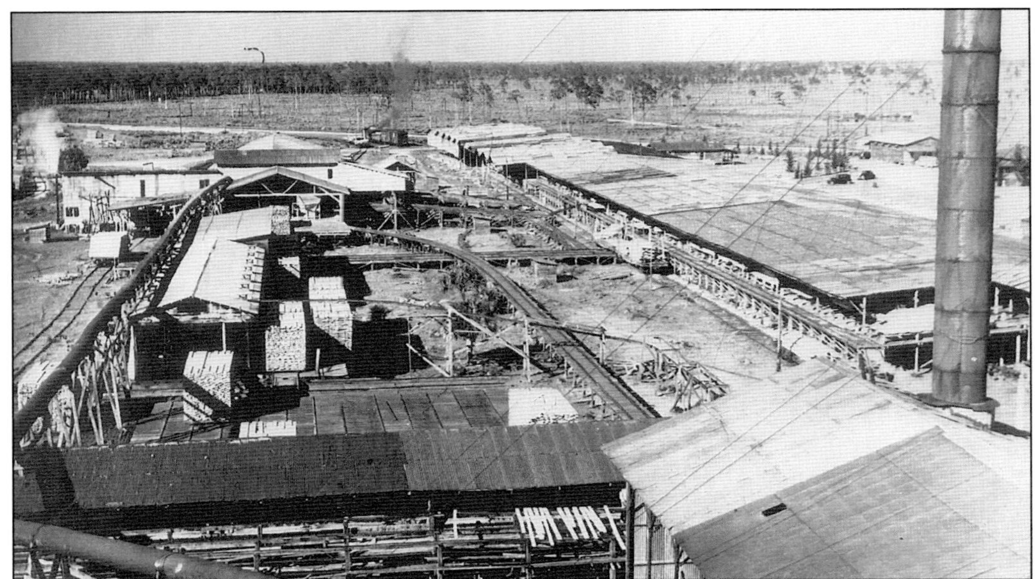

The McWilliams Lumber Mill, located at Slater, ran its own logging railroad. A connection was made here with the Atlantic Coast Line, whose manicured track can be seen in the distance running left to right. In 1925, 50,000 board-feet of lumber was produced daily. Dowling & Camp succeeded in 1929 and operations grew even bigger. (Fort Myers Historical Museum.)

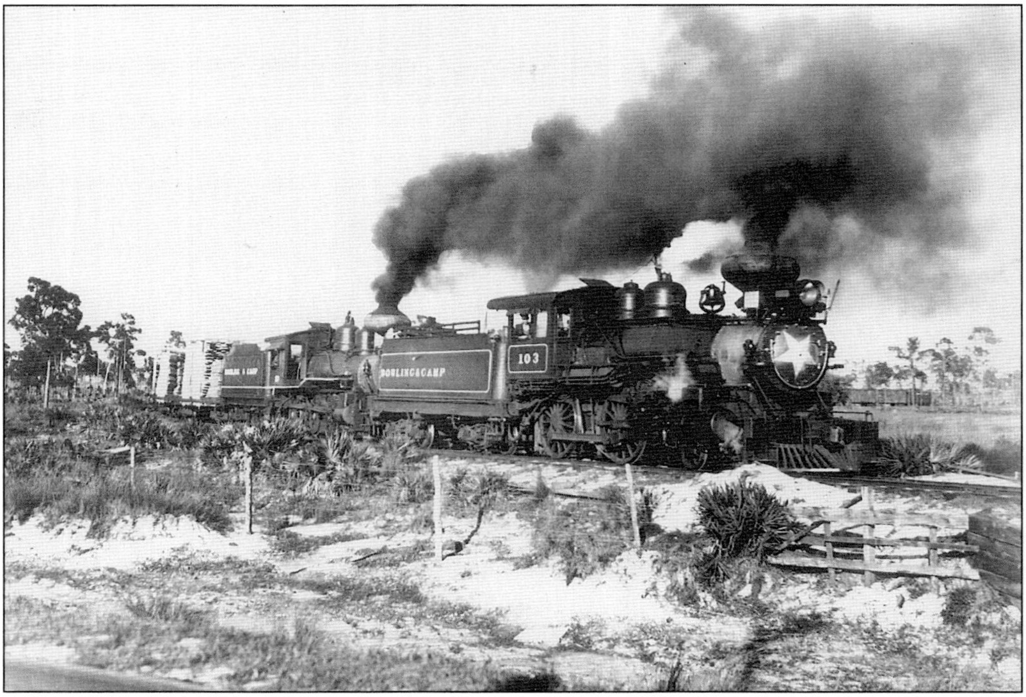

Two Dowling & Camp steam engines—each with cabbage-head stacks—take charge of a 111-car train whose manifest is actually bound for South America. Engine No. 103, built by Baldwin, arrived on the property in 1933. At Slater, D&C connected with the Atlantic Coast Line; at Tamiami City, with the Seaboard. (Fort Myers Historical Museum.)

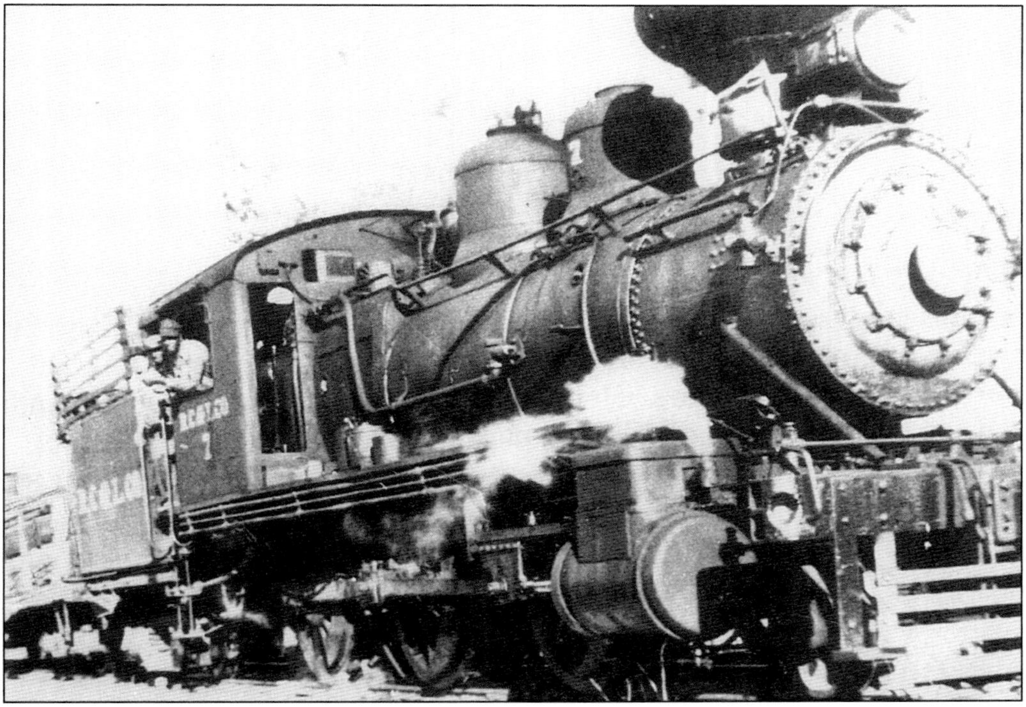

Three wood-burning engines were on the Roux Crate & Lumber roster in Charlotte County. Company rails penetrated the Babcock Ranch property and surrounding area. At Saline—southeast of Cleveland—Roux connected with the Seaboard. Rouxville, a company town, was 4 miles distant. Rails for the Roux line were actually leased from the Seaboard, which demanded $10,000 of business each year. (Charlotte Harbor Area Historical Society.)

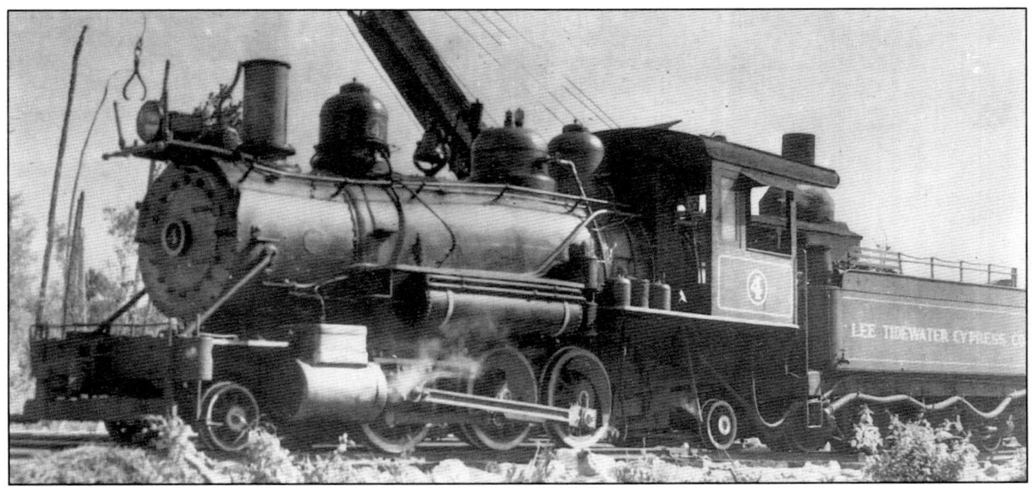

Lee Tidewater Cypress connected with the Atlantic Coast Line at Copeland. Immense tracts of cypress dotted Collier County particularly in the Fakahatchee Strand. Portable rail spurs penetrated its depths and trains loaded with logs came out. Here, Engine No. 4 simmers alongside a log loader, whose hook dangles near the headlight. (Fort Myers Historical Museum.)

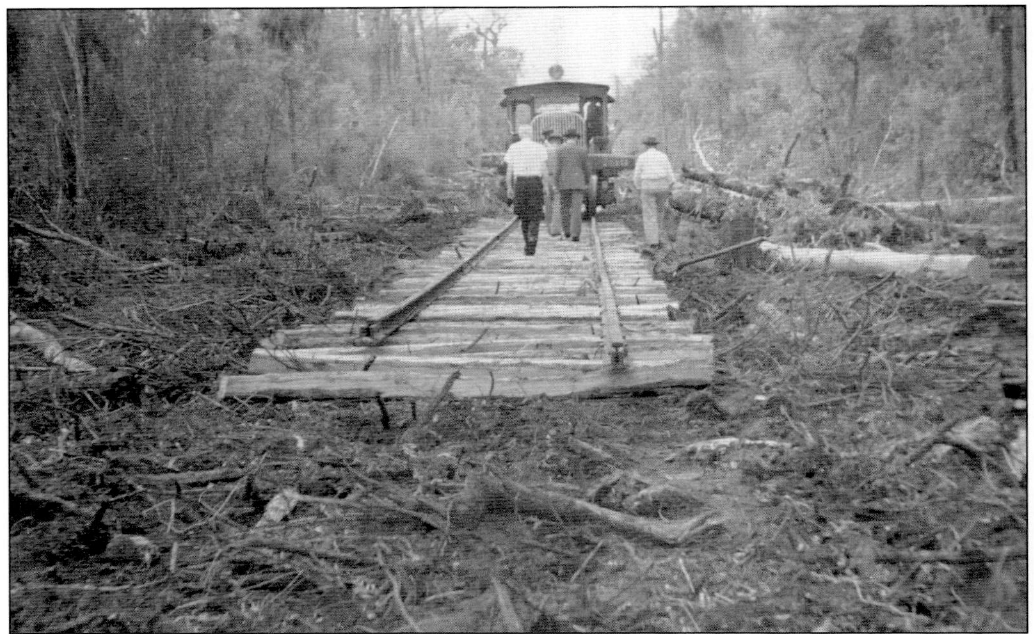

Officials of Lee Tidewater have just inspected a spur track somewhere near Everglades City. Because spurs were temporary, crossties were quickly installed with no ballast. Logging has already taken place in this 1945 scene, and dismantling is about to occur. Once disassembled, the spur will be re-installed elsewhere. (Courtesy of Collier County Museum, Naples, FL.)

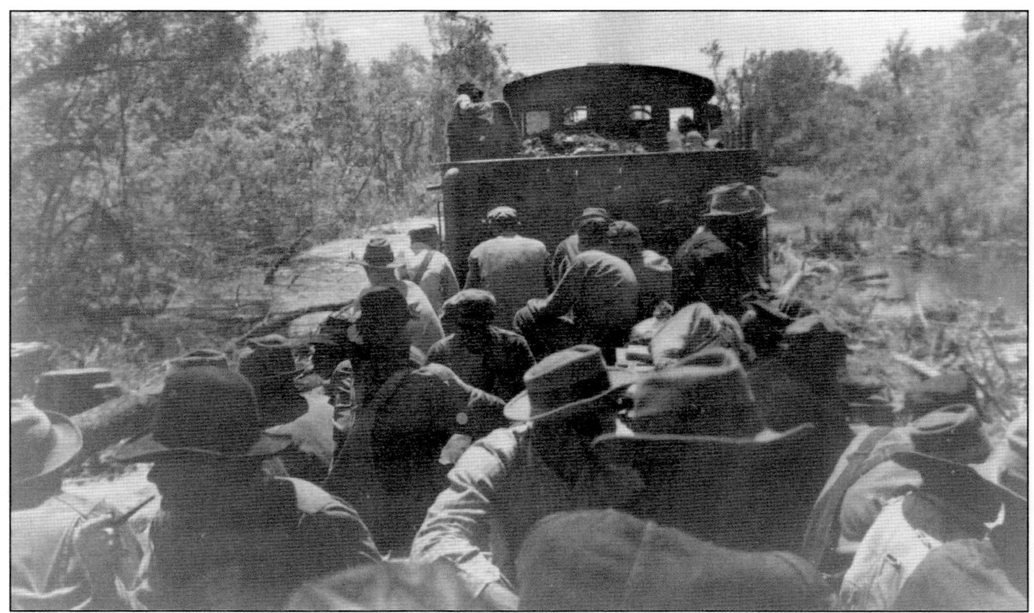

Both black and white workers crowd together for the commute from the Fakahatchee Strand to Lee Tidewater's homebase in Copeland, c. 1947. Long-sleeved shirts and pants, plus headgear, helped protect employees from the sun and mosquitoes. Workers also encountered poisonous snakes, alligators, and crocodiles. (Courtesy of Collier County Museum, Naples, FL.)

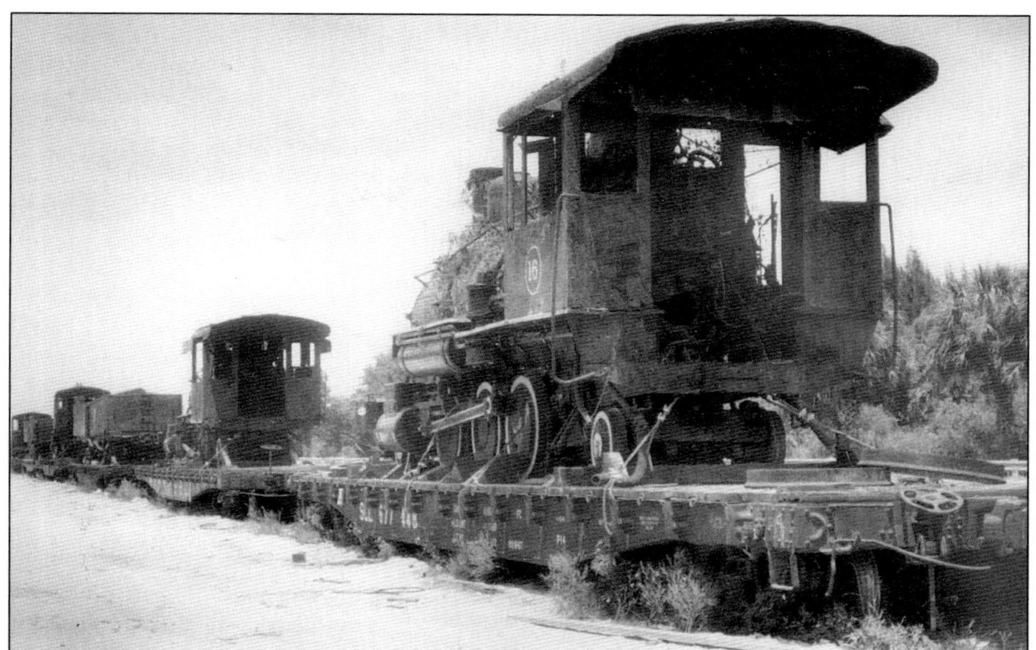

When the great strands of cypress played out, the logging railroad of Lee Tidewater perished. Its engines, all built by Baldwin, were left behind and slumbered from 1957 to 1970. Finally, a collector from Illinois rescued them from the hand of nature. Encrusted with weeds, off they went on Seaboard Coast Line flat cars. (Railroad Museum of South Florida Collection.)

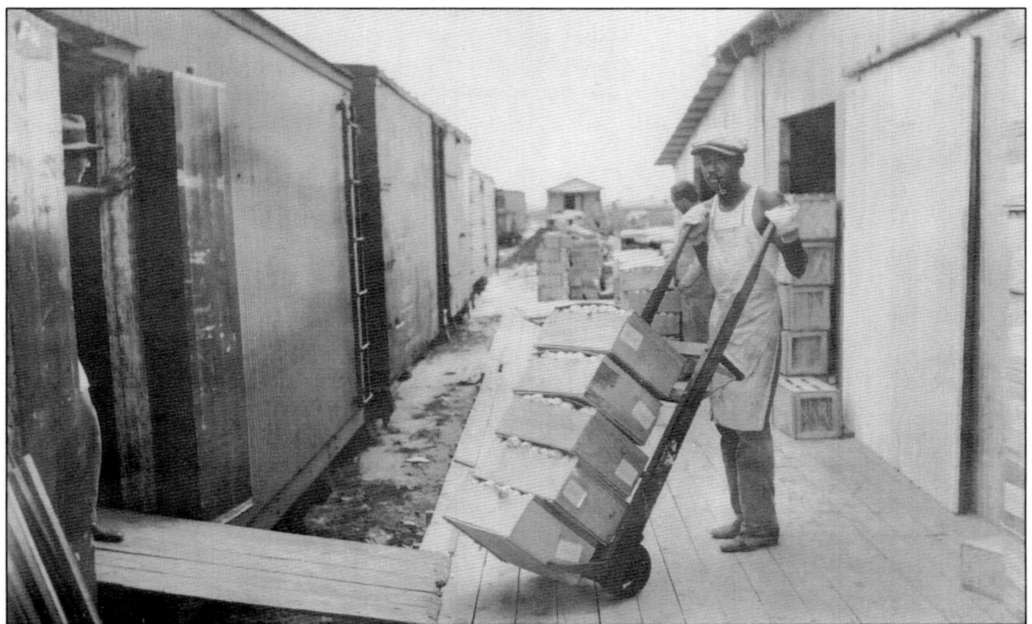

Carnestown, a once thriving vegetable growing area, was located between Copeland and Everglades City. Packing houses existed, and in this 1930 scene we see workmen loading crates of tomatoes into an insulated box car for the trip to northern markets. Eventually, truckers made serious inroads on the traffic. (Courtesy of Collier County Museum, Naples, FL.)

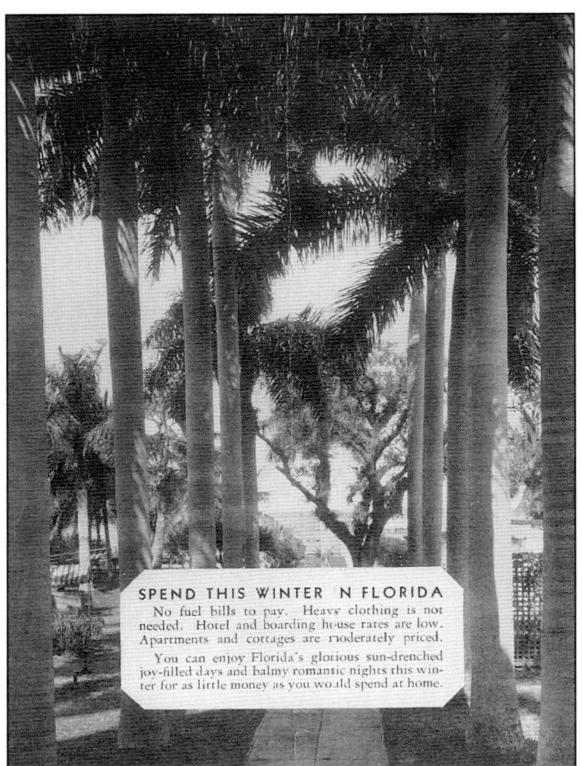

Seductive ads were often run by the railroads. A reader "up north" seeing this copy on a frigid January day may just hop on a Coast Line train and come to the Sunshine State—so the ad men hoped.

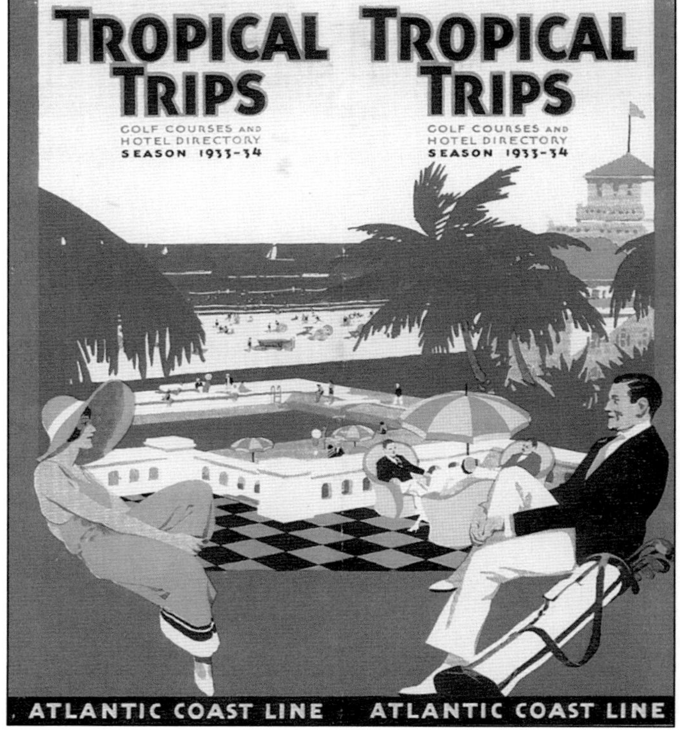

The Coast Line began dispensing its popular "Tropical Trips" brochure during the 1920s. Fifty thousand copies were printed in 1950 alone. It was filled with information about cities and attractions along Coast Line routes, places to stay and where the best golfing and fishing could be enjoyed. The 1933-34 issue of course mentioned nothing about the nationwide Depression that gripped the country.

A small passenger traffic was entertained on the Coast Line's Immokalee Branch. In this 1944 photograph, a solitary combination baggage-coach car is en route to Everglades City, southernmost point on the entire Coast Line system. Thirty-two people could be accommodated, but it lacked air conditioning. Later, a mixed train appeared on a tri-weekly basis which lasted until October 1955. (Courtesy of Collier County Museum, Naples, FL.)

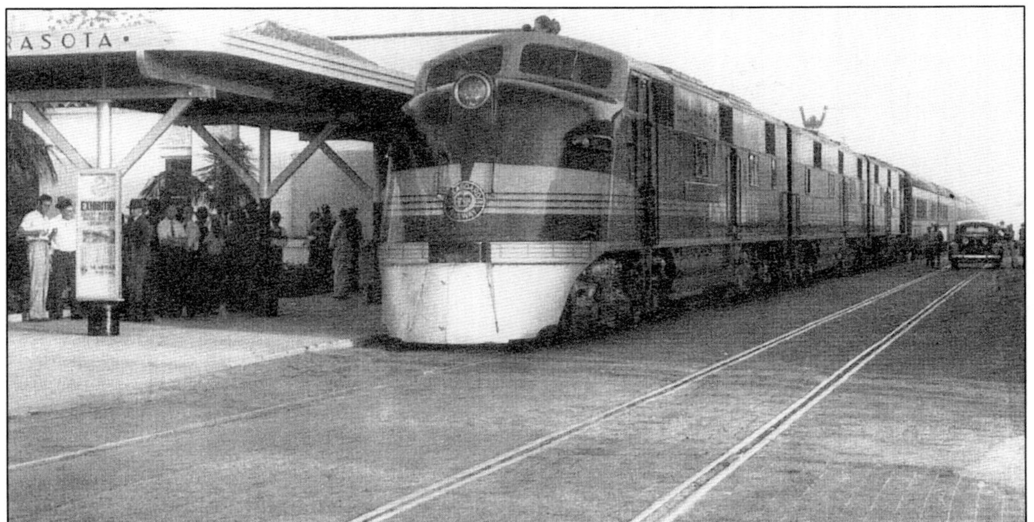

In 1938, the Seaboard acquired its first diesel-electric engines from the Electro Motive Division of General Motors. They boasted 2,000 horsepower and were painted in citrus colors of green, orange, and yellow. Pilot wheels and running gear though sported bright silver. Once received, a Diesel Exhibition Train toured the system, which is seen here at Sarasota. (Railway & Locomotive Historical Society.)

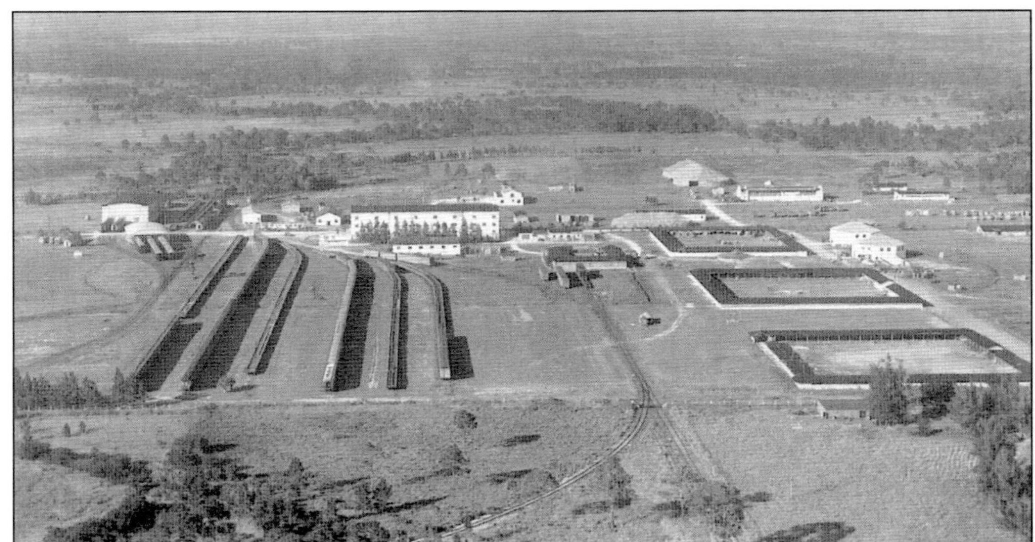

The winter headquarters of Ringing Brothers and Barnum and Bailey Circus was established at Sarasota during the 1920s. Both the Atlantic Coast Line and Seaboard railroads served the facility. Yard tracks accommodated the circus trains, and repair shops can bee seen in the upper left. (Historical Resources, Sarasota County Government.)

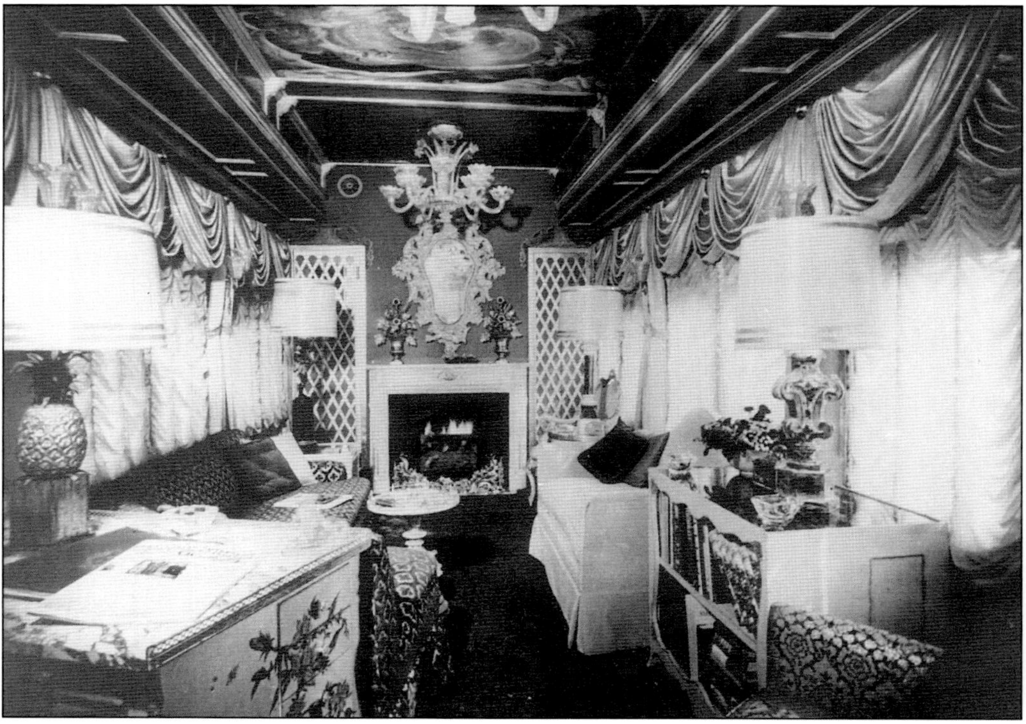

When circus king John Ringling and wife Mabel traveled by rail it was in their private Pullman car named *Jomar.* Their "home on wheels" (not unlike the one seen here) was decorated on the grand scale and even touted a fireplace. Such cars were almost *de rigueur* for bluebloods and 'Captains of Industry.' (The Venice Archives & Area Historical Collection.)

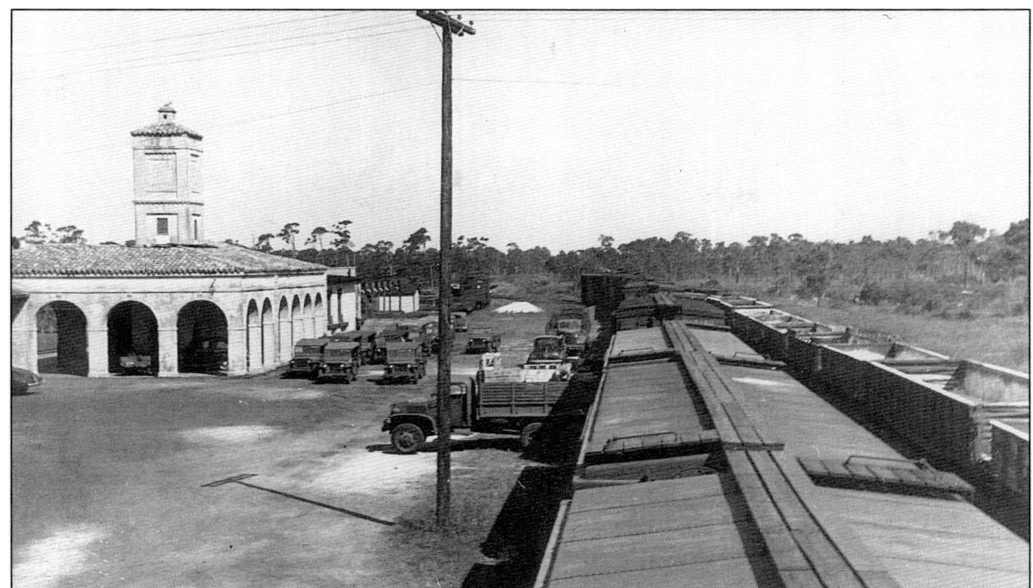

Traffic soared on Florida's railroads during WW II as personnel and materials made their way to and from military installations. An Army Air Base was established in Venice at what became the city's municipal airport. Carloads of supplies arrived at the Seaboard's rail yard, including Jeeps, as this 1942 photograph confirms. The backside of the famed station is at left. (The Venice Archives & Area Historical Collection.)

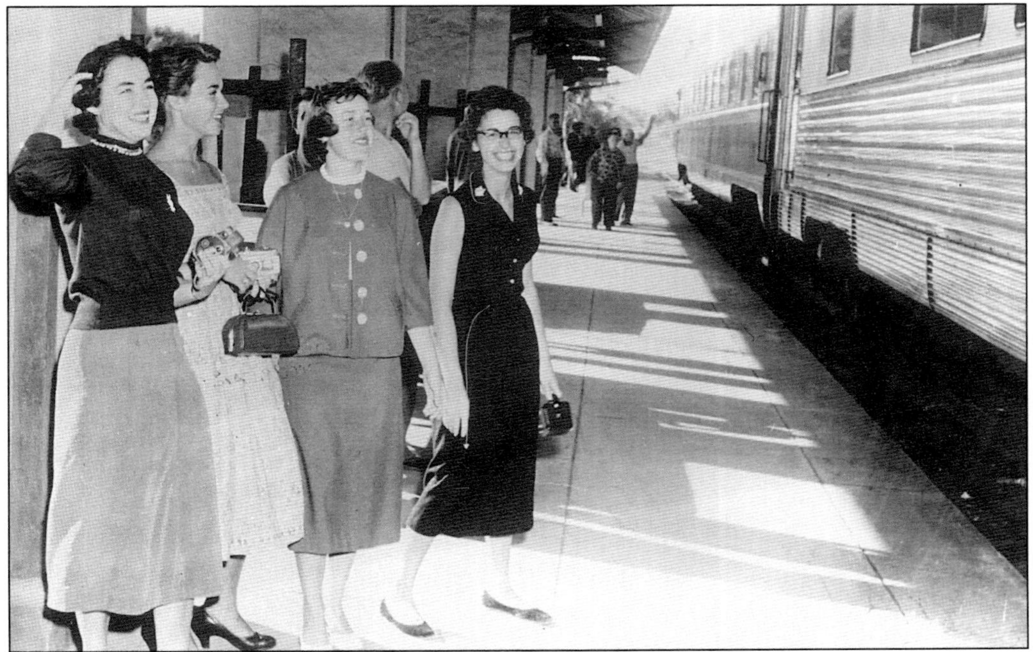

When the Florida land Boom collapsed, so did the economy of Venice. But not for long. The Kentucky Military Institute eventually established its winter campus here in 1931. Before long, the cadets discovered the beautiful girls of Venice. Some are on the station platform wishing beaus a farewell in this *c.* 1950s scene. (The Venice Archives & Area Historical Collection.)

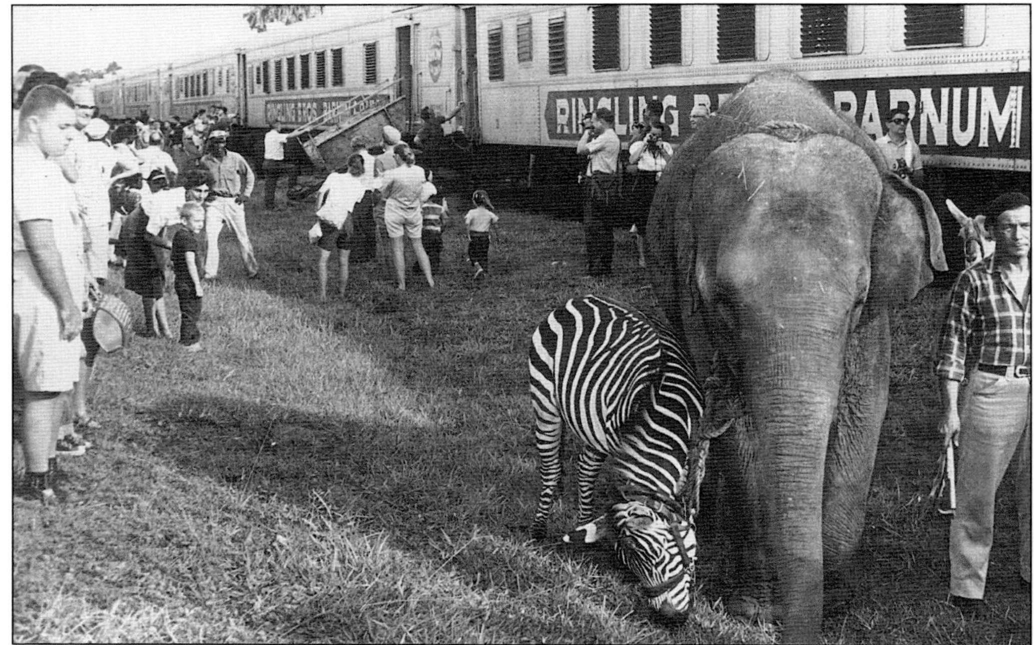

Ringling Brothers moved their winter headquarters to the Venice Airport area, where a 5,000-seat arena was completed for the 1961 rehearsals. Circus trains came down the Seaboard track and halted at Center Road. Then, to the delight of the onlookers, the animals would be unloaded and a procession formed for the near-mile walk to the circus grounds. (The Venice Archives & Area Historical Collection.)

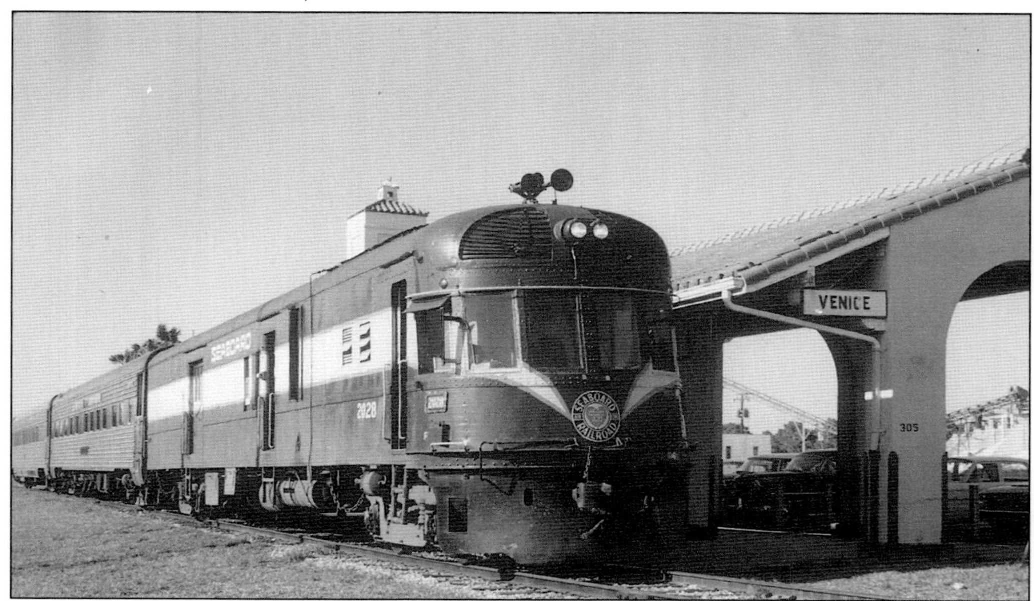

A frequent visitor to Southwest Florida was Seaboard diesel rail car No. 2028, nicknamed "The Doodlebug." Built in 1936 by St. Louis Car and the Electro Motive Corporation, it became No. 4900 on the Seaboard Coast Line roster and ran to the advent of Amtrak in 1971. Here we see it in Venice in April 1964. (Photo by Emery J. Gulash.)

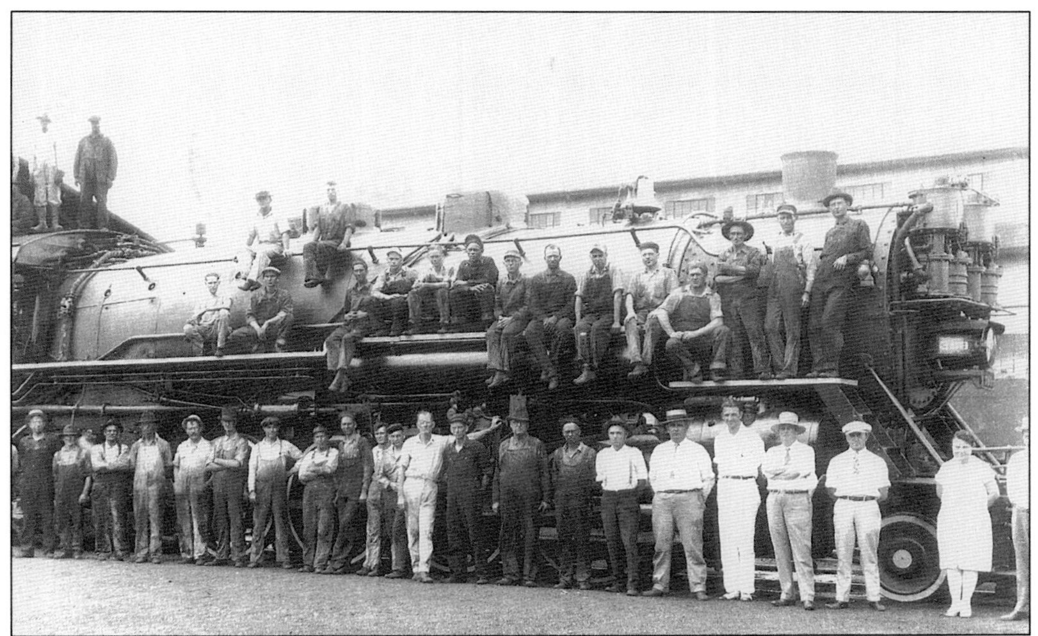

For many years the Seaboard maintained repair shops at Arcadia, just as predecessor Charlotte Harbor & Northern did. In this 1930s scene, shop and office employees pose on Engine No. 388. Built by Alco in 1925, it weighed 300,000 pounds and sported driving wheels 63 inches tall. It was one of the largest steam engines ever to make an appearance in Southwest Florida. (Howard Melton.)

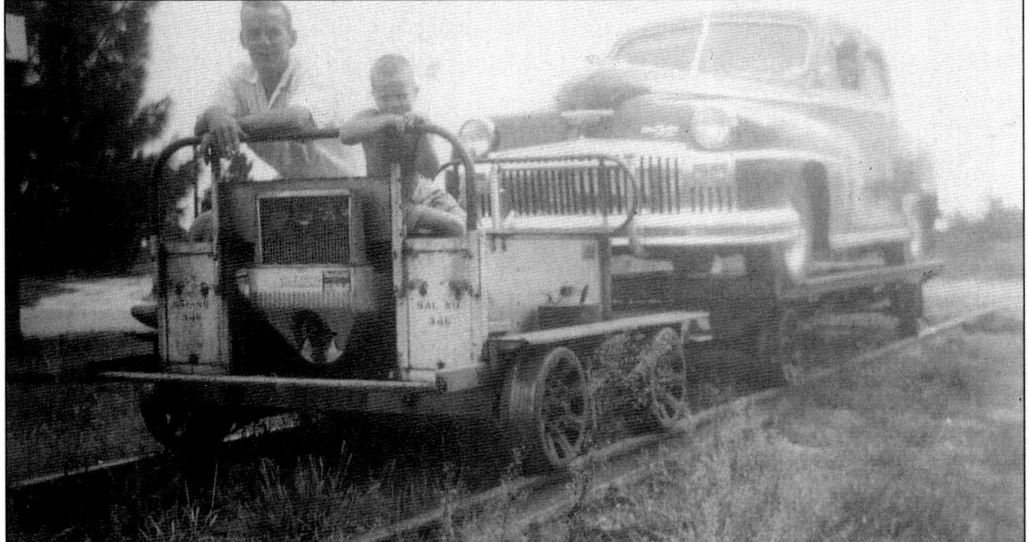

There was a day when cars were brought to Boca Grande by rail. In this 1954 setting, Joseph Saverese Jr. has driven his DeSoto to Placida station where it was ramped onto a flat car. Jim Shea, a Seaboard employee, was at the ready with a motorized section car—nicknamed "The Bull"—which then towed the vehicle to Boca Grande. Mr. Saverese's young son (Joseph III) smiles for the photographer, who happens to be his mother. (Photo by Suzanne Harris Savarese, courtesy of the Boca Grande Historical Society.)

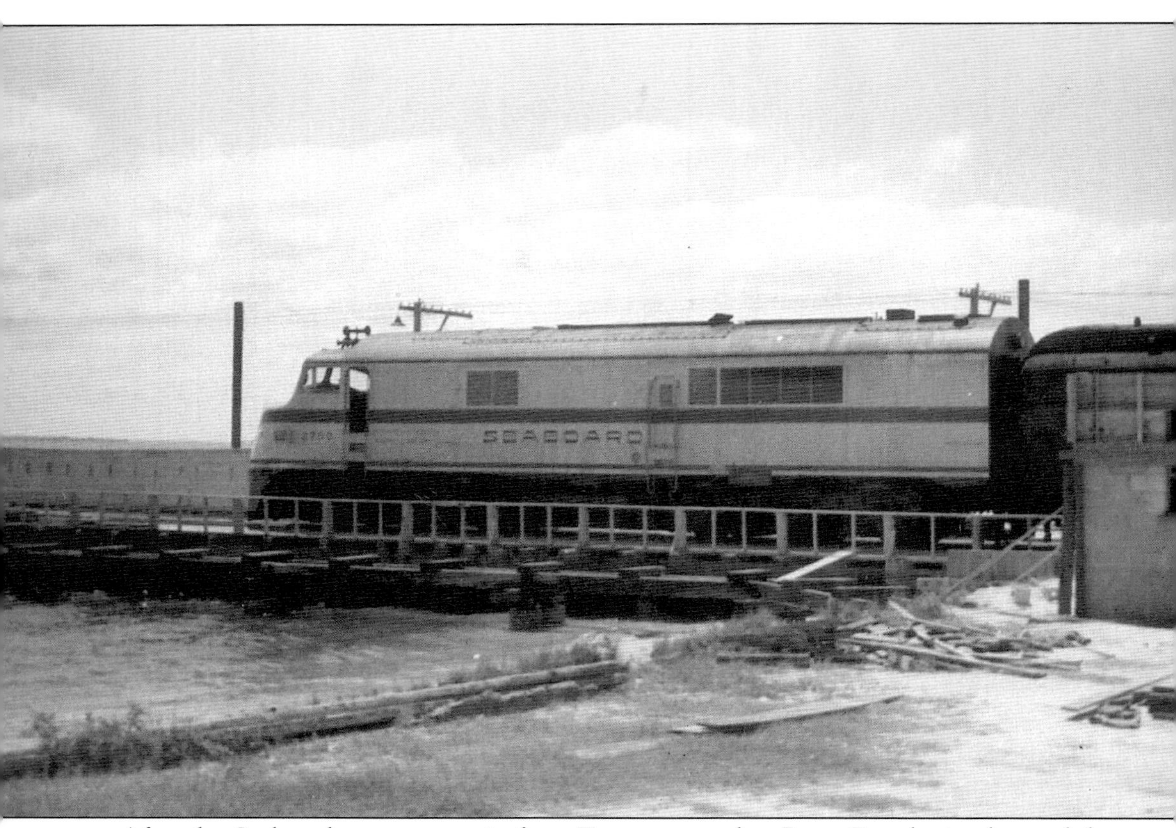

After the Seaboard passenger train from Tampa stopped at Boca Grande, it advanced down to the port area, entered the wye track, and the train was turned around for the northbound journey. In this 1955 scene, Seaboard engine No. 2700 is on the point, one of three built by Baldwin in 1947. The 1,500-horsepower engines had a diminutive front end appearance, and thus were nicknamed "Baby Face" Baldwins. (Boca Grande Historical Society.)

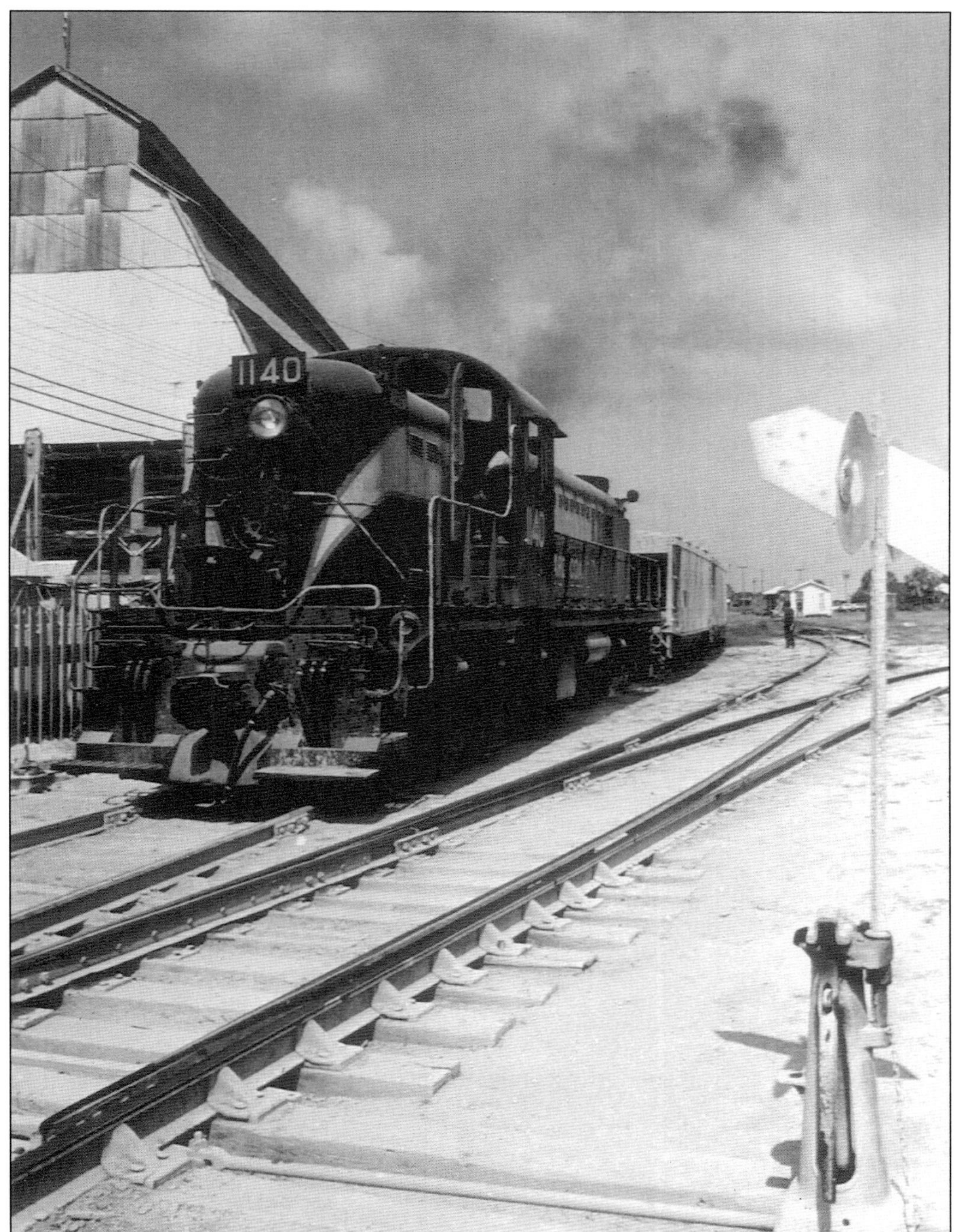

A real workhorse was a road switcher locomotive built by Alco. No. 1140 is shoving hopper cars alongside the huge phosphate storage facility at South Boca Grande. These particular engines could ably handle the stop-and-go routine of switching chores, or pull a consist at speed on the mainline. The track diverging to the far right leads north to Boca Grande proper. (Charlotte Harbor Area Historical Society.)

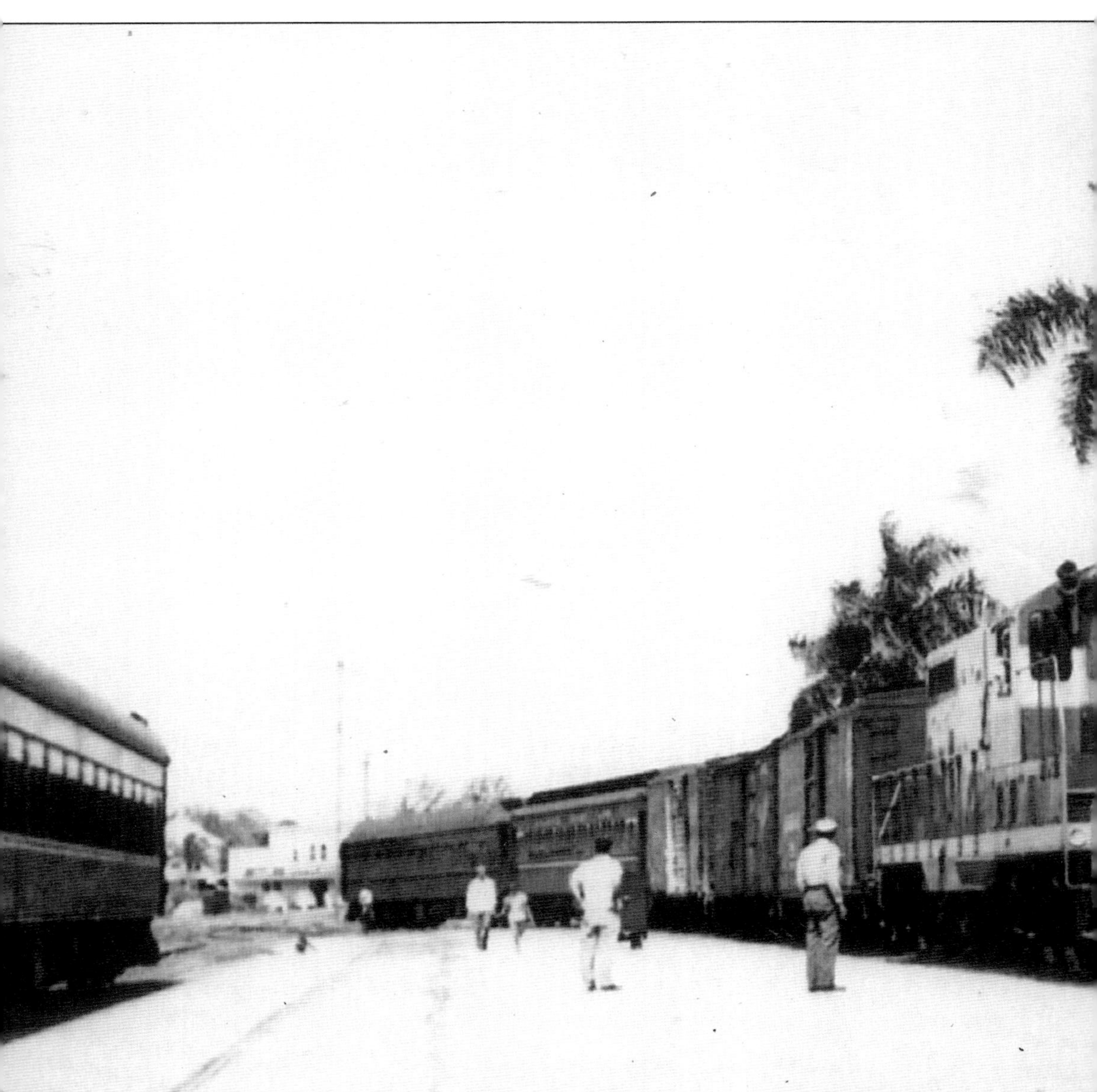

The last "mixed train" (coaches and freight cars) on the entire Atlantic Coast Line system operated between Naples and Fort Myers until November 25, 1957. It was also the only such train that carried a Pullman car in addition to a coach. In this 1951 view, the "mixed" is easing

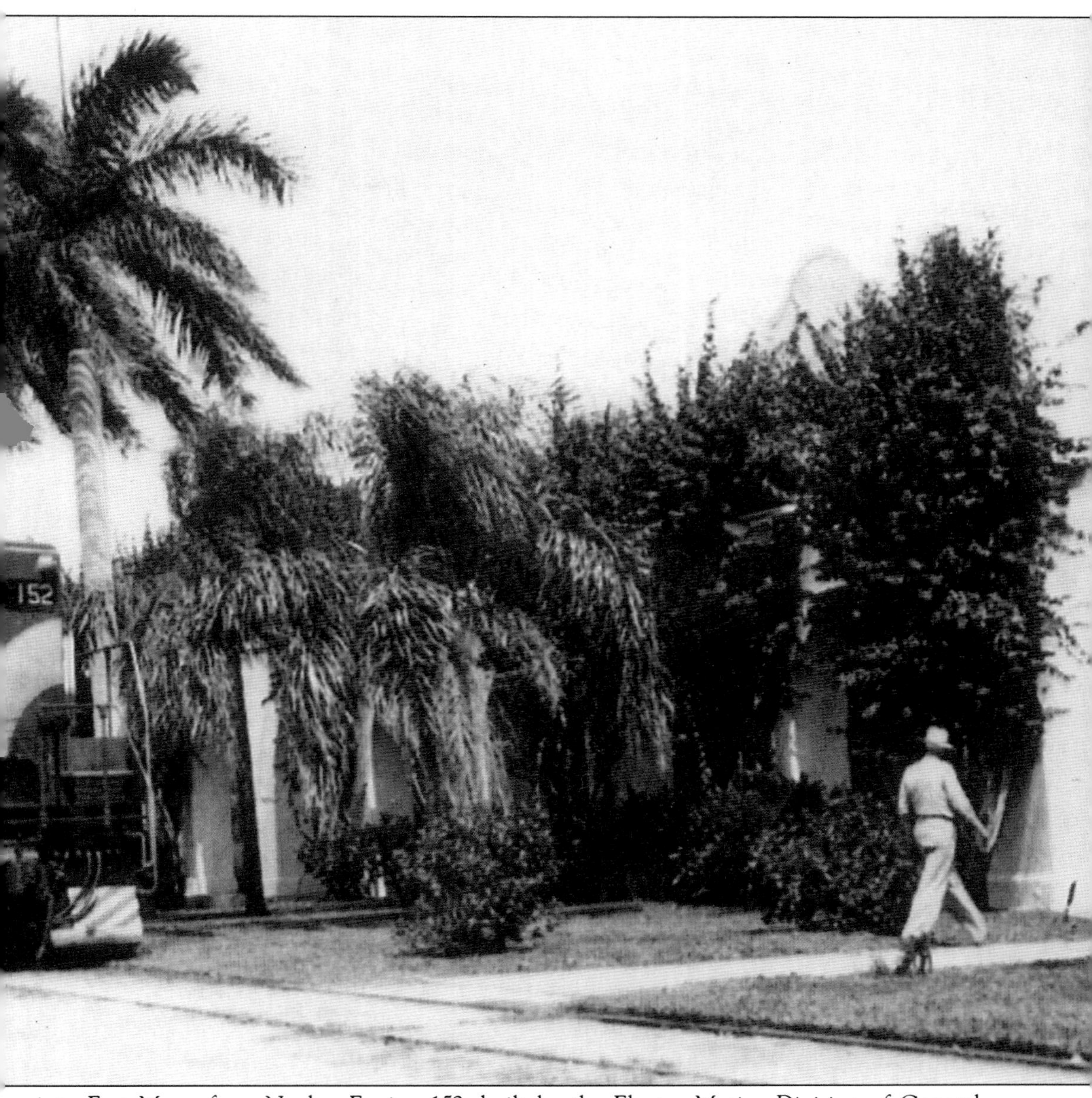

into Fort Myers from Naples. Engine 152, built by the Electro Motive Division of General Motors, was technically called a GP-7. (Photo by William Lenoir courtesy Jim Herron, Herron Rail Video.)

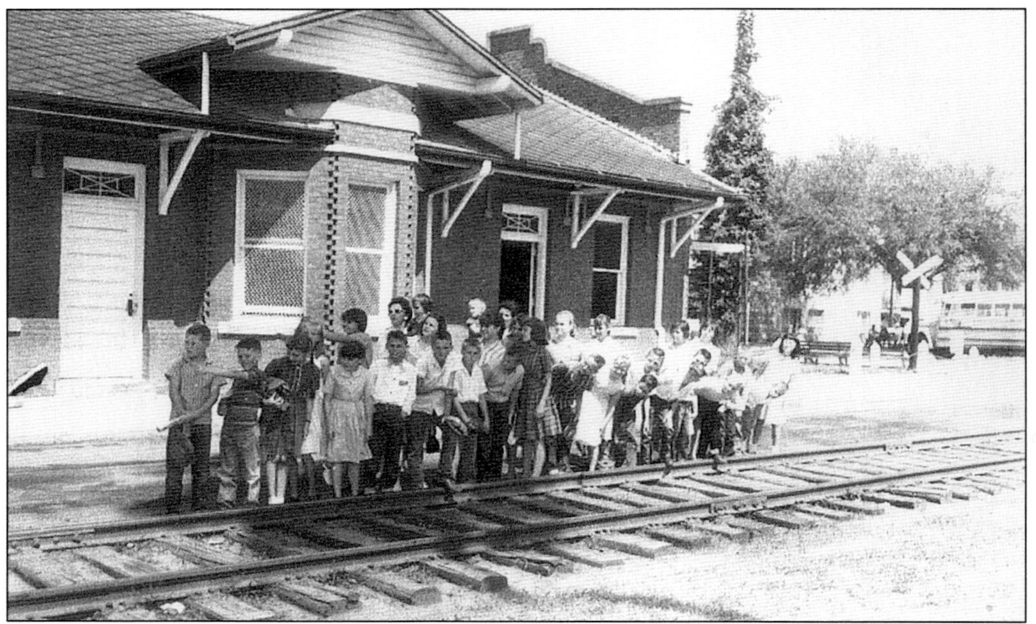

Where's the train? Is it here yet? Can you see it? School kids anxiously await a train ride at Arcadia, Florida, on April 30, 1971. Soon, they will hear a whistle, a locomotive headlight will be seen, and a few minutes later . . .

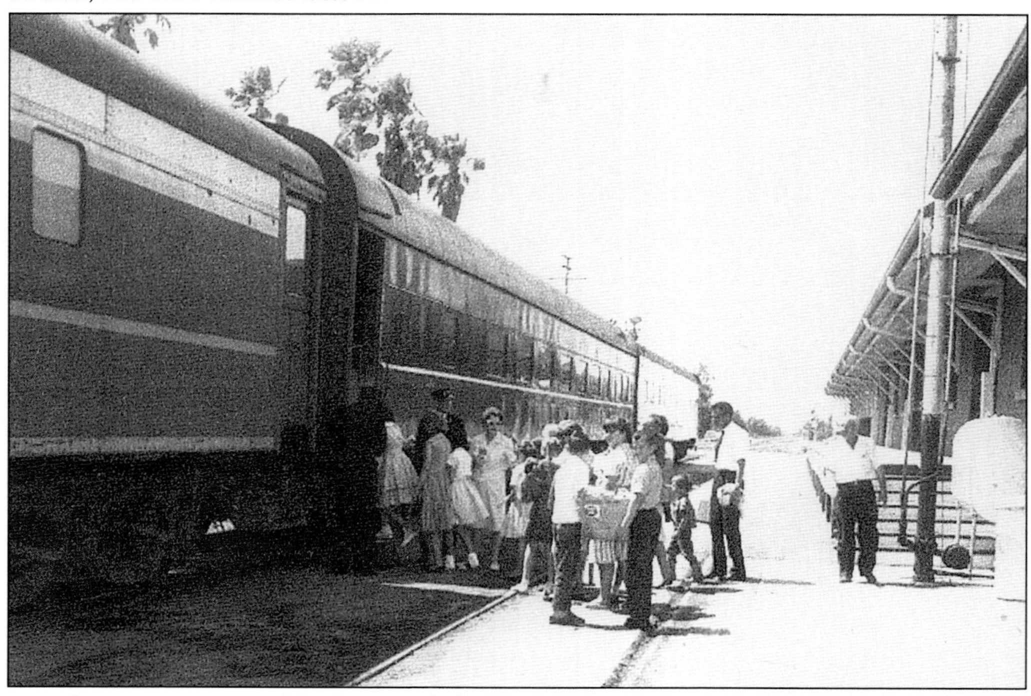

. . . the train arrives and brakes to a halt. Doors open, and a portable step is placed on the ground. Greetings are exchanged, kids and teachers step up, then the legendary call is given: "A-l-l A-h-h-b-o-a-r-d!!" The doors close, two toots on the whistle, brakes are released, and off she goes. (*DeSoto County Times* courtesy of Howard Melton.)

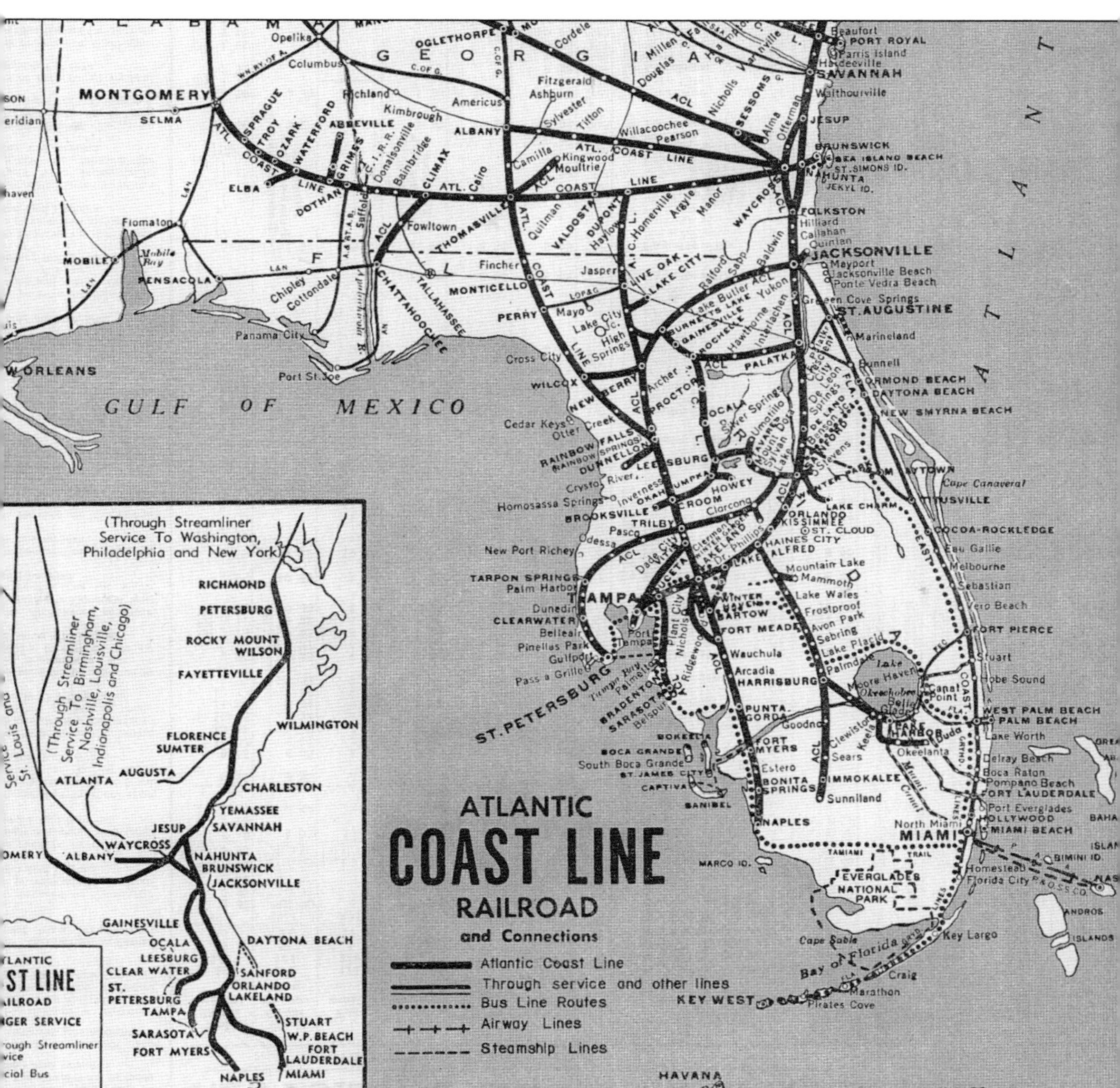

The above map is one of the last issued by Atlantic Coast Line prior to its 1967 merge with the Seaboard. The company still served Southwest Florida, i.e. at Sarasota, from Arcadia to Fort Myers and Naples, from Palmdale to Sunniland, and to Moore Haven and Clewiston. But as the inset map reveals, local passenger train service only existed at Sarasota and in the Arcadia-Fort Myers-Naples corridor.

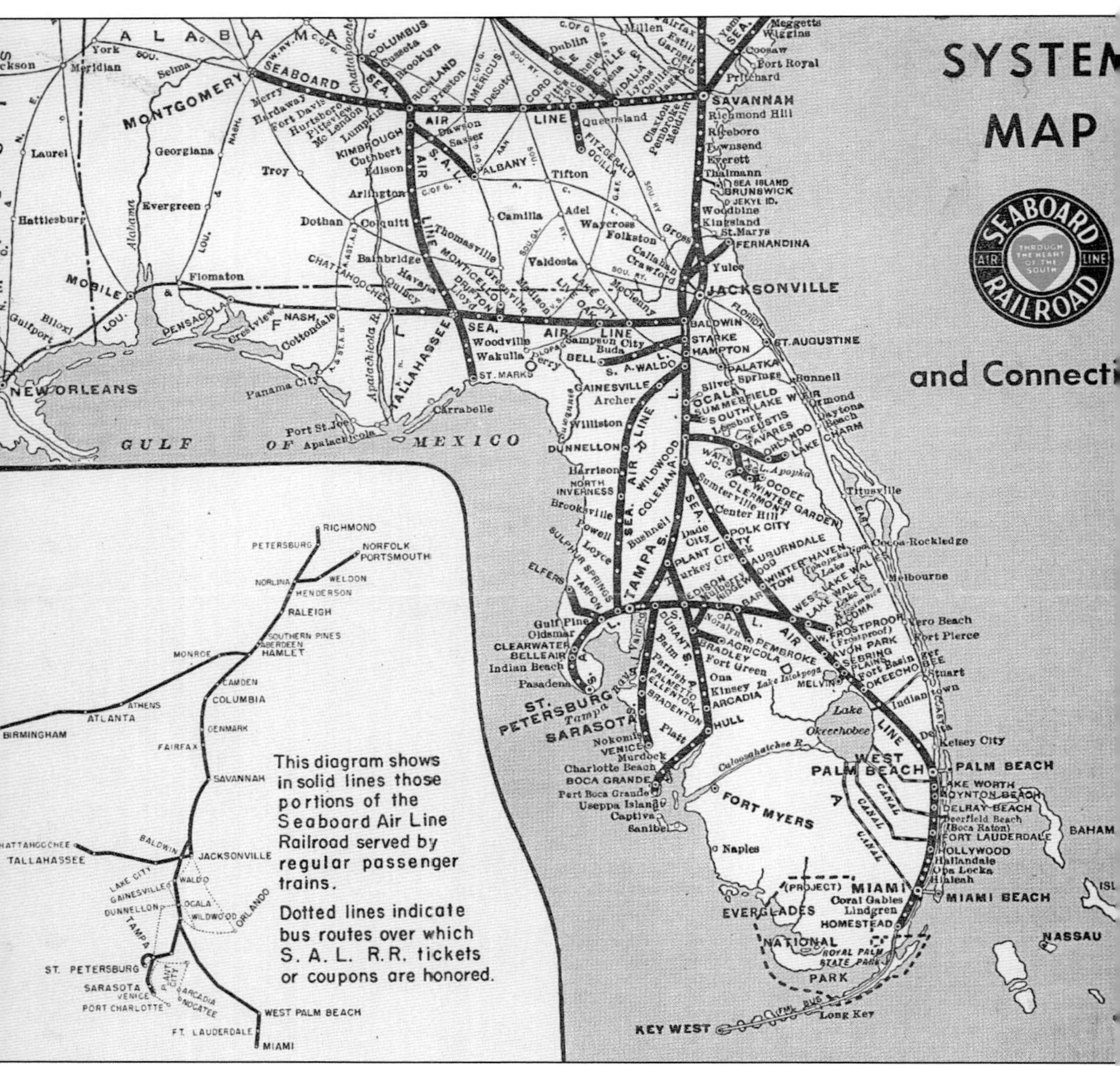

The Florida lines of Seaboard are shown here just before the Seaboard Coast Line merger of 1967. The company's presence in Southwest Florida is limited to the Sarasota-Venice line and the one between Arcadia and South Boca Grande. Passenger trains were run to Sarasota and Venice as the inset map reveals.

Eight

Mergers and Survivors

"We consider ourselves a marketing firm that happens to be in the railroad business."
—Seminole Gulf executives, Fort Myers *News-Press*, January 3, 1988

The Interstate Commerce Commission approved the merger of the Seaboard Air Line and Atlantic Coast Line railroads in December 1963. However, certain other railroads and organizations opposed the marriage and fought the ICC decision. Only after the United States Supreme Court refused to hear any further appeals was the matter laid to rest. The Seaboard Coast Line Railroad came into being July 1, 1967.

Overnight, the Seaboard Coast Line became the eighth largest railroad in the United States with nearly 9,600 miles, 23,000 employees, 62,000 cars, and 1,000 locomotives. Headquarters were established at both Richmond, Virginia, and Jacksonville, Florida. The former president of the Coast Line (W. Thomas Rice) became president of the Seaboard Coast Line, while the former president of the Seaboard (John W. Smith) became its chairman. A holding company—Seaboard Coast Line Industries—was formed in 1968.

In its first year of operation, the merged firm reported a net income of $27.2 million on revenues of $417.3 million. Freight traffic was derived from a variety of commodity groups, which included food, pulp, paper, phosphate, fertilizer, farm products, coal and coke, ordnance; sand, rock, and gravel; lumber and piggyback traffic (truck trailers on railroad flat cars). Over 300 new industries were located along the system that year, which embraced the states of Virginia, the Carolinas, Georgia, Florida, and Alabama. To expedite the handling of Florida phosphate, the company began constructing a state-of-the-art loading facility near Tampa (Rockport) in July 1970.

The National Railroad Passenger Corporation (Amtrak) came into being on May 1, 1971, and its mission was to relieve many railroad companies of passenger train operations. Seaboard Coast Line joined the program, paid an entrance fee of some 30 million dollars, whereupon Amtrak assumed its passenger train responsibilities. (Amtrak, in turn, contracted Seaboard Coast Line to operate its Florida trains.) Unfortunately, service to Southwest Florida was not included in the Amtrak plan and thus was completely eliminated.

Seaboard Coast Line revenues topped the billion dollar mark in 1972, the year it acquired all remaining stock of the Louisville and Nashville Railroad. For several years thereafter, the combined railroads became known as the Family Lines Rail System. Most of the decade was spent in containing the high costs of doing business. Inflation was rampant.

In September 1975, the Seaboard Coast Line sold its Fort Myers depot and downtown land parcels to the city for $806,900. Two years later it installed a new drawbridge over the Caloosahatchee River. During the 1970s, the company also petitioned the Interstate Commerce Commission to abandon other lines in Southwest Florida. Because more and more phosphate traffic was being directed to its newly-built facility at Rockport, the Seaboard Coast Line track from Arcadia to the old phosphate port of South Boca Grande was no longer needed. Also, traffic on the Immokalee Branch had diminished to the extent that the company wanted to remove rails between Sunniland and Immokalee. The ICC approved the requests and the trackage was removed. In 1979, the railroad also obtained authority to remove rails between Naples proper to a point north of Immokalee Road.

In 1979, the Seaboard Coast Line announced that it was going to merge with another big American railroad—The Chessie System. Hearings were subsequently held before the Interstate Commerce Commission which approved the merger in September 1980. The CSX corporation came into existence on November 1 and it instantly became the largest railroad system in the United States with over 27,000 route miles. The transportation giant served 22 states plus Washington, D.C., and the province of Ontario. Seventy thousand employees were on the payroll, and in its first year of operations the new company generated $281.6 million in net income on revenues of $4.8 billion. Its two major railroad units consisted of the Chessie System (based in Cleveland, Ohio) and The Family Lines, which were operated out of Jacksonville and included Seaboard Coast Line. That same year the famous Staggers Act was approved by Congress which provided railroads everywhere with landmark regulatory reforms.

Use of the Family Lines Rail System moniker disappeared in 1982. The Seaboard Coast Line and Louisville & Nashville Railroads were later melded into a new CSX unit called Seaboard System Railroad. On July 1, 1986, all rail properties came under the umbrella of CSX Rail Transportation.

The rail unit of CSX began to restructure itself in December 1985. Nearly 1,500 miles of lightly used lines were sold or abandoned, 13 rail yards were closed, 8 locomotive and car facilities were consolidated, and employment fell to 43,279 persons. Marginal or unproductive assets were also written down, and separation payments were made to certain employees.

CSX Transportation ultimately determined that the railroad requirements of Southwest Florida would be best served by shortline railroads. In November 1987, Bay Colony Railroad of Lexington, Massachusetts, was named the successful bidder for most of the remaining trackage in the region, i.e. between Oneco, Sarasota, and Venice, and from Arcadia south to Vanderbilt (Naples). Bay Colony established Seminole Gulf Railway to operate the lines, and in 1988 the new firm transported 14,500 carloads of freight—10% greater than CSX Transportation did the year before. Later, dinner and excursion trains were inaugurated. At both Oneco and Arcadia, Seminole Gulf connects with CSX transportation to reach the outside world.

In June 1990, CSX trackage between Sebring and Lake Harbor (by way of Palmdale and Moore Haven) was acquired by a subsidiary of Lukens Steel, which subsequently organized the South Central Florida Railroad. In September 1994, the United States Sugar Corporation acquired the shortline, and renamed it the South Central Florida Express. Company headquarters remain at Clewiston, and near Sebring a connection is made with CSX Transportation.

Thus, the railroad heritage of Southwest Florida remains in the hands of two shortline companies. Much has happened in this quadrant of the Sunshine State since railroading began in 1886. Whereas the golden age of railroading has passed, the need for railroad service continues into the new millennium.

Ads like this helped inform the public about the newly created Seaboard Coast Line Railroad. Two diesel engines face one another in the top scene—one from the Seaboard, another from the Coast Line. They merge in the second row, and in the third, initials of the new firm are revealed. The merger became effective July 1, 1967.

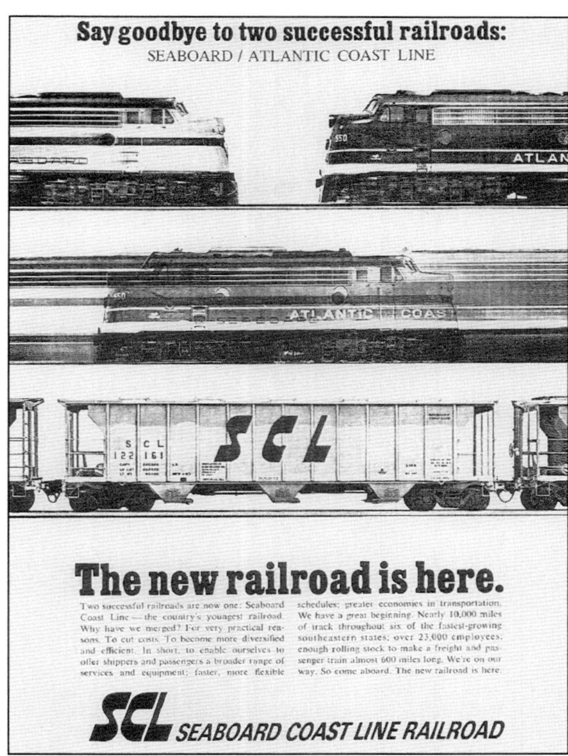

The Florida routes of the Seaboard Coast Line are seen here, and as the legend reveals the black lines with large white "dots" indicate where SCL operated passenger trains in addition to freight.

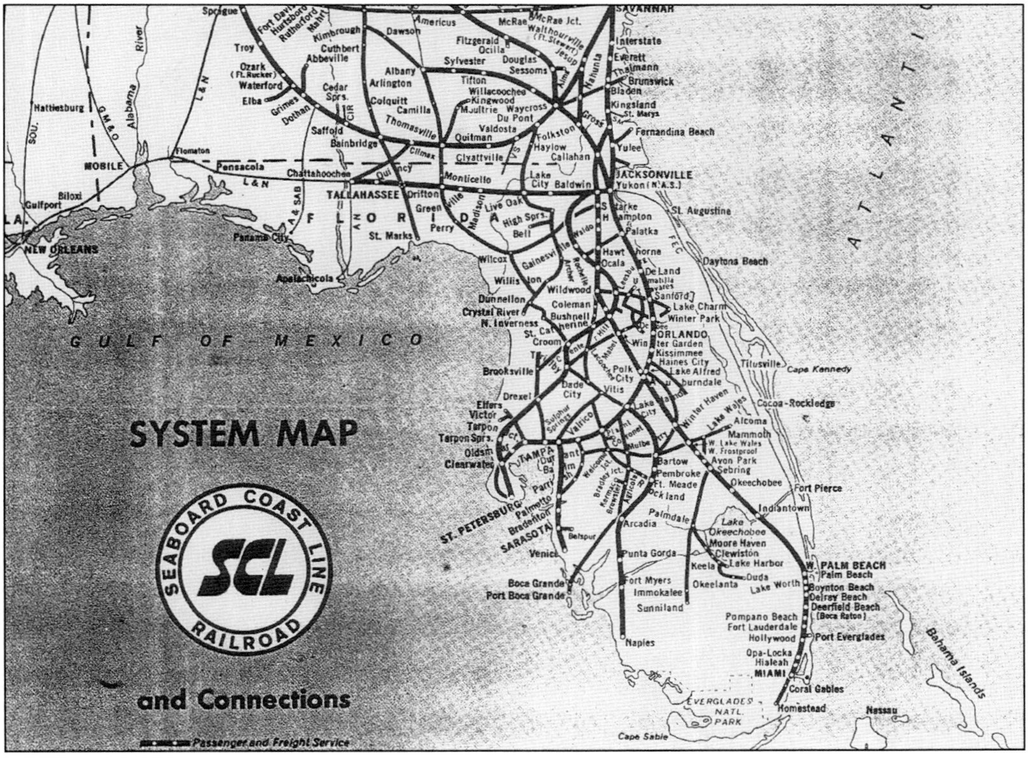

SYSTEM MAP

SEABOARD COAST LINE RAILROAD SCL

and Connections

Passenger and Freight Service

GULF OF MEXICO

ATLANTIC

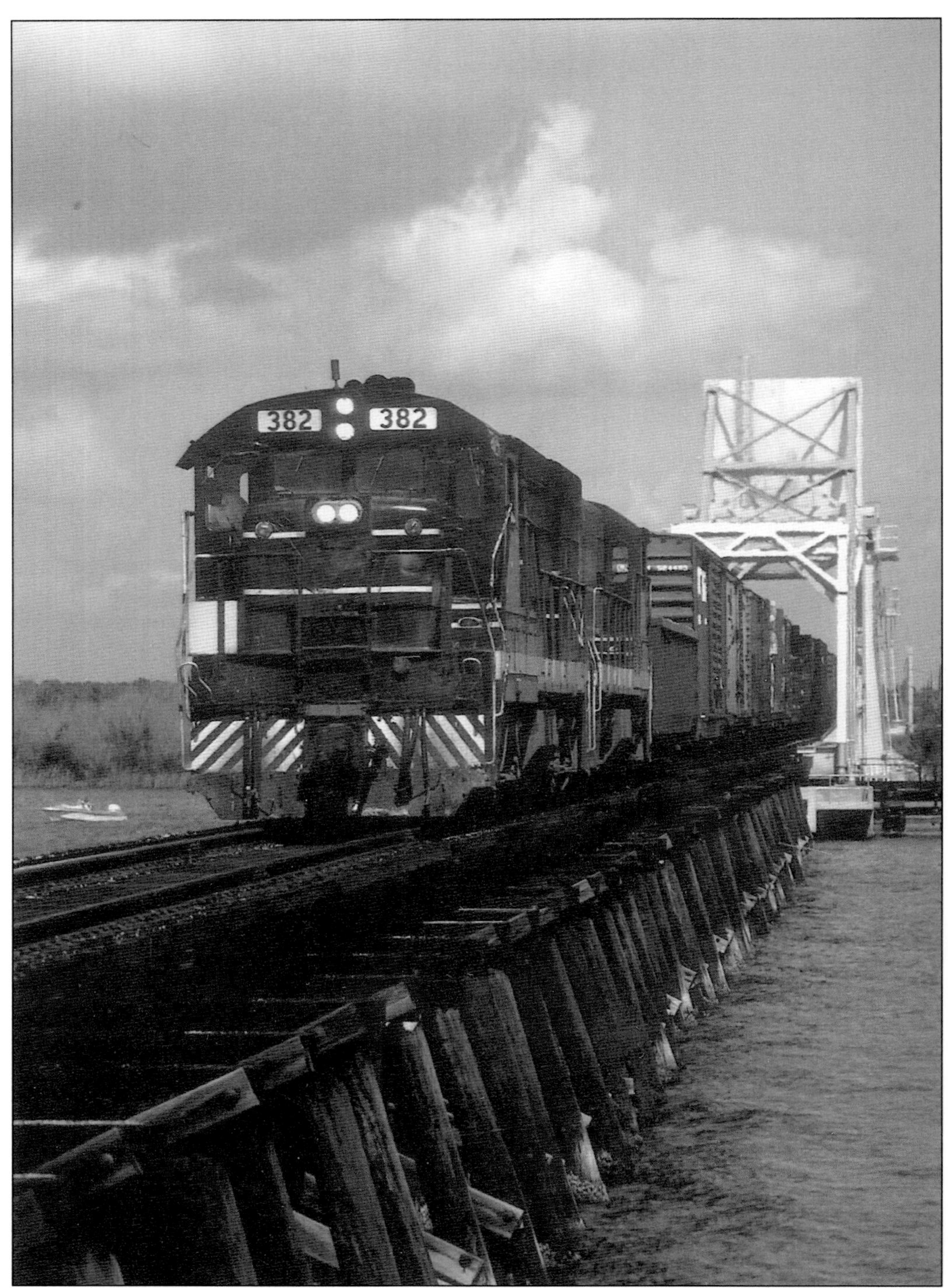

Seaboard Coast Line train 149 eases across the Caloosahatchee River at Tice (Fort Myers) on February 10, 1982. Engines 382 and 380 were built by General Electric as model U18Bs, but in railroad circles they were simply called "U-Boats." The drawbridge is fairly new and was pictured in the company's annual report of 1977. (Scott A. Hartley.)

Hays T. Watkins Jr., one of America's foremost and respected railroad executives, was the architect behind CSX Corporation. After college, the Kentuckian started his career with the Chesapeake & Ohio, and later ran the Chessie System of railroads. When CSX was created in 1980, he was named chairman and CEO. (CSX Corporation.)

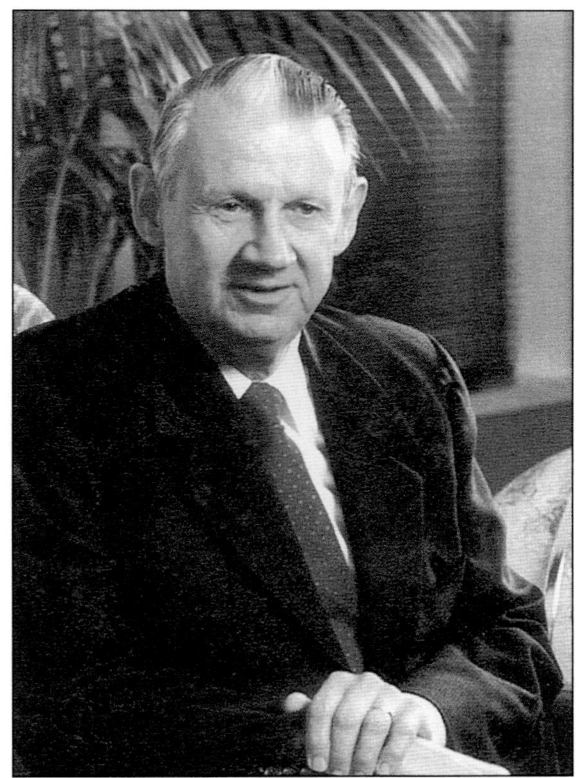

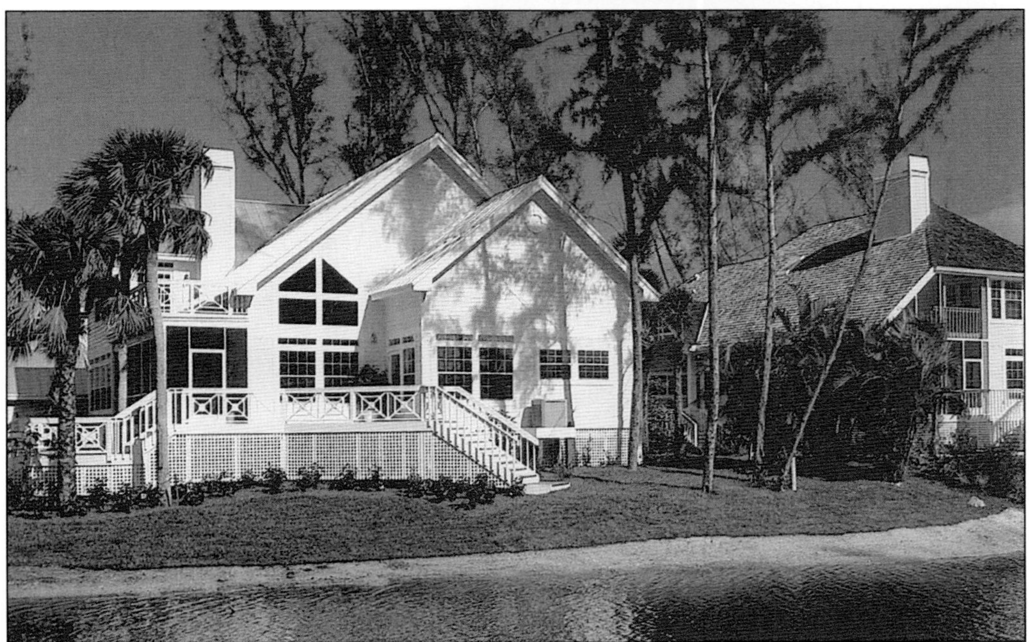

Several business units comprise CSX Corporation of Richmond, Virginia. Its real estate subsidiary, for instance, markets premier properties. The home seen here is part of Boca Bay, a company project located at Boca Grande on Gasparilla Island. (CSX Corporation.)

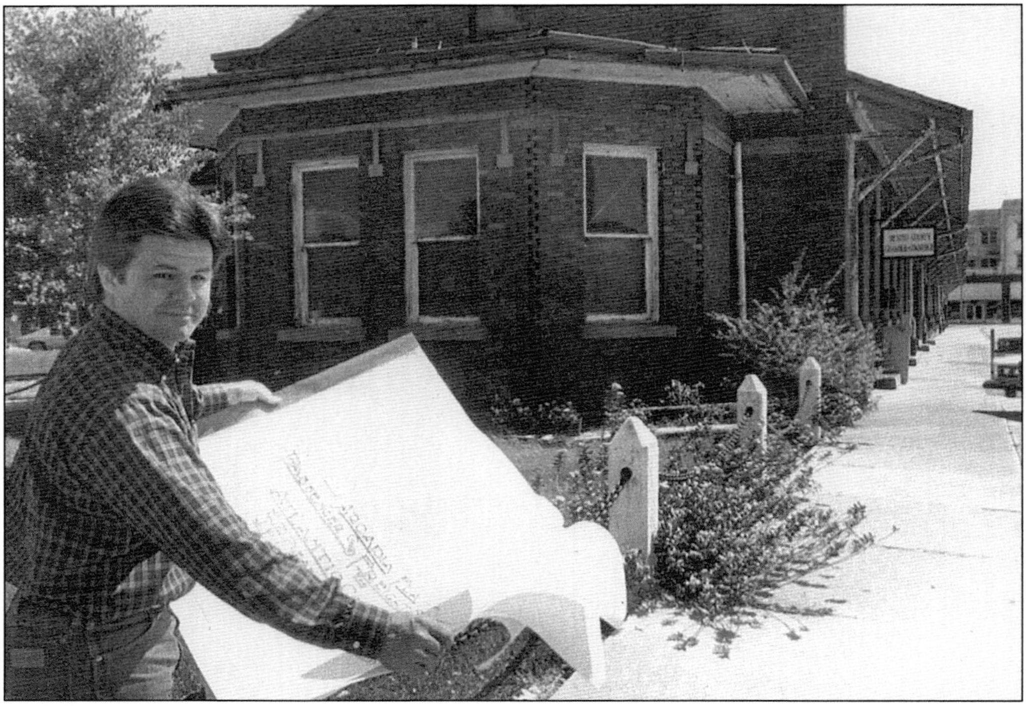

The long brick station at Arcadia was falling on hard times in the 1980s. That is until developer Lee Stevenson appeared on the scene. A comprehensive restoration took place, and today the former Atlantic Coast Line edifice is an asset to the Main Street area. (*DeSoto County Times* courtesy of Howard Melton.)

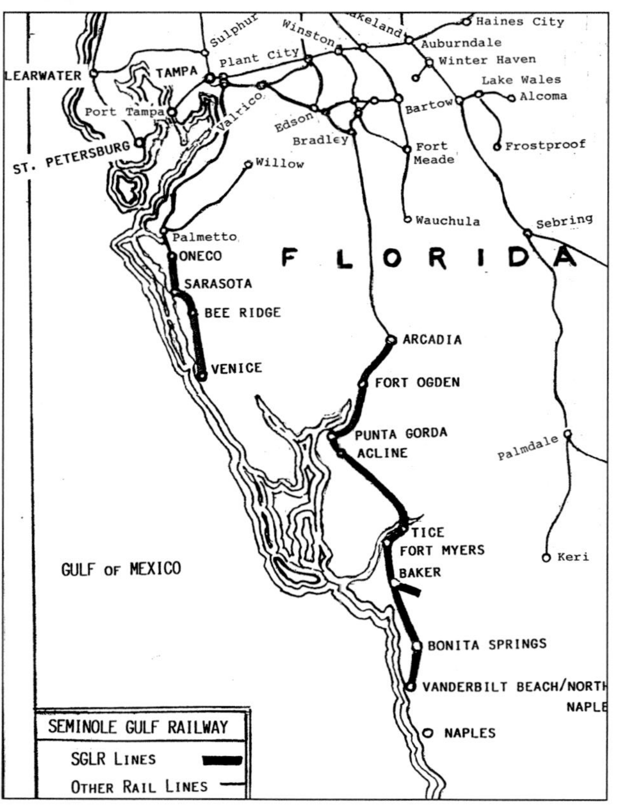

Seminole Gulf began operations in 1987. Its Fort Myers Line stretches from Arcadia down to North Naples, with a spur track at Baker to Florida Rock Industries. Its Sarasota Line ran from Oneco to Venice, with a spur at Sarasota to Matoaka. Both lines connect with CSX Transportation. (Railroad Museum of South Florida Collection.)

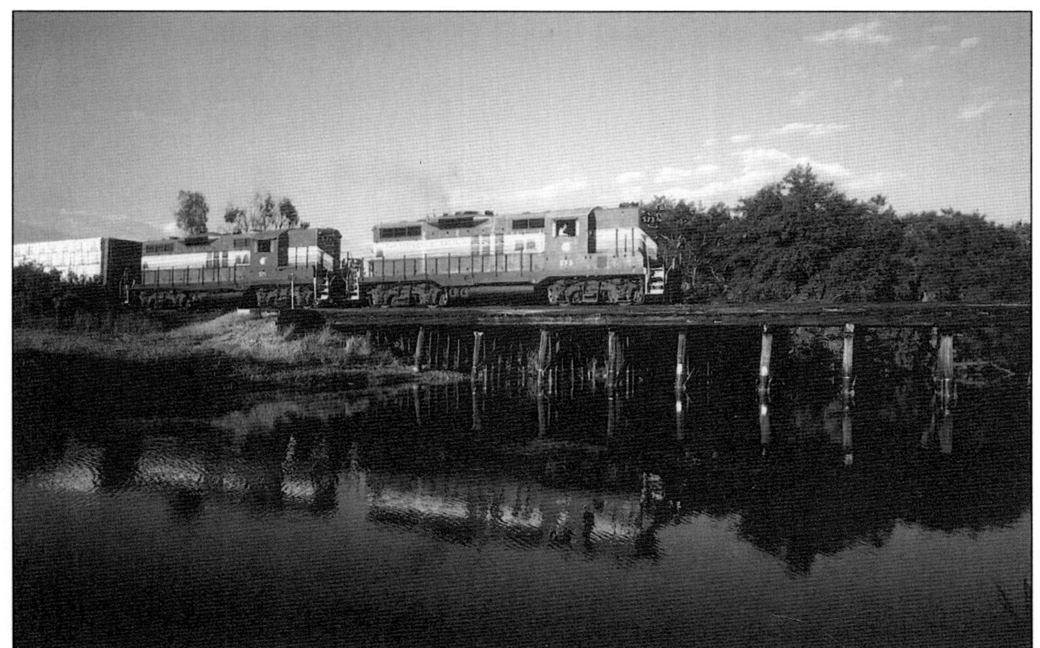

Engines 573 and 571 take a Seminole Gulf freight across Alligator Creek at Punta Gorda Estates, November 20, 1990. To save on start-up costs, many shortlines begin operations with used locomotives. The ones seen here were first owned by the Chesapeake & Ohio and Baltimore & Ohio Railroads respectively. (Scott A. Hartley.)

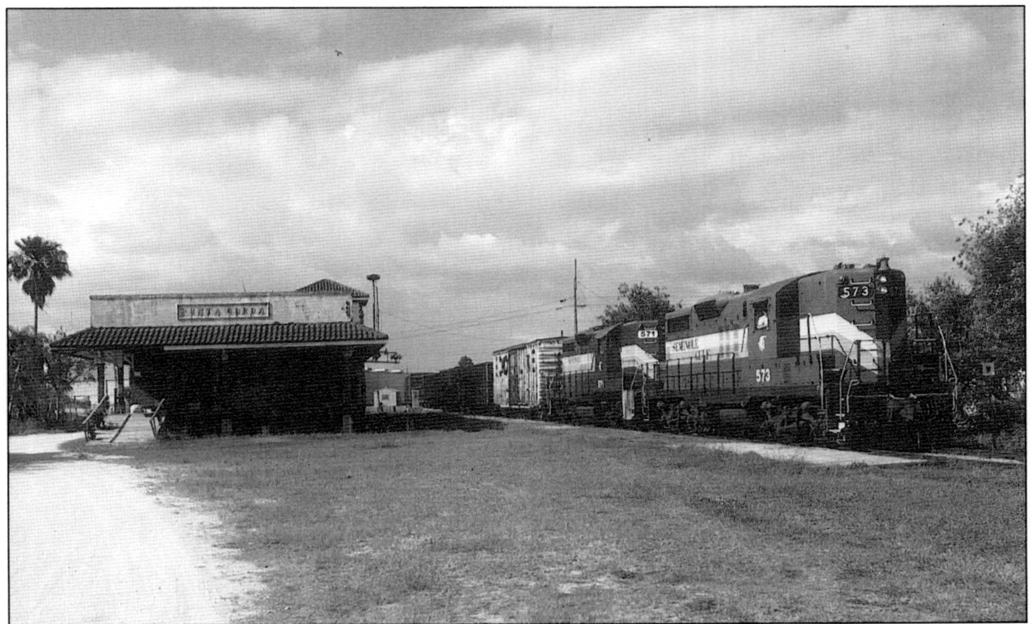

Seminole Gulf engines 573 and 571 were built by the Electro Motive Division of General Motors as GP-9 models—the "GP" standing for "general purpose." In this April 7, 1997 setting, we see them pulling a southbound freight past the historic station at Punta Gorda en route to Fort Myers. (Scott A. Hartley.)

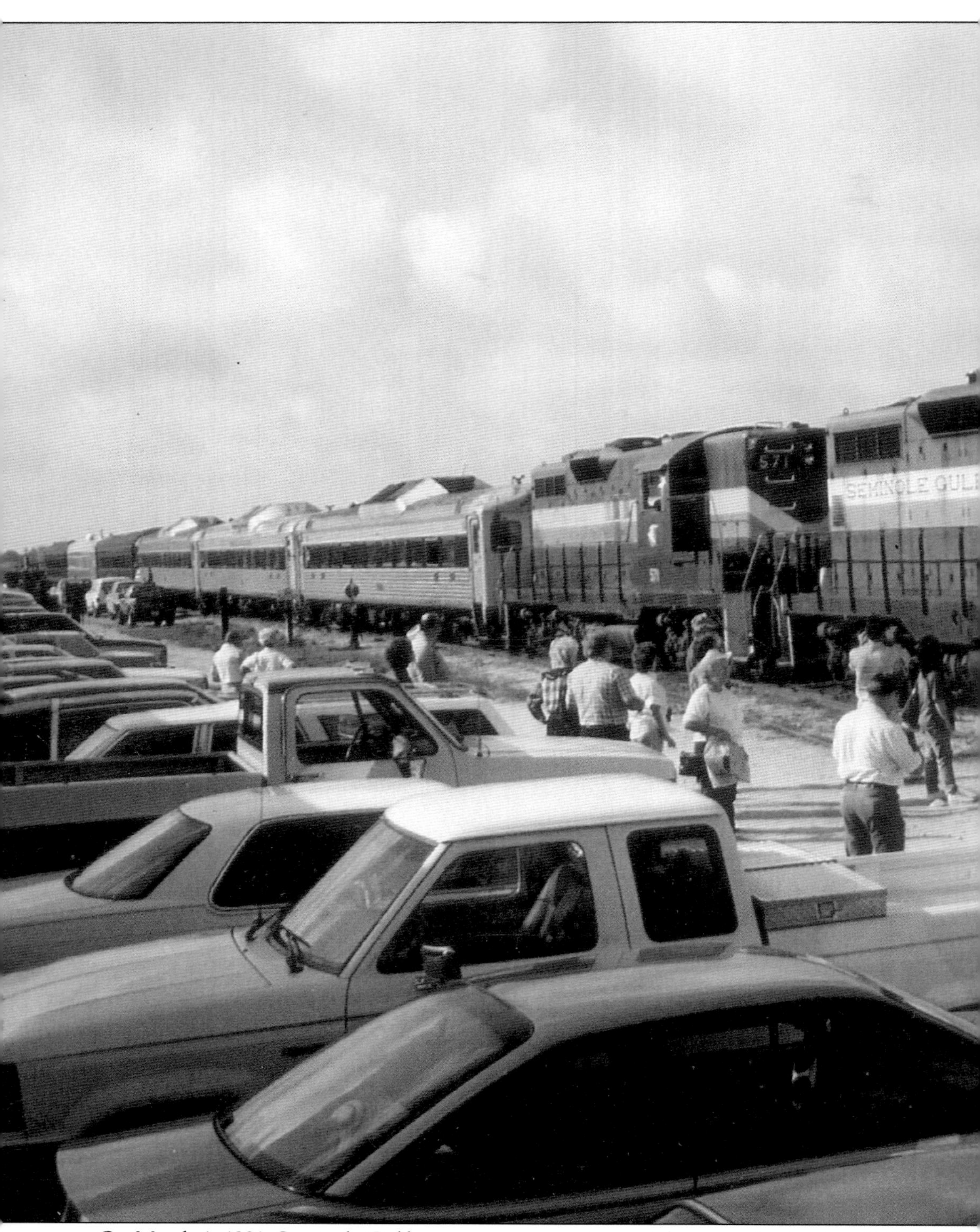

On March 1, 1991, Seminole Gulf ran a passenger train special to Arcadia for the All-Florida Championship Rodeo. More than 400 people rode the train that day, which was the first

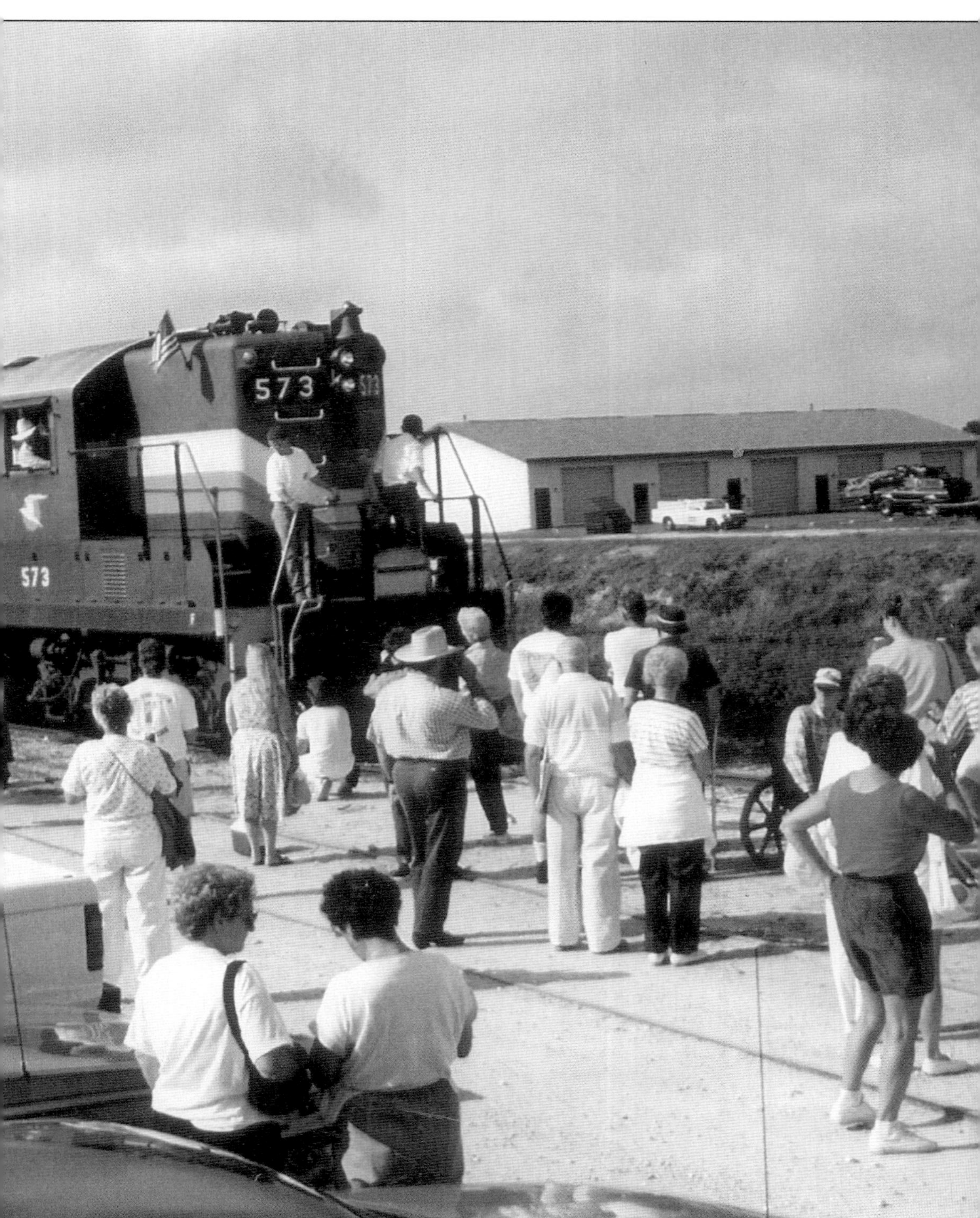

passenger consist to traverse the 78-mile line in almost 20 years. We see it that morning at North Naples, where the trip began. (Photo by Jeanne Hickam.)

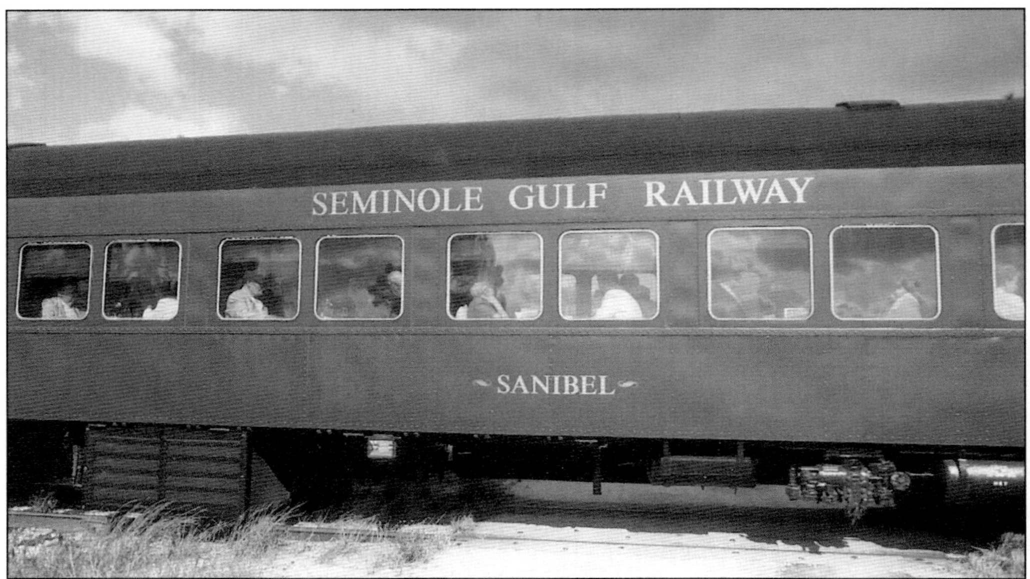

A popular component of the Seminole Gulf operations are its dinner trains. Dining car *Sanibel* was originally built in 1937 as a 64-seat coach for Canadian National Railways. In 1984, it was purchased by Bay Colony Railroad for excursion service in Massachusetts. Then, in the fall of 1990, it was fashioned into a dining car by Seminole Gulf. (Scott A. Hartley.)

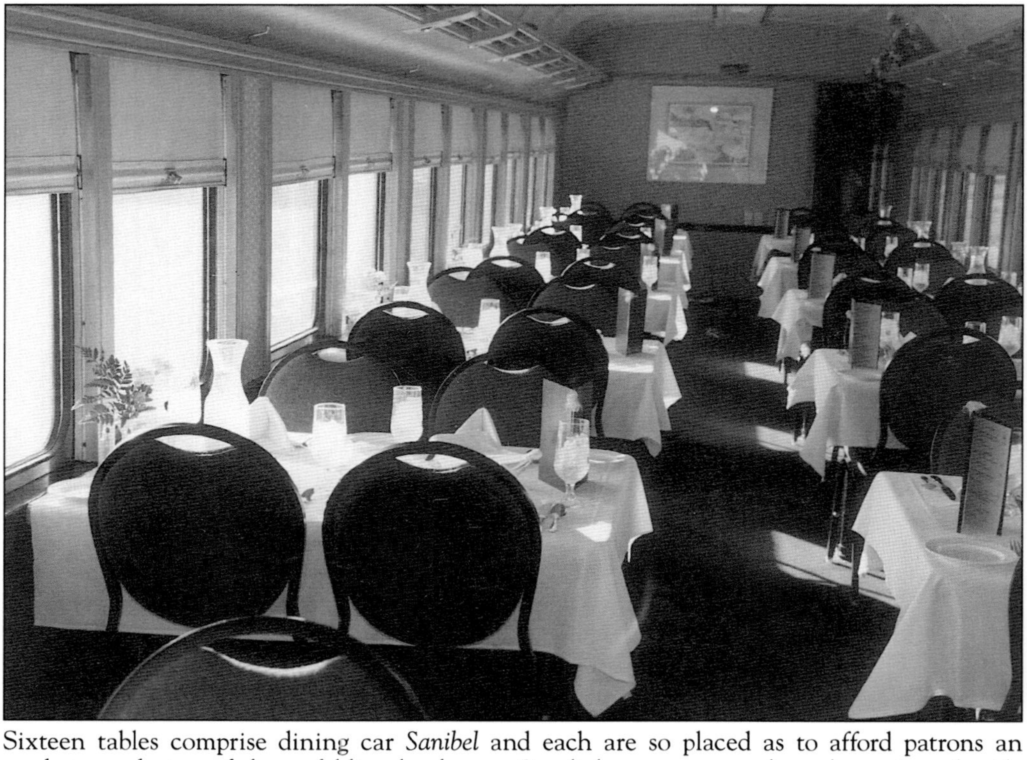

Sixteen tables comprise dining car *Sanibel* and each are so placed as to afford patrons an unobstructed view of the unfolding landscape. Spotlights are mounted on the car's underside which enhance the ride at night. (Photo by Jeanne Hickam.)

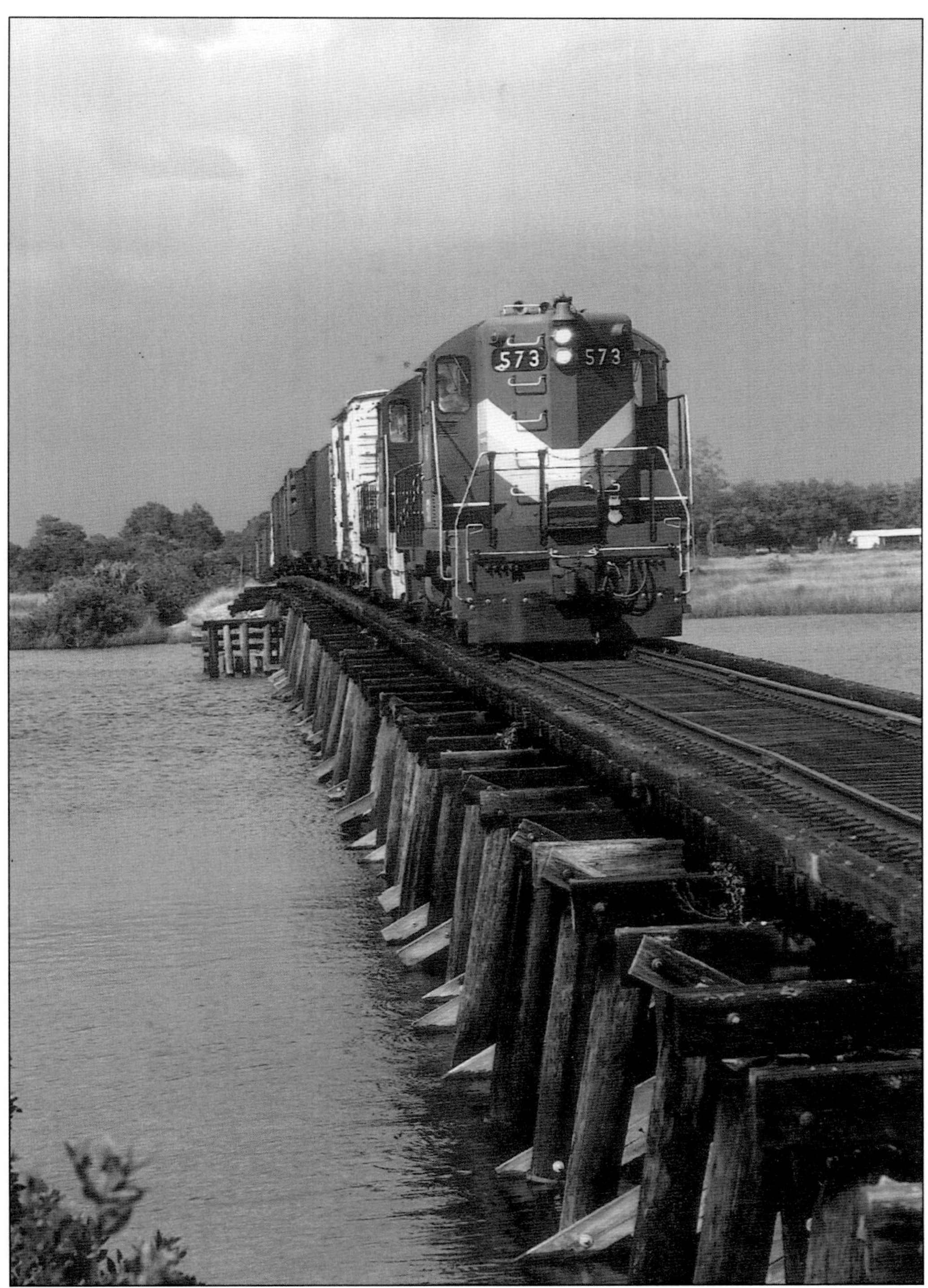

Numerous waterways are encountered along Seminole Gulf's Fort Myers line. At Cleveland, north of Punta Gorda, the track spans Shell Creek on a long wood trestle. On April 7, 1997, we find the company's "DeSoto Turn" in charge of engines 573 and 571. (Scott A. Hartley.)

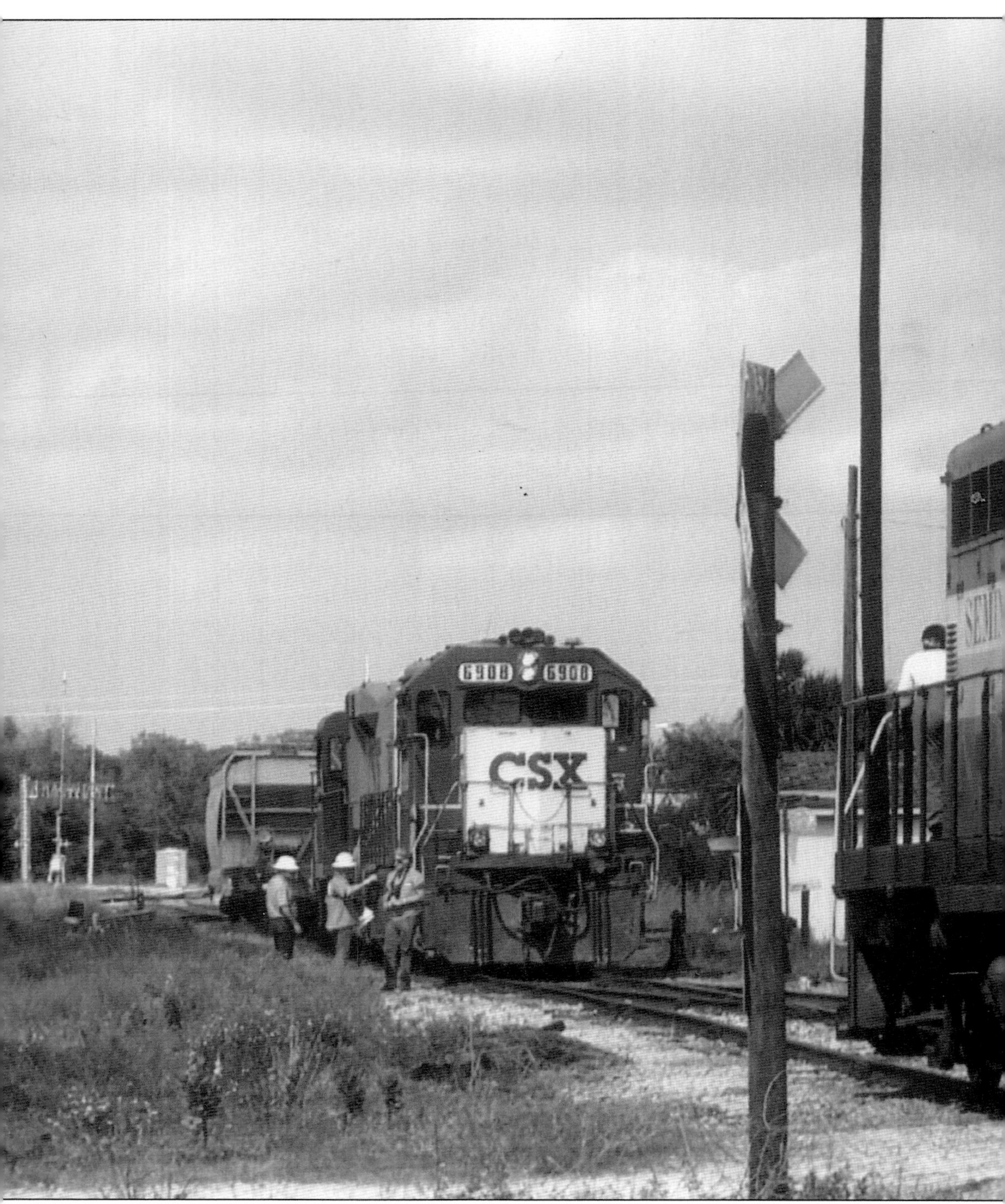

Seminole Gulf connects with CSX Transportation at Arcadia. Cars are exchanged here and trains are made up in the small yard. In this January 30, 1998 setting, composed by nationally-known railroad photographer and author Scott A. Hartley, CSX train 0804 from Mulberry has

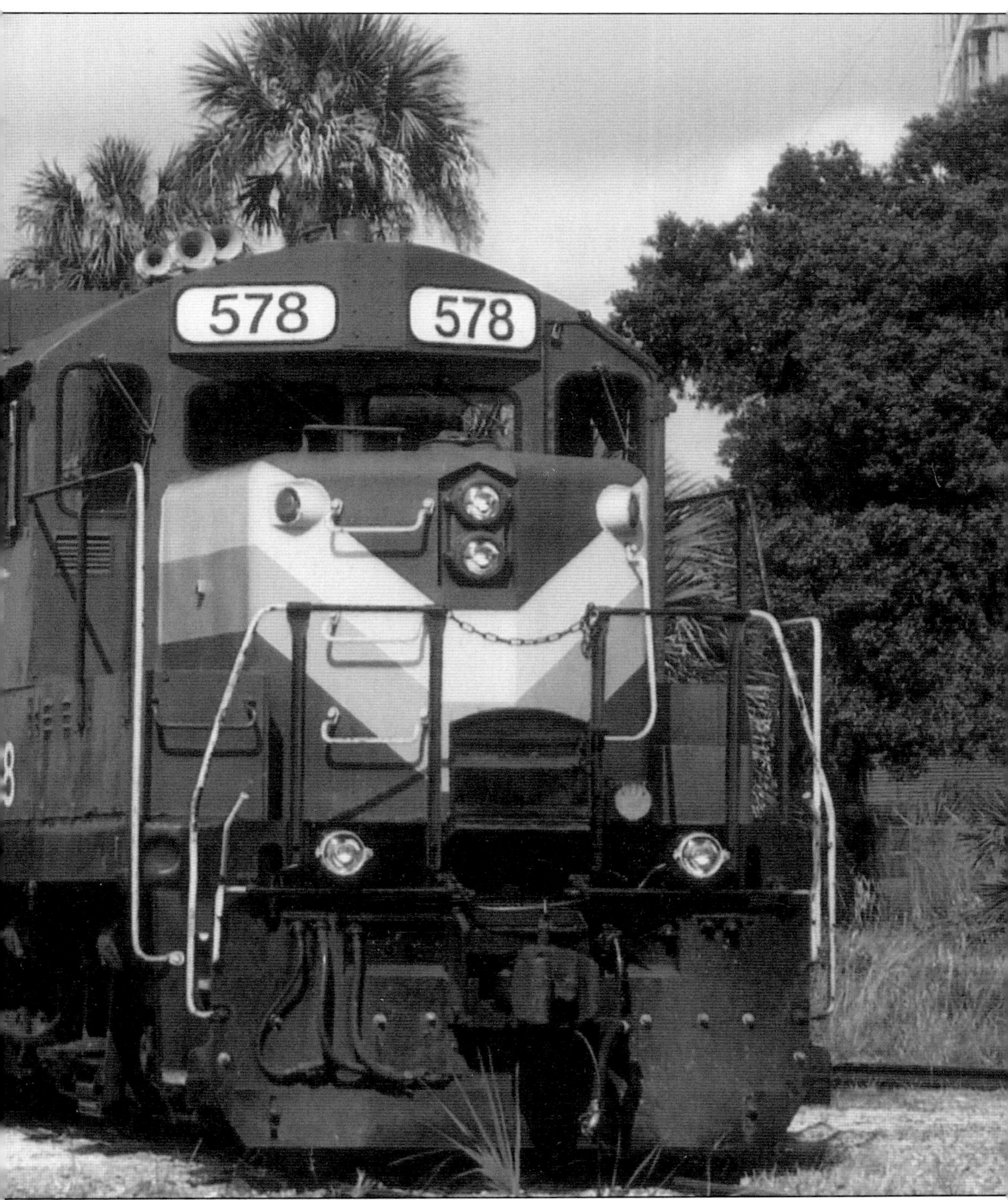

just left a hopper car for the shortline operator. Once engines 6908 and 2296 clear the area, Seminole Gulf engine 578 will retrieve it and the "DeSoto Turn" will head back to Fort Myers.

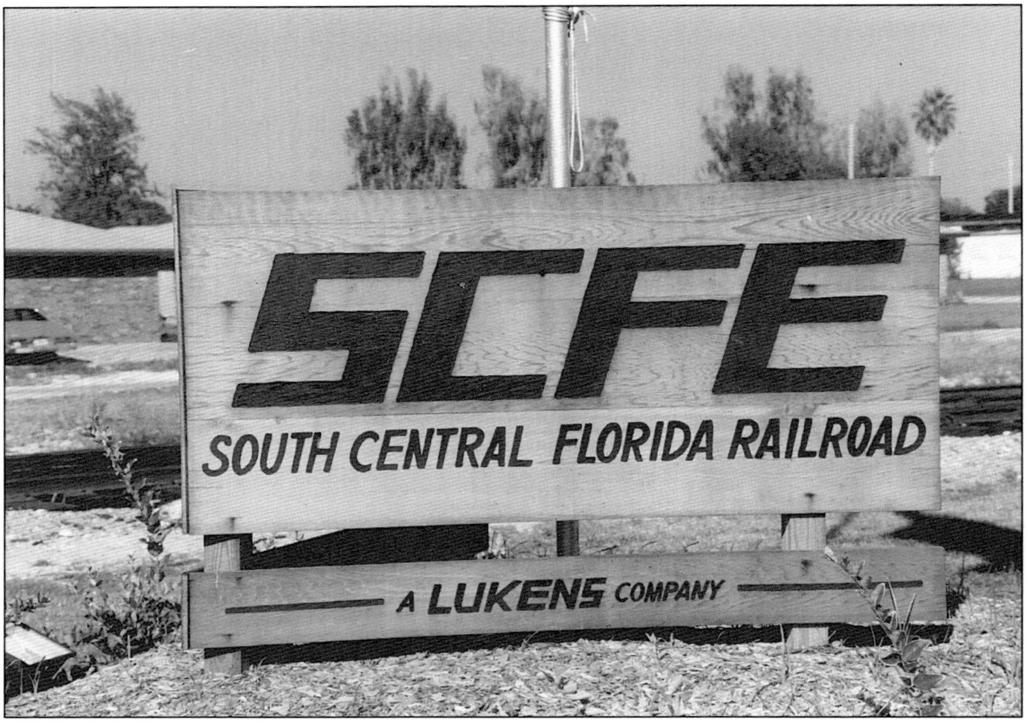

In 1990, CSX Transportation spun-off trackage between Sebring and Lake Harbor to Brandywine Valley Railroad, a subsidiary of Lukens Steel. The South Central Florida Railroad was created, and this signboard graced headquarters at Clewiston. Four years later, Lukens sold the shortline to U.S. Sugar which re-christened it South Central Florida Express, Inc. (Photo by Jeanne Hickam.)

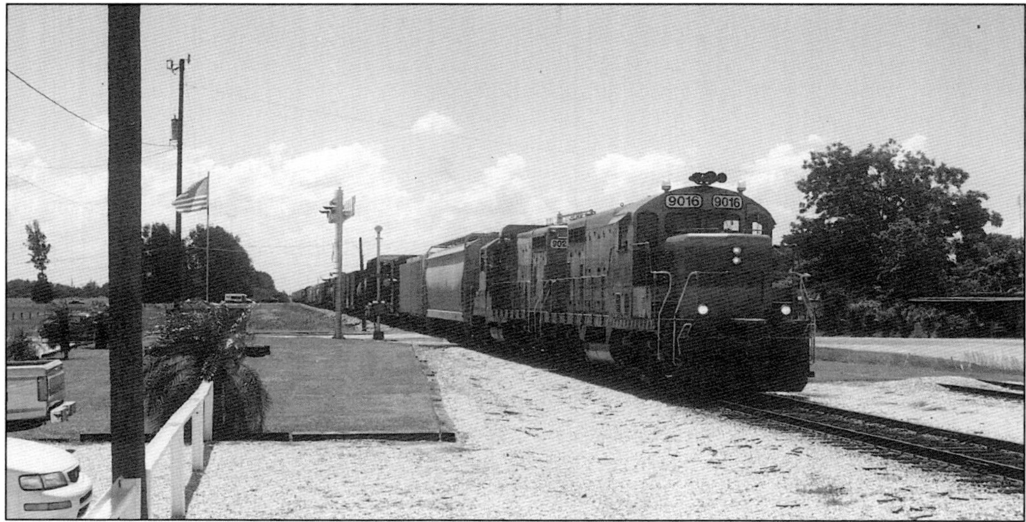

A train of the South Central Florida Express is seen here passing company headquarters at Clewiston. Engine No. 9016 was built by the Electro Motive Division of General Motors in 1951 for another railroad, and rebuilt in 1980 as a model GP-16. The paint scheme is "pumpkin" orange and blue. (South Central Florida Express.)

Twenty-six customers are identified on this South Central Florida Express map. The successful shortline connects with CSX Transportation at Sebring, plus it operates the Florida East Coast's "K-Line" branch between Lake Harbor and Fort Pierce. Revenues in 1998 were $8.4 million. Principal commodities hauled include cut cane, sugar, fertilizers, molasses, LPG, pulpwood logs, rolled paper, and farm equipment. (South Central Florida Express.)

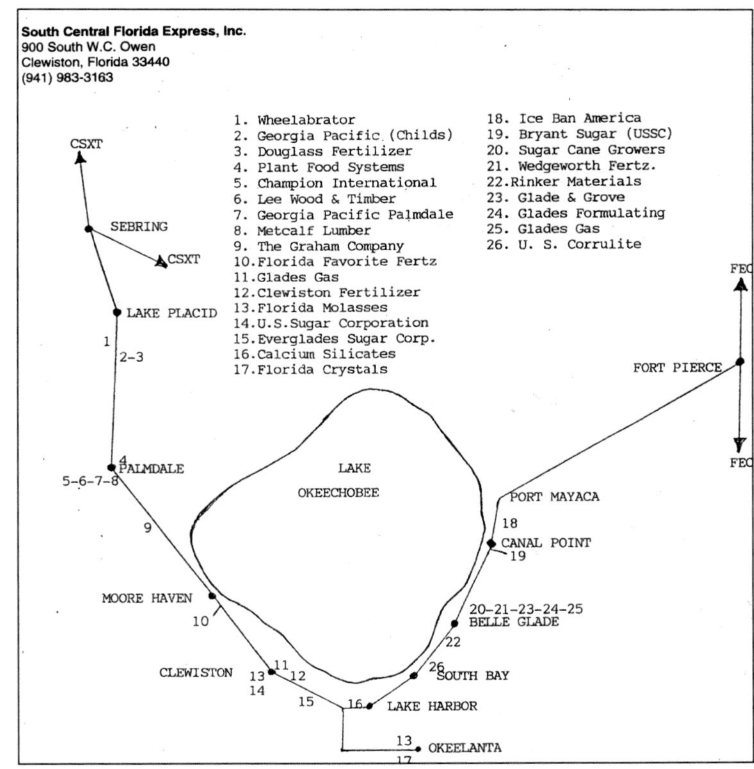

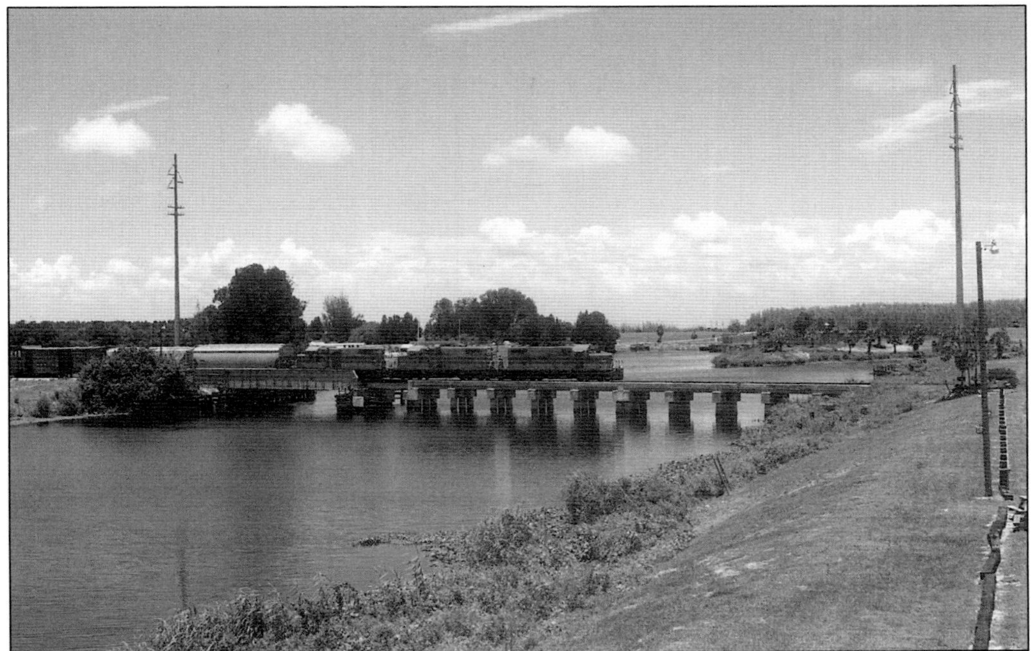

A South Central Florida Express train eases across the Okeechobee waterway canal at Moore Haven. Locks are visible in the distance. The railroad itself is a subsidiary of U.S. Sugar, which is based in Clewiston. (South Central Florida Express.)

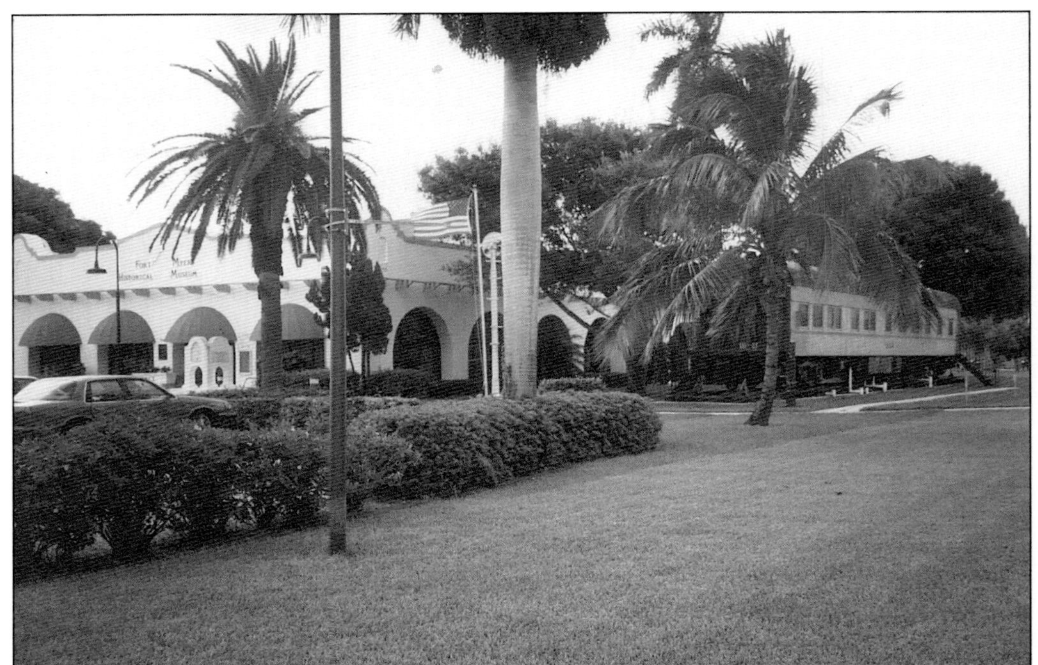

Superb exhibits attract young and old to the Fort Myers Historical Museum, located in the beautifully restored Atlantic Coast Line station on Peck Street. A museum store is operated as well as a research facility. The private Pullman car *Esperanza* can also be toured.

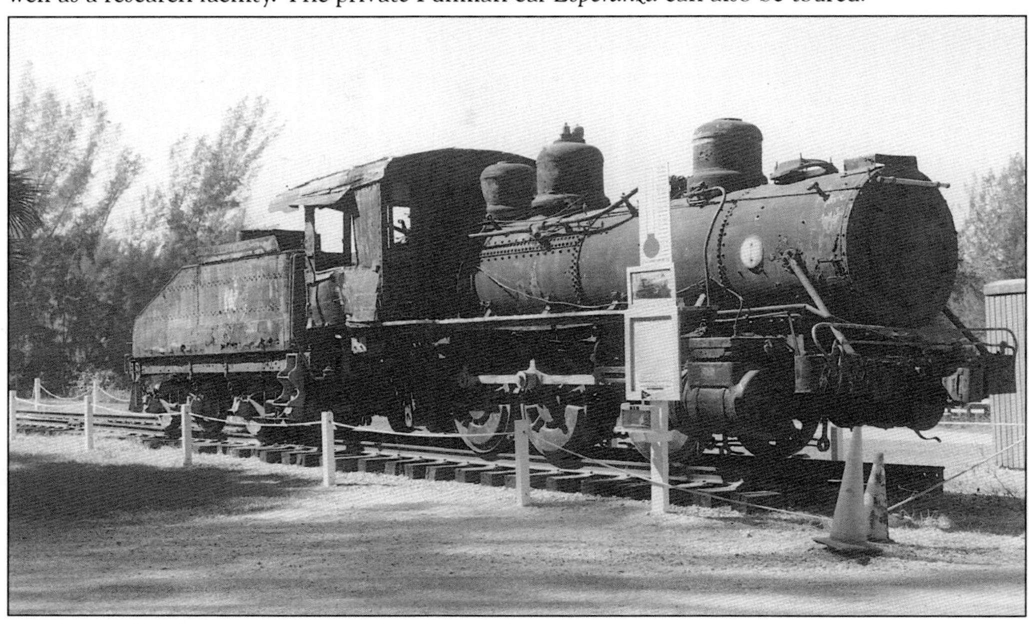

The Railroad Museum of South Florida, based in Fort Myers, operates a museum store at the famed Shell Factory. At Lakes Regional Park, engine 143 (seen above) is displayed. Built by Baldwin (1905) for Atlantic Coast Line, it was sold to Agrico (1944) and worked the phosphate district at Pierce (Mulberry) until 1959. Restoration is occurring, thanks to contributions and a grant from Florida's Division of Historical Resources. (Photo by Jeanne Hickam.)

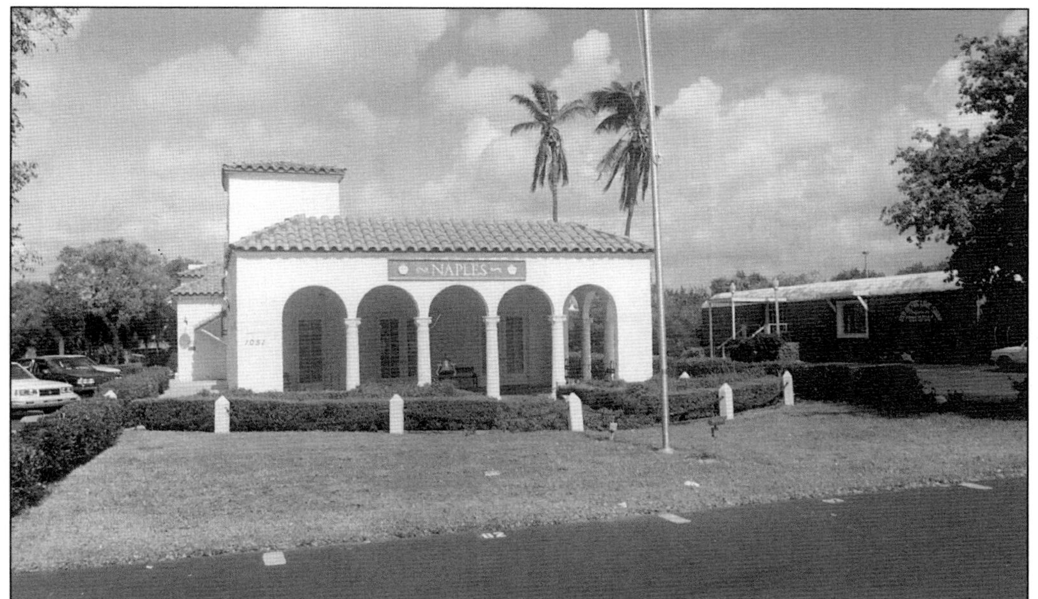

The splendid Seaboard depot at Naples is beautifully restored and serves as community arts center and railroad museum. Several rail cars adorn the property; one houses a railroad gift store. (Photo by Mike Mulligan.)

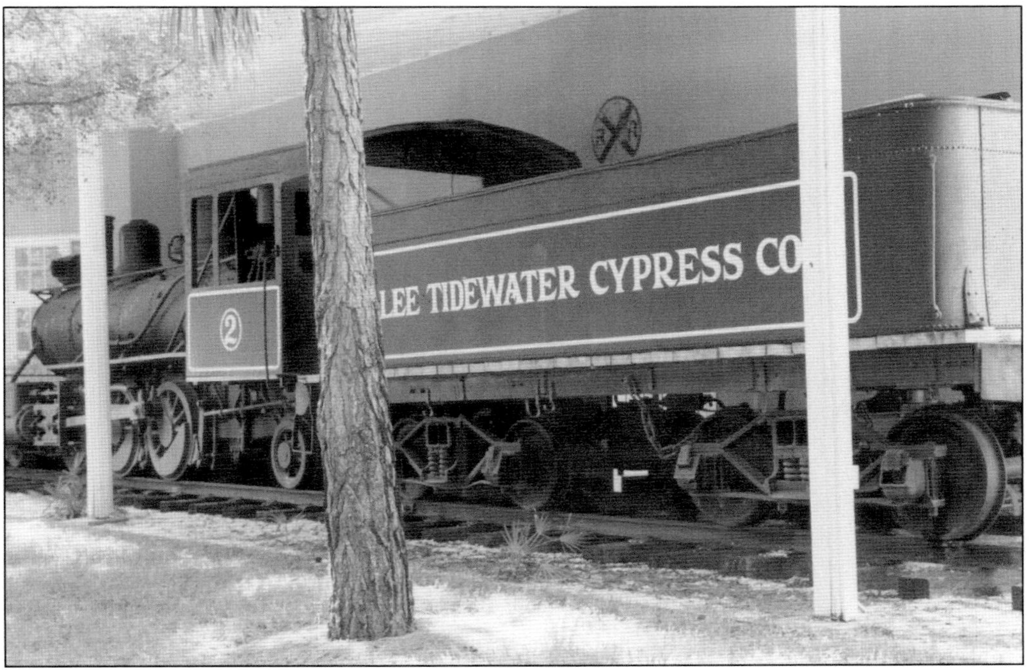

Visitors to the Collier County Museum in Naples can see a real logging locomotive. No. 2—The Deuce—was a coal burner built by Baldwin in 1913 and one of five that hauled log trains of Lee Tidewater Cypress at Copeland. Chicago train collector John Thompson donated it in 1987. One of its sisters appeared in the movie *Winds Across the Everglades.* (Courtesy of Collier County Museum, Naples, FL.)

FURTHER RAILROAD READING

Goolsby, Larry. *Atlantic Coast Line Passenger Service: The Postwar Years*. Lynchburg, Virginia: TLC Publishing, Inc., 1999.

Griffin, William E. Jr. *Seaboard Air Line Railway*. Lynchburg, Virginia: TLC Publishing, Inc. 1999.

Hoffman, Glenn, Ph.D. *A History of the Atlantic Coast Line Railroad Company*. Edited by Richard E. Bussard. Richmond, Virginia: CSX Corporation, 1998.

Johnson, Robert Wayne. *Through the Heart of the South: The Seaboard Airline Railroad Story*. Erin, Ontario: Boston Mills Press, 1995.

Peeples, Vernon E. "Charlotte Harbor Division of the Florida Southern Railroad." Vol. 58, *Florida Historical Quarterly*. Melbourne, Florida: Florida Historical Society, 1980.

Pettengill, George W. Jr. "The Story of Florida Railroads." Bulletin No. 86, Railway & Locomotive Historical Society, 1952. (Reprinted May 1998 by Southeast Chapter of R&LHS, PO Box 664, Jacksonville, Florida 32201.)

Shrady, Theodore and Arthur M. Waldrop. *Orange Blossom Special: Florida's Distinguished Winter Train*. Valrico, Florida: The ACL & SAL Historical Society, 1996.

Sulzer, Elmer. *Ghost Railroads of Sarasota County*. Sarasota, Florida: Sarasota Historical Society, 1971.

Warren, Bob and Fred Clark Jr. *Seaboard Coast Line*. Newton, New Jersey: Carstens Publications, 1985.

Welsh, Joseph M. *By Streamliner: New York to Florida*. Andover, New Jersey: Andover Junction Publications, 1994.